LAW AND SOCIETY IN ISLAM

LAW AND SOCIETY IN ISLAM

Devin J. Stewart
Baber Johansen
Amy Singer

Markus Wiener Publishers
Princeton

For information write to: Markus Wiener Publishers
114 Jefferson Road, Princeton, NJ 08540

Library of Congress Cataloging-in-Publication Data

Stewart, Devin J.
Law ans society in Islam: three essays/by Devin J. Stewart, Baber Johansen, and Amy Singer.
(Princeton Series on the Middle East)
Includes bibliographical references
ISNB 1-55876-123-3
1. Islamic law—History. I. Johansen, Baber. II. Singer, Amy. III. Series.
Law <Islam 7 Stew 1995>
340.5'9'—dc20 95-46698
CIP

Markus Wiener Publishers books are printed in the United States of America on acid-free paper, and meet the guidelines for permanence and durability of the committee on production guidelines for book longevity of the council on library resources.

Contents

Introduction

For the medieval and early pre-modern periods of the Islamic world of the Middle East, the use of texts and literature that are primarily religious in nature for social and other secular historical subjects and themes is in its early stages. This remains so in spite of the exceptional richness, both in quantity and quality of such sources.

In terms of sheer quantity, works of Islamic religious law are probably the most prominent genre or class of writings to come down to us from the pre-modern period. Given the claim of Islamic law to regulate virtually every aspect of personal, social, economic as well as religious life, this body of texts is not only copious, but also comprehensive and covers a wide range of subjects of fundamental interest to the social and other historians.

For the historian (other than legal historians), one of the main problems with this rich and vast body of literature, has been its theoretical character. That is, it is a lawyer's literature; even worse, it is a religious lawyer's literature that sees itself as an elaboration of a divine law whose goal is to establish a set of rules intended to help the believer attain salvation on the day of judgement.

It has been clear for some decades now that these legal materials, if properly exploited, could yield important insights on a variety of historical topics, topics that are frequently inaccessible from other sources. Some such work has been done, but not nearly enough.

The present collection of articles not only exemplifies an impressive confirmation of the preceding proposition, but also represents a measure of methodological innovation and advance in this regard. Two of the articles—those of Baber Johansen and Amy Singer—use Islamic legal material (albeit of very different kinds) to explore areas of life and thought for which this material was not previously utilized. The third study, that of Devin Stewart, utilizes theological and hagiographic texts to illuminate fundamental aspects of social interaction and presentation. The great merit of all three articles in this volume is that they pose unexpected questions to a genre of material that we would not prima facie expect to provide appropriate or relevant answers.

Virtually all students of medieval Islamic culture and society have recognized both its doctrinal and its practical capacity to deal with diversity and differences in its midst. This characteristic is particularly striking when we compare the medieval Islamic world to medieval Christian Europe. If, to formulate it very schematically, the *dhimma* was the doctrinal framework for dealing with the continued existence of non-Muslim communities in the domain of Islam (Christians, Jews and many others), it was the doctrine of *taqiyya* that was one of the doctrinal means that made possible the remarkable diversity of religious ideas and practices within the *ummah*, the Islamic community itself. The doctrine of *taqiyya* (usually translated by the English 'dissimulation') permits Muslims (Sunnīs as well as Shiʿīs), living under adverse circumstances, to go so far as to deny their faith and to violate explicit requirements of Islamic religious law in order to protect their lives and wellbeing. Accepting this principle made possible, in theory at least, the avoidance of stark confrontations. In this manner, not every doctrinal difference, or variation in practice and approach had to be converted into a question of heresy and apostasy. Heresies could be dissimulated, overlooked and ultimately, tolerated without schisms or painful social and communal dislocation.

Working with this norm of religious behavior, Devin Stewart translates its implications on a variety of social and cultural levels. In effect, it is via the practice of *taqiyya* that he is able to illuminate basic aspects of identity and communication in Islamic societies from the Middle Ages through the early 20th century.

The 'text' for his exposition is the journey effectuated by Bahā' al-Dīn al-ʿĀmilī, one of the foremost Shiʿite scholars of the early Safavid period, in Sunnī-Ottoman terriory between the years 1583-1585. Politically and religiously these were unsettled times between Ottomans and Safavids and between Sunnīs and Shiʿīs. Only by concealing his real identity and religious preference was Bahā' al-Dīn safely able to undertake this journey whose itinerary included a pilgrimage to Mecca as well as study-visits at a number of centers of Sunnī learning (Aleppo, Damascus, Jerusalem and Cairo). Stewart does not focus on the religious and theological differences that separated al-ʿĀmilī from his Sunnī confreres. Rather, it is the behavior, the gestures and the strategies adopted by Bahā' al-Dīn in order to conceal one identity and project another that are at the center of the author's attention in this study. By approaching the account of his journey from a tangent, as it were, Stewart is able to identify the basic devices of self-presentation in the early modern Islamic world. So, for example, we observe how Bahā' al-Dīn manipulated not only his true convictions, but also his clothing, his name and even a spurious genealogy in order to perform the *taqiyyah* necessary to assure his safety while 'pursuing knowledge' from the leading Sunnī scholars of his day.

Beyond the career of this sixteenth ʿālim, Stewart expands the relevance of the study by introducing illuminating social science insights (Goffman and Simmel) and by chronologically extending its implications to include such figures as the nineteenth century religious reformer Jamāl al-Dīn al-Afghānī and by referring to the Imam Khomeinī's treatment of this subject, thereby demonstrating the vitality and relevance of this form of religious behavior in more recent times on a political rather than on a social level.

What is the value of the human body in Islamic religious law? Indeed, what are the norms and principles that govern the status of the human body in medieval Islamic society? Through a skillful and extraordinarily perceptive interrogation of classical texts of Islamic religious law (primarily those of the Hanafī school), Baber Johansen reveals to us an unsuspected treasure trove of insights.

Johansen's starting point is an examination of the rules governing "the circulation of persons and goods," that is, virtually all categories of exchange, in Muslim Sunnī law. Within this broad framework he had the simple but inspired idea of distinguishing between the rules of commercial exchange and those of symbolic or social exchange (e.g., marriage, clientage, slavery). A systematic exploration of this distinction reveals that the status of the human body in Islamic religious legal doctrine is 'cuturally constructed' and that permissible behavior with respect to the body (one's own body, but especially that of another person) changes according to a number of major social categories, primarily those of gender, kinship, religion and free or servile status. One is continually surprised and impressed by the direct, lucid awareness of medieval Muslim legal writers (especially the eleventh century Sarakhsī) of the social and cultural elements that come into play in this regard and one is particularly appreciative of their crisp formulations, which Johansen cites liberally and to good effect.

This study is a very promising beginning for investigations on this and related subjects in the Islamic Middle East both for pre-modern and modern times. Indeed, the author concludes his article precisely by indicating areas of inquiry that could prove fruitful and that he was unable to treat in this pioneering and most stimulating presentation.

Amy Singer's contribution is based on quasi-legal material of a markedly different kind than that utilized by Baber Johansen. Her data derives not from the legal and social commentaries of learned and articulate scholars of Islamic religious law, but from the more modest but no less eloquent (historically speaking) administrative records of late sixteenth century pious endowments (*evkāf*) in Jerusalem, endowments that derived their income from the agricultural villages around the town of Ramle to the west of Jerusalem. In addition to the agricultural revenues that covered most of the expenses of the mosque, hostel and public kitchen of the Jerusalem endowment, there was also, as it turned out, a supplementary source of income generated both by marriage fees as well as by fines and penalties levied on those villagers who from time to time violated the norms of civil behavior.

From the data provided by a single such list found in Istanbul and covering a four month period in 1586, Amy Singer is able to propose a number of stimulating insights and hypotheses about aspects of rural life at that time that are otherwise very difficult of access, even indirectly. She is able skillfully to transform the neutral, micro-information of this document into reinterpretations of the local as well as the imperial realities relating to rural life. On the very local level, for example, this single document "confirms that villages could and did differ enormously from each other even within a very small area." (p.150) On the level of the fiscal realities of the Ottoman Empire, the data from these lists suggests "that the collection of revenues was not unidirectional toward Istanbul, with expenditures flowing uniquely in the opposite direction. Rather, revenue was collected and disbursed in a system of micro-economies, interconnected through the command chain of authority which distributed the jurisdiction over them." (ibid.)

These are original observations of far-reaching significance for our understanding of pre-modern Middle Eastern rural society.

A.L. Udovitch
Princeton University

Taqiyyah as Performance: The Travels of Bahā' al-Dīn al-'Āmilī in the Ottoman Empire (991-93/1583-85)

DEVIN J. STEWART

As Ignaz Goldziher has observed, Islamic sects occupy a precarious legal position. The intermediate status afforded to Christians and Jews is, at least in theory, unavailable to Muslim sectarians. A Muslim sectarian is either accepted as a believer (*mu'min*), in which case he is accorded full rights in the community, or rejected as an unbeliever (*kāfir*), in which case all his rights are forfeited, his property is to be confiscated, and he is to be executed.[1] Some jurists allow that he should be given the opportunity to repent before being executed, but others do not allow him that opportunity, on the grounds that the oath of an avowed heretic cannot be accepted.[2] Islamic law recognizes no middle ground because heresy within Islam is tantamount to apostasy, and apostasy is a capital offense. Bernard Lewis notes that the practice of Islam concerning the punishment of heretics has in general been less severe than its theory,[3] and such scholars as al-Ghazālī advised their colleagues to refrain from accusing fellow Muslims of heresy whenever possible.[4] Nevertheless, the trial and execution of Muslim sectarians has not been a rare phenomenon in the history of Islam. For example, a number of Shiites were executed in Mamlūk Damascus, including the prominent jurist Muḥammad b. Makkī al-Jizzīnī, known in the Shiite scholarly tradition as al-Shahīd al-Awwal (The First Martyr), who was tried and executed as a heretic in 786/1384. In the square just below the citadel, he was put to death by sword, and his body crucified, stoned, and, finally, burned.[5]

Given the danger involved in accusations of heresy, it is not surprising that Islamic sects developed a variety of methods to protect themselves by concealing doctrinal differences and heterodox allegiances from the majority. One such method is the establishment of a hierarchy in which only those initiated into the higher levels may gain access to the esoteric teachings of the faith, as found in the Ismāʿīlī *daʿwah*, its historical off-shoots in the Levant, the ʿAlawīs or Nuṣayrīs and the Druze, and also, perhaps, in early Imāmī Shiism. Adherents of the Druze religion, for instance, are divided into two distinct categories, *juhhāl*, or "ignorant ones," and *ʿuqqāl*, or "sages," only the latter being allowed to read the sacred texts of the religion and attend the *khalwah*, or secret ceremony of worship. Another such method is *taqiyyah* (literally, "caution"), the principle of precautionary dissimulation, whereby Muslim sectarians are allowed to deny their beliefs when to do otherwise would put them in danger. The group most widely recognized for the use of this particular method is that of the Twelver Shiites.

Taqiyyah is an accepted principle in both Sunni and Shiite Islam.[6] Its use is based on the interpretation of several Koranic verses, including verse 16:106 in particular: "Whoever expresses disbelief in God after having accepted belief [will suffer greatly]—except him who is forced while his heart is still at peace in belief ..." This verse is taken to refer to ʿAmmār b. Yāsir, a Companion of the Prophet who outwardly denied Muḥammad's prophecy and worshipped pagan idols in order to protect himself while in Mecca. The verse is generally interpreted to mean that a Muslim may deny his faith or violate Islamic law if his life is threatened.[7] For Twelver Shiites, *taqiyyah* has had more extensive applications, and many have seen *taqiyyah* as a crucial doctrine and fundamental characteristic of Shiism.[8]

Discussions of Twelver Shiite *taqiyyah* in modern scholarship have concentrated on a limited number of issues treated in *ḥadīth* and legal texts. Investigators agree that the principle of *taqiyyah* allows one to do two things: to deny one's faith or to violate individual points of law to follow majority practice, as in performing prayer or ritual ablutions. The substance of *taqiyyah* is generally seen as being limited to expressions of belief and ritual practices.[9] The study of *taqiyyah* in Islam is still rudimentary; theoretical discussions of the concept, including a substantial independent treatise on the topic by Khomeini,[10] have not been extensively analyzed, nor has the material on *taqiyyah* in legal compendia and responsa been fully examined. Furthermore, even a thorough examination of theoretical texts treating the issue would leave many important questions unanswered. *Taqiyyah* is not merely an abstract principle buried in legal texts to be exercised only by those who have extensive familiarity with the law. It is an important part of daily life for many Muslim sectarians, a method which must be performed not only in a legally correct manner, to avoid sinful acts, but also in a convincing manner, to avoid bodily harm and promote the economic success and social welfare of the sectarian community. While it is important to understand the theory behind the principle, it is clear that the theoretical texts leave a great deal unsaid. A moment's reflection on the social problems minorities generally face suffices to alert the investigator to the fact that a different approach may provide a more extensive understanding of *taqiyyah* as a dynamic principle.[11] For a Shiite to pretend to be a Sunni takes more than a simple statement to that effect. It requires a sustained performance which might require hundreds of individual statements and actions of different types, many of which might have little to do with expressions of belief or ritual practice *per se*. The juridical texts say something about the circumstances under which *taqiyyah* should be performed, but very little about how one is to do this in such a sustained and convincing manner, should the need arise. To gain a more complete understanding of the principle of *taqiyyah*, it is important to examine specific historical examples of its use.

Little attempt has been made to examine *taqiyyah* as practice in scholarship to date; notable exceptions include Aharon Layish's study on some uses of *taqiyyah* among the Druze in modern Israel and L. P. Harvey's discussion of the North African Sunni jurist al-Wahrānī's 910/504 *fatwā* permitting Muslims in sixteenth-century Spain to adopt Christianity outwardly out of *taqiyyah*.[12] The following study attempts to provide an outline of practical *taqiyyah*, drawing both on theoretical texts and on a particular historical performance of *taqiyyah*, that of Bahā' al-Dīn al- 'Āmilī (953-1030/1547-1621) during his travels through the Ottoman Empire between 991/1583 and 993/1585. This scholar, also known in the sources by his Persian poetic *takhalluṣ* Bahā'ī or as al-Shaykh al-Bahā'ī, had the curious fortune to be recognized by many Sunnis as a fellow Sunni while at the same time serving as one of the foremost juridical authorities in the officially Shiite Safavid empire. After establishing as complete and accurate a text of Bahā' al-Dīn's journey as the available sources allow, this study then analyzes Bahā' al-Dīn's performance of *taqiyyah* in the course of his journey. Coupled with material from theoretical discussions of *taqiyyah* as well as other historical examples of its use, the analysis of Bahā' al-Dīn's performance aims to provide an outline of *taqiyyah* as a social practice.

* * *

Bahā' al-Dīn Muḥammad was born in Ba'labakk on 27 Dhū 'l-Ḥijjah 953/16 February 1547 to Ḥusayn b. 'Abd al-Ṣamad al-'Āmilī, a native of the town of Juba' in Jabal 'Āmil, the predominantly Shiite region in what is now southern Lebanon. When Bahā' al-Dīn was still a young boy, his father emigrated to Iran with the entire family. The Safavid Shah Ṭahmāsb (930-84/1524-76) eventually summoned Ḥusayn to court and appointed him *shaykh al-islām*, or chief jurisconsult, in Qazvin, then the capital. After having served as *shaykh al-islām* in Qazvin, Mashhad, and Herat for roughly twenty years, Ḥusayn left Iran to perform the pilgrimage, leaving his son behind. He died on 8 Rabī I 984/5 June 1576, in Baḥrayn, several months after completing the pilgrimage. Bahā' al-Dīn soon after assumed the post of *shaykh al-islām* of Isfahan. The importance of his post was greatly enhanced when Shah 'Abbās I (996-1038/1587-1629) made Isfahan the Safavid capital in 1005/1597, and Bahā' al-Dīn became the foremost religious authority in the empire for most of Shah 'Abbās' reign. He died in Isfahan in 1030/1621.[13]

It is well known that Bahā' al-Dīn made a number of long journeys in the Middle East, and anecdotes about these journeys figure prominently in many of the biographical notices about him. Scholars have over-estimated, however, the extent of Bahā' al-Dīn's travels outside the Safavid Empire. One source of this confusion is a statement by 'Alī Khān Ibn Ma'ṣūm al-Madanī (d. 1117/1705), the author of the poetic anthology *Sulāfat al-'aṣr fī maḥāsin shu'arā' kull miṣr*, to the effect that Bahā' al-Dīn traveled for thirty years.[14] The twentieth-century Shiite biographers Muḥsin al-Amīn and Āghā Buzurg al-'Ṭihrānī take this statement literally, and al-Amīn laments the fact that Bahā' al-Dīn did not record his thirty years of travels in Turkey, the Levant, and other areas, which, he supposes, would have surpassed those of Ibn Baṭṭūṭah and Ibn Jubayr in extent and quality.[15] In actuality, Bahā' al-Dīn's trips outside Safavid territory did not approach anywhere near thirty years in length. Ibn Ma'ṣūm's statement seems to be an exaggeration for literary effect, perhaps intended to link Bahā' al-Dīn with the famous Persian poet Sa'dī (d. 691/1292), also renowned as having traveled for thirty years.[16] Other estimates of the length of the journey are more reasonable. Tunkābunī (d. ca. 13101892) suggests that Bahā' al-Dīn traveled for four years and spent two in Egypt.[17] Nafīsī, Newman, and Ja'far al-Muhājir date Bahā' al-Dīn's trip correctly to 991-93/1583-85.[18]

Bahā' al-Dīn undertook his journey through Ottoman territory at a time of sectarian strife. Literally traveling through a war zone, he had good reason to practice *taqiyyah*. The death of Shah Ṭahmāsb in 984/1576 and the murder of his son and successor Shah Ismā'īl II (984-85/1576-77) in Ramaḍān 985/November 1577 had left the Empire prey to factional rivalry. The Ottomans were quick to take advantage of the weak Safavid central authority to make advances into the western border provinces. The Ottomans first launched their campaign in Muḥarram 986/March 1578, subduing most of Georgia and northern Azerbaijan, and taking Tiflis, Shirvan, and Erivan in that same year. In 987/1579, they rebuilt the frontier fortress at Qārṣ to serve as a base, and in the following years they fortified the other citadels under their control. Although Safavid forces gained some temporary victories, they lost a major battle in Rabī' I 991/May 1583, allowing the Ottomans to maintain their hold on the region. In 993/1585, the Ottomans advanced once more, capturing Tabriz, the provincial capital, in Ramaḍān/September of that year and occupying all of Azerbaijan. The occupation lasted until Shah 'Abbās reconquered the province over twenty years later. When Bahā' al-Dīn set out on his trip into Ottoman territory ca. 991/1583, the Ottomans had already been in Azerbaijan for several years, although they would not capture Tabriz until after his return.

Sectarian tension within the Safavid empire had reached new heights just a few years before Bahā' al-Dīn's journey during the short and bloody reign of Shah Ismā'īl II, who unsuccessfully attempted to implement many pro-Sunni policies, outlawing the cursing of Abū Bakr and 'Umar, and removing references to 'Alī from the coinage. This tension was aggravated by the ensuing Ottoman campaigns in Azerbaijan. Given that Ḥusayn b. Ḥasan al-Karakī (d. 1001/1593), *shaykh al-islām* of Qazvin and leading religious authority of the Empire at the time, declared all non-Twelvers unbelievers,[19] it is difficult to imagine that travelling in Sunni Ottoman territory was encouraged during this period. Writing in Jumādā II 989/July 1581,[20] just two years before Bahā' al-Dīn's journey, Mīrzā Makhdūm al-Sharīfī al-Shīrāzī (d. 995/1587), the renegade *ṣadr* or head of the religious institution[21] of Shah Ismā'īl II who had escaped to the Ottoman Empire after the latter's murder, predicted on astrological considerations that either A.H. 990 or A.H. 991 would be a propitious year to rid the world of Shiism, obviously, in this context, coterminous with the Safavid state.[22] While Mīrzā Makhdūm's prediction was as much an effort on his part to curry favor with the Ottoman Sultan Murād III (982-1003/1574-95) as an expression of popular opinion, it must have been calculated to harp on sentiments current at the time. Because Shiism was associated with the Safavid political threat, the position of Shiites in Ottoman territory had become increasingly difficult.

Many possible motives may be attributed to Bahā' al-Dīn in deciding to make this journey, and it is difficult to unravel the various strands of evidence available, let alone conjecture what facts remain hidden from view. The Safavid court chronicler Iskandar Beg Munshī states that Bahā' al-Dīn made the trip for pious reasons, both to perform the pilgrimage and to adopt a more ascetic lifestyle, giving up his power and exalted position for higher spiritual goals. Bahā' al-Dīn indeed performed the pilgrimage and refers to the journey specifically as a trip to Mecca in several autograph notes. One should also note the title of the poetry collection he wrote on the way, *Sawāniḥ safar al-Ḥijāz* "Thoughts on the Journey to the Ḥijāz" as well as the mystical content of the poems themselves. Other evidence confirms that he had a propensity for mysticism and that he expressed a desire to distance himself from Safavid Shahs for reasons of piety.[23] In addition, though, it is likely that Bahā' al-Dīn would have wanted to visit Jabal 'Āmil, the land of his ancestors, which he had not seen since his early childhood and about which he had doubtless heard a great deal from his parents, relatives, and other acquaintances. He also seems to have intended to partake in the long Shiite tradition of study and debate with Sunni scholars. Together with al-Shahīd al-Thānī ("the Second Martyr") Zayn al-Dīn al-'Āmilī (d. 965/1558), Bahā' al-Dīn's father, Ḥusayn, had traveled to Damascus, Cairo, and other cities in Ottoman territory to study with Sunnis, but Bahā' al-Dīn had not been able to take part in this tradition himself. He had grown up in the officially Shiite Safavid Empire, where Sunnis were persecuted and where it was difficult for Sunni learning to survive except in fields unmarked by doctrinal considerations such as grammar, astronomy, mathematics, and so on. Mīrzā Makhdūm, for example, considered one of the Shiites' great heresies the fact that they rejected outright the six well known compilations of Sunni *ḥadīth*, including the *Ṣaḥīḥs* of al-Bukhārī and Muslim.[24] He states that it was impossible to study Sunni *fiqh*, *ḥadīth*, or *tafsīr* in Iran ever since the establishment of Safavid rule in 907/1501, and makes the exaggerated claim that if a Sunni work on one of these subjects were found in someone's house, the entire house would be burned down along with the book.[25] Many of the accounts of Bahā' al-Dīn's journey show great persistence on his part in engaging in exchanges with Sunni scholars as adversaries in debate, colleagues, and students, following, almost literally, the footsteps of his father and al-Shahīd al-Thānī. The fields he studied and discussed during his travels included not only those which were doctrinally neutral, such as poetry and mathematics, but also fields which were marked for sect, such as *ḥadīth*. That Sunni learning had a considerable effect on Bahā' al-Dīn's thinking is indicated by many passages in his later works, including a statement in his work on *ḥadīth* criticism, *al-Wajīzah* ["*The Succinct Treatise*"], in which he made it clear that he was familiar with Sunni as well as Shiite *ḥadīth*: "The *ḥadīths* transmitted from [the Imams] contained in the books of the Shiites are many more than those in the six *Ṣiḥāḥ* of the Sunnis, as is clear to anyone who has examined the *ḥadīths* of both groups."[26] Bahā' al-Dīn is of course not alone in the phenomenon of studying with Sunnis, but statements such as this one indicate that a desire to do so may have been one of the motives for his travels.

The evidence available suggests that Bahā' al-Dīn had all four of the above motives in mind when he set out on his journey. None of them, however, would explain why he undertook the journey at this particular juncture. Perhaps only at this time was he able to obtain the Shah's permission; he had been denied the permission to perform the pilgrimage when is father left Iran in 983/1585.[27] Perhaps he decided to leave in order to escape some political problem in Iran, involving either the Shah or some other important political figure. The fact that he traveled in disguise may have facilitated his exit from Iran as much as his safety in Ottoman territory. Perhaps Bahā' al-Dīn even intended to escape married life temporarily. Since he was posing as an ascetic dervish, it seems inconceivable that his wife accompanied him on this journey, which kept him away from their home in Isfahan for nearly two years. One can only surmise what combination of pressures or desires prompted him to leave Iran to undertake this journey in 991/1583 in particular. His exact intentions for embarking on this trip, however, are not of primary concern here, and in the final analysis, the crucial motive for the journey may simply have been wanderlust or curiosity. It is clear, nevertheless, that he intended to pass as a Sunni in the course of his travels, and in doing so used methods which, though geared to his specific surroundings and circumstances, have served, *mutatis mutandis*, other Shiites—whether scholars, merchants, or commoners—throughout Islamic history.

Bahā' al-Dīn's Journey through Ottoman Territory

It is possible to sketch Bahā' al-Dīn's journey by piecing together information from *ijāzah* documents and Bahā' al-Dīn's own writings with accounts from chronicles, biographical works, and unpublished manuscripts. Although several anecdotes concerning Bahā' al-Dīn's journey are well known, a degree of confusion has surrounded previous accounts of the trip, specifically with respect to the order and dating of events.[28] The composite account presented below attempts to provide as comprehensive and detailed a picture of the trip as possible. The analysis of Bahā' al-Dīn's performance of *taqiyyah* will follow the composite account.

In 991/1583, Bahā' al-Dīn decided to make an extended trip into Ottoman territory. At this time he was an established scholar in his late thirties and held the post of *shaykh al-islām* of Isfahan, then an important provincial capital. He enjoyed the prestige of descent from a long line of

Shiite scholars, enhanced by the fact that he had inherited, as it were, the learning of al-Shahīd al-Thānī through his father, Ḥusayn, one of the foremost religious authorities of the previous generation. Bahā' al-Dīn began his trip by giving up his post as *shaykh al-islām* of Isfahan expressly in order to perform the pilgrimage.[29] He wrote a marginal note in Isfahan on 20 Rajab 991/9 August 1583 and adds the phrase "during the days when I decided to journey to God's Sacred House" (*ayyāma 'l- azmi alā 't-tawajjuhi ilā bayti 'Llāhi 'l-ḥarām*).[30] Just prior to his trip, Bahā' al-Dīn was probably in Isfahan: he had completed his *Risālah fī taḍārīs al-arḍ* there in Dhū 'l-Ḥijjah 990/December 1582-January 1583.[31] This probably involved obtaining permission from the reigning Shah, Muḥammad Khudābandah (985-95/1578-87), at the Safavid capital, then Qazvin. Safavid chronicler Iskandar Beg Munshī describes how Bahā' al-Dīn set out on his trip as follows.

> Then the longing to gain the happiness of pilgrimage to the House of God and the yearning for travel prevented him from performing such duties [as *shaykh al-islām* of Isfahan]. He set out upon a journey blessed by the steps of his predecessors. After he had experienced the greatest joy [of performing the pilgrimage],[32] the longing for abstinence and the life of a mendicant became preponderant in his noble temperament, and he chose to travel in the garb of dervishes. He traveled through Iraq of the Arabs, Syria, Egypt, the Ḥijāz, and Jerusalem for a long time, and during the days of his travel, he benefited from the company of many scholars, wise men, great Ṣūfī leaders, traveling dervishes, the people of God and asceticism—the chosen ones of God. Through accompanying them he came to share in their abundant blessings, and obtained both worldly and spiritual perfections.[33]

While this account seems to say that Bahā' al-Dīn traveled as a dervish only after performing the pilgrimage itself, other accounts imply that he had adopted dervish's garb for the entire trip. He apparently did not want to draw attention to himself and intended to remain incognito in order to travel safely in Ottoman territory.

It was usual, in this period, for pilgrims from Iran and Transoxania to follow the trade route Tabriz-Van-Amid-Aleppo-Damascus, passing through an Ottoman checkpoint at Amid.[34] Bahā' al-Dīn mentions that in Amid he wrote a poem in Persian for his book *Sawāniḥ safar al-Ḥijāz*, and then describes his unpleasant stay there in somewhat exaggerated terms.

> These verses were brought forth by my slow, unresponsive mind during my stay in the town of Amid. I was in a tormented mood, with my heart grieving and my tears flowing, because fate had disappointed me, destiny had taken away my loved ones, and the stay of the caravan had drawn on to the point of boredom and misery. This was due to the prevention of the officials, who wanted, out of their greed, to take some of our goods. I remained there for twelve days, without eating or sleeping at all, until, when we had just about given up our souls, God made it possible for us to leave.[35]

It is clear that these were Ottoman customs officials, Amid, the capital of the province of Diyār Bakr, lying then deep within Ottoman territory. It seems clear as well, though he does not say so explicitly, that he was leaving Iran at the time, for he mentions his separation from loved ones rather than homesickness or hopes of the anticipated return to his home in Isfahan.

After the delay, Bahā' al-Dīn continued on to Aleppo, where he had an altercation with a local Sunni scholar. Abū al-Wafā' al-'Urḍī (d. 1071/1660) reports that Bahā' al-Dīn arrived in Aleppo during the reign of the Ottoman Sultan Murād III (982-1003/1574-95) and relates the following incident, which occurred when Bahā' al-Dīn appeared at the lesson of al-'Urḍī's father, 'Umar b. Ibrāhīm (d. 1024/1615).

> He came to Aleppo in secret during the reign of the late Sulṭān Murād, seeking to join the noble pilgrimage caravan and changing his appearance to that of a dervish. He attended the lesson of my father, the Master, without revealing that he was a scholar until my father had finished the lessons. Then [Bahā' al-Dīn] asked about the

> proofs that al-Ṣiddīq [Abū Bakr] was superior to al-Murtaḍā ['Alī]. [My father] mentioned the *ḥadīth* "The sun has neither risen nor set on anyone after the prophets better than Abū Bakr." and many other similar *ḥadīths*. Then Bahā' al-Dīn answered my father, the Master, and began to cite many things which required admission of the superiority of al-Murtaḍā. My father insulted him, calling him a Shiite heretic[36] and cursing him. Bahā' al-Dīn remained silent, but later ordered one of the Persian merchants to hold a banquet and invite both my father and himself. Al-Khōjah Fatḥī held a banquet and invited them both. He told [my father], "This is al-Munlā[37] Bahā' al-Dīn, the scholar of the Land of Persia."
>
> [Bahā' al-Dīn] said to my father, "You insulted us."
>
> [My father] replied, "I did not know that you were al-Munlā Bahā' al-Dīn, but mentioning these things in front of the common people is not proper."
>
> Then [Bahā' al-Dīn] said to my father, "I am a Sunni and I love the Companions, but what can I do? Our Sultan is a Shiite and kills Sunni scholars."
>
> He had written a piece on *tafsīr* in the name of Shah 'Abbās,[38] but when he entered Sunni territory, he tore out the introduction, replacing it [with a new one] stating that he had written it in the name of Sultan Murād. He told my father, "I fear that the government officials (*umarā' al-dawlah*) will find out about me. I wrote the introduction in the name of Murād so that if they question me, I will say that I have fled from the Shah to the Sultan. If they do not ask me, I will go on the pilgrimage and then return to Persia."
>
> When the people of Jabal Banī 'Āmilah [i.e. Jabal 'Āmil] heard of his arrival, they came to see him in droves. He feared that he would be discovered, and left Aleppo.[39]

While this account should be treated with some caution, it shows, among other things, that Bahā' al-Dīn had close relations with members of the

Persian merchant community, and was probably traveling with a caravan of Persian merchants as well. Able to have banquets held at his request, he was clearly not living the life of an ascetic dervish.

From Aleppo Bahā' al-Dīn went on to Karak Nūḥ, near Ba'labakk, Lebanon, where it is reported that he met al-Ḥasan (d. 1011/1602), the son of al-Shahīd al-Thānī, who may have heard of his arrival from Iran and come north from Jabal 'Āmil to meet him before he reached Damascus.[40] After this meeting, Bahā' al-Dīn must have continued on to Damascus in order to join the caravan there to make the pilgrimage of 991/1583-84. In the period after the Ottoman conquest of Syria and Egypt in 922-23/1516-17, the pilgrimage route from Baghdad was closed, and pilgrims from Iran and Transoxania regularly joined the Damascus pilgrimage caravan.[41] The caravan usually left Damascus between the fifteenth and the twentieth of the month of Shawwāl,[42] so that Bahā' al-Dīn must have arrived there by Shawwāl 991/November 1583. He would have been in Mecca performing the rites of the pilgrimage in Dhū 'l-Ḥijjah 991/December 1583, and he records that he was composing a short treatise on *tafsīr* during his stay in Mecca itself.[43]

After performing the pilgrimage, Bahā' al-Dīn apparently did not return to Damascus, but traveled with the Egyptian caravan to Cairo instead. He would have arrived there in late Ṣafar 992/mid-March 1584.[44] In his anthology *al-Kashkūl*, he mentions that while in Cairo in 992/1584 he copied a poem from Muḥammad al-Bakrī al-Ṣiddīqī (d. 993/1585), the leader of the Bakrī Ṣūfī order, and visited the tomb of al-Shāfi'ī.[45] The contemporary Damascene litterateur Muḥammad Darwīsh al-Ṭāluwī (d. 1014/1605) reports that Bahā' al-Dīn met often with al-Bakrī during his stay in Cairo and composed a forty-line *qaṣīdah* in his praise.[46] Abū 'l-Wafā' al-'Urḍī also mentions that Bahā' al-Dīn met al-Bakrī during his stay in Cairo:

> When he arrived in Cairo the protected, he met with the gifted Master and consummate scholar Muḥammad al-Bakrī—may God bless his soul. Al-Bakrī honored him immensely, and Bahā' al-Dīn said to him, "Oh Master, I am a poor dervish. How is it that you honor me?" [Al-Bakrī] said, "I smell in you the scent of learning (*faḍl*)."[47]

In meeting with this scholar Bahā' al-Dīn was carrying on a family tradition. His father had traveled to Cairo with al-Shahīd al-Thānī in 942-43/1535-37 and had studied *tafsīr* and *fiqh* there with the leader of the Bakrī Ṣūfī order, Abū l-Ḥasan al-Bakrī (d. 953/1546-47), the father of Muḥammad al-Bakrī.[48] Bahā' al-Dīn did not always find what he sought. Part of the poem he wrote in praise of Muḥammad al-Bakrī expresses his disappointment with the general state of learning in Egypt, indicating his expectations of higher standards of scholarship there, due, perhaps, to his father's accounts of his own stay in Egypt. Bahā' al-Dīn wrote,

> Egypt, God bless you! You are a paradise; your fruit is ripe and easy to pick.
> Its soil is like gold in its fineness, its water like pure silver.
> Egyptian breeze puts musk to shame, its flowers make ambergris seem cheap. . . .
> Whoever wants to live happily there, blessed and content,
> Should put aside scholarship and its bearers, and adopt ignorance as a veil.
> Medicine and logic to one side, syntax and exegesis in a corner,
> He should leave off study and teaching, and abandon text and commentary along with the gloss.
> How long, O time, until when will your days make my life miserable?
> You grant the hopes of some out of sympathy, yet you disappoint mine.
> This is what you do to every learned man with high expectations. . . .
> Yet if you consider me one of them, then by my life you are mistaken.
> Leave off annoying me, lest I report you to His Highness.[49]

Here Bahā' al-Dīn extols the natural beauty of Egypt while apparently complaining about the standards of scholarship and the neglect of serious academic study there. His last remark about "His Highness" (*dhī 'l-ḥaḍrati 'l-'āliyah*) probably refers to the Ottoman governor of Egypt, and is perhaps intended as a jibe against the Egyptians' sycophantic behavior toward the Ottoman authorities.

The eleventh/seventeenth-century Iraqi Shiite scholar Niʿmat Allāh al-Jazāʾirī (d. 1112/1701) relates another account concerning Bahāʾ al-Dīn's stay in Cairo.

> I would like to relate a discussion which took place between Our Master Bahāʾ al-Dīn—God bless his soul—and a scholar of Egypt, one of the most learned and respected scholars there. Bahāʾ al-Dīn had led this scholar to believe that they shared the same faith. He asked Bahāʾ al-Dīn, "What do the Shiites who were before you say of the Two Shaykhs [Abū Bakr and ʿUmar]?"
>
> Bahāʾ al-Dīn—God have mercy on him—answered, "They mentioned two *ḥadīth*s to me, and I was unable to answer them."
>
> He asked, "What do they say?"
>
> I said, "They say that Muslim transmitted in his *Ṣaḥīḥ* that the Apostle of God—God bless him and his descendants—said, 'Whoever wrongs Fāṭimah has wronged me as well as God, and whoever wrongs God is an unbeliever." and that Muslim also related, five pages after this *ḥadīth*, that Fāṭimah—Peace be upon her—left this world angry with Abū Bakr and ʿUmar. I do not know how to reconcile these two *ḥadīths*."
>
> The scholar said to him, "Let me examine this tonight." When it was morning, the scholar came and said to Bahāʾ al-Dīn, "Didn't I tell you that the Shiites lie in their transmission of *ḥadīth*? Last night I examined the book and found that there were more than five pages between the two *ḥadīth*s."
>
> This was his excuse for the contradiction of the two *ḥadīths*.[50]

Niʿmat Allāh does not give the name of the Sunni scholar in question here and does not cite a specific source for this account. If the account is not apocryphal, the original source must have been Bahāʾ al-Dīn himself. An oral account may have reached Niʿmat Allāh from Muḥammad Bāqir al-Majlisī, from his father Muḥammad Taqī al-Majlisī, who was a student of Bahāʾ al-Dīn.

From Cairo, Bahā' al-Dīn headed back to Damascus, stopping at Jerusalem on the way. He reports that in Jerusalem in 992/1584 he read *Mujallī al-afrāḥ*, a commentary by Badr al-Dīn al-Zarkashī (d. 794/1392) on *Talkhīṣ al-miftāḥ*, the famous manual of rhetoric by al-Khaṭīb al-Qazwīnī (d. 739/1338), itself an abridgement of *Miftāḥ al-'ulūm* by al-Sakkākī (d. 626/1229).[51] He also met 'Umar Ibn Abī 'l-Luṭf al-Maqdisī (d. 1003/1595), the Ḥanafī *muftī* of Jerusalem, to whom he sent a poem.[52] Bahā' al-Dīn's poem, meant as an amiable display of philological erudition and scholarly trivia, presents a riddle, the answer to which is the word *al-Quds* ("Jerusalem"). Umar reciprocated by sending Bahā' al-Dīn a similar poem.[53] Al-Ṭāluwī's poetic anthology *Sāniḥāt dumā al-qaṣr* includes the following account of Bahā' al-Dīn's arrival and stay in Jerusalem, which he heard from Muḥammad Raḍiyy al-Dīn b. Yūsuf Ibn Abī 'l-Luṭf al-Maqdisī (d. Jumādā II 1028/May-June 1619), a young relative of 'Umar.[54]

> A man venerable in appearance arrived here from Egypt and stayed in Jerusalem in the open area surrounding the sanctuary. In him were the signs of piety, and he had adopted the garb of traveling mystics. He avoided people and preferred to be alone, without company. He would go frequently from the sanctuary to the courtyard of the mosque of al-Aqṣā. All the while he stayed there, no one could attribute any fault to him. It occurred to me that he was one of the greatest scholars, one of the most brilliant Persian masters. I kept trying to please him and avoid that which he did not like, until he grew accustomed to me and trusted me. Then his situation became apparent to me. He was one to whom students journey that they might study under him and transmit *ḥadīth* from him. He was named Bahā' al-Dīn Muḥammad al-Hamdānī al-Ḥārithī al-Qazwīnī. Thereupon, I asked him if I could study some sciences with him, and he said "On the condition that this be kept secret (*maktūm*)." I agreed to this, and read some astronomy and mathematical sciences, including geometry, with him. Then he proceeded to Damascus, heading towards the land of the Persians, and I heard nothing more of him."[55]

In Jumādā I 992/11 May-9 June 1584, in Jerusalem, Bahā' al-Dīn received an *ijāzah* or certificate of study from the Shāfi'ī *muftī* of Jerusalem, Muḥammad Ibn Abī 'l-Luṭf al-Maqdisī, the brother of 'Umar, the Ḥanafī *muftī* of Jerusalem mentioned above.[56] The *ijāzah*, which will be discussed in greater detail below, was issued both to Bahā' al-Dīn and to his brother—or to someone else posing as his brother—and the text of the document indicates that they were both claiming to be Sunnis and, in particular, descendants of the famous Sunni scholar al-Ghazālī. This is another case where Bahā' al-Dīn specifically sought out the descendants of the scholars his father and al-Shahīd al-Thānī had met in their own travels over forty years before. In 948/1542, al-Shahīd al-Thānī, probably accompanied by Ḥusayn, had made a short trip from Jabal 'Āmil to Jerusalem and obtained an *ijāzah* from Shams al-Dīn Ibn Abī 'l-Luṭf al-Maqdisī.[57]

From Jerusalem, Bahā' al-Dīn proceeded to Damascus. Al-Ṭāluwī reports that Bahā' al-Dīn passed through Damascus in 992/1584, after performing the pilgrimage and passing through Cairo and Jerusalem.[58] He recounts,

> When I returned [from Cairo] to Damascus, I asked someone who knew of such things about [Bahā' al-Dīn], and he informed me that [Bahā' al-Dīn] had stayed in Damascus fewer than three nights. [The informant] had met with him on one of these nights and held valuable discussions with him. This was in the company of Mawlānā al-Ḥāfiẓ al-Ḥusayn al-Karbalā'ī of Qazvin or Tabriz, who had settled in Damascus, and was the author of *al-Rawḍāt* [59] on the shrines of Tabriz, because of the brotherly friendship which had existed between them in those lands [Iran]. [The informant] asked [Bahā' al-Dīn] to recite some of his short poems [*maqāṭī'*] and other poetry. He inquired about [Bahā' al-Dīn's] name and patronym, and about his experiences in his travels. Bahā' al-Dīn mentioned to him that his *nisbah* [al-Ḥārithī] referred to Ḥārith of the Hamdān tribe, and that this ancestor of his was the man whom ['Alī b. Abī Ṭālib], the Commander of the Faithful, used to address as "*yā Ḥāri Hamdān*." He then related some anecdotes about [Ḥārith].[60]

Najm al-Dīn al-Ghazzī (d. 1061/1651), in his biographical notice on Muḥammad b. Abī ’l-Ḥasan al-Bakrī, cites the panegyric Bahā’ al-Dīn wrote for al-Bakrī and provides a short account of Bahā’ al-Dīn’s journey, perhaps based on that of al-Ṭāluwī.

> Among those who praised the Master [al-Bakrī] in poetry is the learned literateur, Muḥammad b. al-Ḥusayn al-Ḥārithī, who is Shāmī in origin and Khurāsānī by birth. He performed the pilgrimage and returned to Egypt. Then he visited Jerusalem, then entered Damascus, and left quickly from there for Iraq. He used to reside in Qazvin at the court of the king of Persia, Shah ‘Abbās, but I do not know whether he is alive now or has died.[61]

Another account of Bahā’ al-Dīn’s stay in Damascus, possibly also related to al-Ṭāluwī’s account, is given by the later Damascene scholar al-Muḥibbī (d. 1111/1699) in the biographical dictionary *Khulāṣat al-athar.*

> When he arrived in Damascus, he stayed in the quarter of al-Kharāb[62] with an important merchant. Al-Ḥāfiẓ al-Ḥusayn al-Karbalā’ī al-Qazwīnī al-Tabrīzī, the author of *al-Rawḍāt* on the holy places of Tabriz, who was staying in Damascus, met with him and asked him to recite a great deal of poetry.
>
> I have often heard that he asked to meet with al-Ḥasan al-Būrīnī. The merchant with whom he was staying summoned al-Būrīnī for him by inviting al-Būrīnī to his house and entertaining him most elegantly, along with most of the important men of his quarter. When al-Būrīnī came to the gathering, he saw Bahā’ al-Dīn there in the garb of a wandering dervish (*bi-hay’ati ’s-suyyāḥ*) at the head of the gathering, with all the others staring at him in extreme reverence. Al-Būrīnī was amazed at this, for he neither knew this person nor had ever heard of him. So he paid no attention to him, pushed him out of his place, and sat without turning to him.
>
> He started, as was his custom, to display the intricacies of his knowledge, [and continued] until they prayed the evening prayer. Then they sat down, and Bahā’ al-Dīn began to relate some anecdotes and hold some scholarly discourses,

> bringing forth a recondite discussion on *tafsīr*. He [at first] spoke on this topic with simple expressions which everyone present understood, then used more and more complex expressions until al-Būrīnī was the only one remaining who could understand what he was saying. Then he used even more obscure expressions, and all those present, including al-Būrīnī, remained silent, not moving, and not knowing what he was saying other than that they were listening to statements, objections, and replies which boggled the mind. Thereupon, al-Būrīnī jumped to his feet and said "If this is the case, then you must be al-Bahā' al-Ḥārithī, for there is no one today equal to this but he!" They embraced, and after that began reciting the most precious [poetry] they knew by heart. Bahā' al-Dīn asked al-Būrīnī to keep his presence a secret (*kitmān amrih*). They parted that night, but Bahā' al-Dīn did not linger, and left for Aleppo.[63]

This story, though perhaps exaggerated for dramatic effect, is not far-fetched in its basic outline. Al-Būrīnī (d. 1024/1615) himself relates that al-Ḥusayn al-Karbalā'ī al-Tabrīzī—known as Ibn al-Karbalā'ī—moved from Tabriz to Damascus shortly after making the pilgrimage in 988/1580-81, and stayed there until his death in Sha'bān 997/June 1589,[64] so that it is quite likely that Bahā' al-Dīn met him there in 992/1584. Al-Būrīnī reports that he and Ibn al-Karbalā'ī became very close friends and would often stay together continuously for three days and nights. Ibn al-Karbalā'ī taught al-Būrīnī Persian and calligraphy, as well as a great deal about the history and legends of the kings of Persia.[65] That al-Būrīnī was interested in Iran and things Persian is clear. He himself wrote poetry in Persian and Turkish in addition to Arabic. It is likely that he would have known who Bahā' al-Dīn was, not only because of his stature as a religious authority, but also because of his fame as a scholar and poet. The similarities between the two accounts, together with the fact that al-Būrīnī was a close friend of Ibn al-Karbalā'ī, suggests that al-'Ṭāluwī's unnamed informant may have been al-Būrīnī himself.

These last accounts show that Bahā' al-Dīn left Damascus for Aleppo after a brief stay, heading back to Iran.[66] Bahā' al-Dīn mentions that he wrote a poem in Persian expressing his homesickness for Isfahan on the road from Aleppo to Amid.

> You have brought life, oh morning breeze;
> One would say that you have come from the land of Persia!
> You have renewed the pain of longing;
> One would say that you have come from the land of Iraq!
> You could bring a soul dead for a hundred years back to life;
> If you can, pass over Isfahan.[67]

In an autograph note Bahā' al-Dīn records that he composed another Persian *ghazal* in the town of Van—north-east of Amid in what is now eastern Turkey—on 5 Ramaḍān 992/10 September 1584 "on the return trip from Mecca the Venerable" (*ayyāma 'l-mu āwadati min makkata 'l-musharrafah*)."[68]

> In this world, each wise soul is bound by the chains of love's mad passion.
> No lotus and camphor for my death shrouds!—I prefer the dust and clay of my beloved's path.
> Many people are ready to pay with their lives, but—may I die your ransom!—how much is a kiss from you?
> Our discussions of formal learning in these sinful abodes are but incense to ward off the evil eye.
> Though Bahā'ī is returning from the Ka'bah, he is still the same intoxicated penitent.[69]

A note in *al-Kashkūl* places him in Tabrīz, back in Safavid territory, on Friday, 20 Ṣafar 993/21 February 1585,[70] but he probably had arrived several months before. The entire journey took less than nineteen months, being bound by the dates 20 Rajab 991/9 August 1583 and 20 Ṣafar 993/21 February 1585. He arrived in Isfahan later that year, perhaps after visiting the court at Qazvin. He related a *ḥadīth* to his student Sayyid Ḥusayn b. Ḥaydar al-Karakī in Isfahan on 2 Ramaḍān 993/28 August 1585.[71] Bahā' al-Dīn spent the subsequent years in Isfahan and resumed his duties as *shaykh al-islām* of the city.[72]

The Practice of *Taqiyyah*

Accounts of Bahā' al-Dīn's travels reveal a great deal about the actual process of *taqiyyah*, providing valuable clues for the examination of other examples of *taqiyyah* within Twelver Shiite and other Islamic traditions. The following outline of the practice of *taqiyyah* draws primarily on the case of Bahā' al-Dīn but in addition uses other historical evidence as well as theoretical discussions of the topic in Shiite legal literature. The theoretical basis for the discussion is the assumption that religious dissimulation is a process of social interaction, and as such, may be treated using the methods of Erving Goffmann, who analyzes various types of everyday social interaction as series of performances, using the language and concepts of theater.[73] His work *Stigma: Notes on the Management of Spoiled Identity* is of particular relevance here in that it treats the social pressures members of stigmatized minorities face and discusses the types of behaviors which develop as a result of their distinct position in society. The following remarks will not attempt to recover the original circumstances surrounding early Shiite *ḥadīth* material, recount the history of Shiite discussions of *taqiyyah*, or provide a faithful record of standard Shiite doctrine. Rather, the intention here is to use both historical and theoretical material to construct an outline of *taqiyyah* as a social practice. In many instances, this view of *taqiyyah* follows closely the lines set forth in Shiite legal literature, and many of the terms and concepts used in the latter lend themselves to an analysis of *taqiyyah* from this perspective. In other instances, however, the two approaches diverge, for a variety of reasons. One need only look at the rituals Shiites perform to commemorate the martyrdom of Ḥusayn on 'Āshūrā' to realize the often wide divergences between Shiite legal theory and Shiite practice, however strongly they may be related. The goal here is not to present Shiite legal theory or discuss its historical development, but rather to describe how *taqiyyah* is actually used in everyday life.

I. THE PURPOSES AND TYPES OF *TAQIYYAH*

Taqiyyah is a principle of social interaction developed by a minority community with stigmatized status surrounded by a discriminatory and potentially oppressive majority. Many scholars, both Muslim and

Western, viewing *taqiyyah* as an article of faith and generally from the perspective of the Sunni majority, overlook the fact that similar strategies are quite common in many other societies, and see *taqiyyah* as a doctrine encouraging dishonesty and duplicity. Perhaps influenced by hostile Sunni polemics, Von Grunebaum gives an extremely unsympathetic portrayal of *taqiyyah* as practiced by the Twelver Shiites, equating it with hypocrisy and lack of moral conviction:

> Intransigence and intolerance are made particularly unpleasant by the doctrine of *taqiyya*. . . . The Shiite is bidden to act like a Sunni when dominated by a Sunni government. The injunction met with sufficient responsc to imbue medieval Shiism with a most unattractive flavor of moral ambiguity. The Shiite in non-Shiite territory lives the life of a conspirator. He curses in private whom he joins in public. The laws of morality are valid only within the conventicle. . . . A blend of self-pity and self-righteousness, unmeasured hatred and unmeasured devotion, made up the atmosphere surrounding the Friends of the Household.[74]

Von Grunebaum has little sympathy for this persecuted minority, and fails to see that *taqiyyah* embodies a natural response to social, economic, and political oppression or discrimination and the legal consequences of heresy in Islam. He further sees *taqiyyah* as the most characteristic feature of Shiism, though Kohlberg has suggested that it is far from clear that *taqiyyah* is a fundamental article of Shiite faith, and holds that one must take a more nuanced view of the topic.[75] This sort of dissimulation is not unique to Shiism; *taqiyyah* is also an accepted principle in Sunni Islam, and, as Kohlberg aptly notes, similar strategies have been adopted by various other religions as well.[76] One can generalize even further; it is in fact a pattern of behavior employed by many stigmatized groups, whether they be religious, ethnic, or other minorities, in a wide variety of societies. The Shiite scholar Muḥsin al-Amīn voices an opinion about *taqiyyah* quite opposed, as one would expect, to that of von Grunebaum. Interpreting the career of Jamāl al-Dīn al-Afghānī (d. 1314-1897) as an example of *taqiyyah*, he gives the following assessment of al-Afghānī's concealment of the fact that he was Iranian:

> Were it not for this, he would not have been called "the Sage of Islam" or "the Philosopher of the East," nor would he have attained such great fame, nor would the Grand Vizier ʻAlī Pasha have received him in Istanbul with such unprecedented respect and honor, nor would ministers and princes have honored him so, nor would he have been appointed a member of the Academy of Sciences (*majlis al-maʻārif*), nor would the Egyptian government have paid him a monthly stipend of one thousand Egyptian piasters, nor would al-Shaykh Muḥammad ʻAbduh have been able to associate with him, study under him, or adopt him as a spiritual mentor and close friend.[77]

Al-Amīn's main point here is that al-Afghānī's use of *taqiyyah* was nothing more than a natural response to the systematic discrimination against Shiites in societies dominated by a Sunni majority.

It cannot be denied that Shiites have suffered on account of their faith during many periods of Islamic history and in many regions of the Muslim world. *Taqiyyah* developed as a method by which they could promote the welfare of the minority community and stave off harm from a potentially hostile majority while avoiding assimilation or the abandonment of sectarian religious convictions. In periods of great danger for the Shiites, *taqiyyah* assumed an important role in defining the minority community, providing its solidarity and even making its survival possible. Many of the twenty-three *ḥadīth* reports which make up the section on *taqiyyah* in *al-Kāfī*, the earliest of the four standard collections of Shiite *ḥadīth,* compiled by Muḥammad b. Yaʻqūb al-Kulaynī (d. 329/941), stress the importance of *taqiyyah* and its central position in Shiite faith.[78] They include such statements as "*Taqiyyah* is part of God's religion" (*at-taqiyyatu min dīni 'Llāh*); "*Taqiyyah* is part of my religion and that of my ancestors" (*at-taqiyyatu min dīnī wa-dīni ābāʼī*); "In *taqiyyah* lie nine tenths of the religion" (*inna tisʻata aʻshāri 'd-dīni fī 't-taqiyyah*); and "He who has no *taqiyyah* has no faith" (*lā īmāna li-man lā taqiyyata lah*). The Imams are depicted as exhorting the believers to practice *taqiyyah*. Jaʻfar al-Ṣādiq is reported as asking the rhetorical question, "What pleases me more than *taqiyyah*?" (*wa-ayyu shayʼin aqarru li-ʻaynī min at-taqiyyah*) and stating "By God, nothing on the face of the earth is more pleasing to me than *taqiyyah*" (*wa 'Llāhi mā 'alā wajhi 'l-arḍi shay'un aḥabbu ilayya min at-taqiyyah*). *Taqiyyah* is portrayed in such reports as a crucial obligation of the believer and a necessary part of the religion.

The twentieth-century scholar Khomeini suggests that the *ḥadīth*s of the Imams which stress *taqiyyah* to such an extreme degree refer to *kitmān*, "secrecy," in particular, one of four types of *taqiyyah* he distinguishes.[79] *Kitmān*, he holds, is that type of *taqiyyah* which is required for its own sake (*maṭlūbah li-dhātihā*) as opposed to other types, which are required for other reasons (*maṭlūbah li-ghayrihā*).[80] These reports seem to emphasize the character of Shiism as a secret and potentially revolutionary organization. The first duty of any member in the organization is *kitmān* "secrecy," i.e., concealment of the organization's existence and particularly the position of its leader, and the worst possible sin he can commit is *idhā'ah*, "spreading the secret," i.e, to reveal the organization or betray its leader. The safety of the entire group depends on this obligation of secrecy. Several *ḥadīth*s stress that *taqiyyah* is crucial for preservation of the sectarian community, particularly regarding hiding allegiance to the Imam. Ja'far al-Ṣādiq is reported as addressing the following warning to his followers:

> You among the generality of the people are like bees among birds. If the birds only knew what lay hidden inside the bees, they would not leave any of them uneaten, and if the people only knew what lay hidden inside you, that is, that you love the descendants of the Prophet, they would eat you with their tongues and heap invective upon you, both in secret and in the open.[81]

Many other *ḥadīth*s in al-Kulaynī's section on *taqiyyah* as well as the following section on *kitmān* stress the importance of concealing the identity of the Imam from outsiders. Ja'far al-Ṣādiq is reported as saying, "He who broadcasts our situation is like he who denies us."[82] In another *ḥadīth*, Ja'far al-Ṣādiq praises a believer for pretending not to recognize him in public.[83] The type of system this seems to reflect is described by the sociologist Georg Simmel as a "secret society"[84] and recalls the medieval Ismā'īlī *da'wah* organization. Khomeini holds that *kitmān* is enjoined when one lives under an illegitimate regime (*dawlat al-bāṭil*) waiting for the advent of legitimate rule (*dawlat al-ḥaqq*).[85] He states that the purposes behind *kitmān* "are both political and religious—were it not for (this type of) *taqiyyah*, the sect would have become subject to disappearance and extinction."[86] In Twelver Shiism, however, such prescriptions have long since lost much of their relevance, for with the Imam in occultation, the immediate threat to Sunni government was reduced and Twelver Shiism lost much of its potential revolutionary character.[87]

Khomeini distinguishes two main types of *taqiyyah* used in the non-revolutionary situation. One of these is *taqiyyah mudārātiyyah*, "conciliatory *taqiyyah*," used to attract the Sunnis' good will and prevent the spread of discord among the Muslim community for the sake of internal harmony and solidarity against outside threats.[88] This interpretation of *taqiyyah* finds support particularly in a *ḥadīth* where Ja'far al-Ṣādiq urges the Shiites to pray in the gatherings of the Sunnis, visit their sick, and attend their funerals—in short, to participate in their social life.[89] Thus, Shiites are urged to blend as completely as possible into the Sunni community, and even to act as exemplary members of it. The Imam adds, "Do not let them do any good before you, for you are more worthy of it than they."[90] Khomeini remarks that such behavior is highly laudable, reporting that praying in the front row among Sunnis is like praying behind the Prophet.[91] This type of *taqiyyah* is different from other types in that it is not undertaken as a reaction to duress or the anticipation of harm, that is, it is not seen as a defensive measure adopted out of fear of attacks on the part of Sunnis, but rather as a positive measure undertaken to avoid antagonizing opponents and improve relations between Muslims.

The remaining type of *taqiyyah* is *taqiyyah iḍṭirāriyyah*, or "*taqiyyah* out of compulsion." Khomeini distinguishes two sub-categories, *taqiyyah ikrāhiyyah*, or "*taqiyyah* by coercion," and *taqiyyah khawfiyyah* or "*taqiyyah* out of fear." He discusses *taqiyyah ikrāhiyyah* in another work, his *Risālah fī al-makāsib al-muḥarramah*, in connection with the question of being appointed to an office by an illegitimate ruler against one's will.[92] *Taqiyyah khawfiyyah* is used when one fears harm; this is the main category of relevance to the present discussion, for it has to do with the everyday behavior of the Shiite believer in a potentially hostile environment.

The primary purpose of *taqiyyah* is to avoid harm to one's person (*daf' al-ḍarar*),[93] and the seventeenth-century Iraqi scholar Niʿmat Allāh al-Jazāʾirī holds that Shiites who do not use *taqiyyah* risk suffering harm (*yataḥammalūna 'ḍ-ḍarar*).[94] While *taqiyyah* is deemed important for an individual's safety, as seen in the *ḥadīth* "*Taqiyyah* is the shield of the believer and his fortress,"[95] a key idea in the use of *taqiyyah* is that the actions of any member of the community potentially reflect on all other members. The faithful must be careful to avoid acts that might put co-religionists in a compromising position. One *ḥadīth* attributed to Jaʿfar al-Ṣādiq states this explicitly, drawing a comparison between the Shiite community and a family: "Take heed not to do anything for which they will reproach us, for the bad son brings blame upon his father through his actions. Be an adornment for him to whom you have sworn allegiance, and not a mark of shame."[96] In sociological terms, this *ḥadīth* emphasizes the fact that Shiism is a tribal stigma, which Goffman sees to include race, nation, and religion.[97] Unlike stigma such as physical deformities or blindness, sectarian allegiance, like ethnic identity in general, is usually viewed as running in families, and as propagating less through conversion than through *taqlīd al-ābāʾ* "following the ways of one's ancestors." The harm one fears in a situation where one decides to use *taqiyyah* need not be directed against oneself. Khomeini holds that one may use *taqiyyah* if there is an expectation of harm to (1) one's self, the honor of one's women, one's property or belongings; (2) one's fellow believers, close relatives or companions; or (3) the Muslim community in general.[98] In fact, one of the Shiites' main justifications for the obligatory use of dissimulation is that it not only protects the individual performing dissimulation, but also reduces the risk to his co-religionists, the sectarian community at large.[99]

The harm one seeks to avoid through *taqiyyah* can be of various types. Khomeini mentions as examples of duress imprisonment or the payment of a fine.[100] The seventeenth-century scholar al-Ḥurr al-ʿĀmilī reports instances of the execution of Shiites in this regard.[101] Bahāʾ al-Dīn was of course aware that his father's teacher and close friend al-Shahīd al-Thānī had been killed by Ottoman officials less than thirty years before. Al-Jazāʾirī also includes as possible types of harm beating (*ḍarb*), other forms of physical abuse (*adhā*), and verbal abuse (*ihānah*), implying that the most prevalent of these forms in everyday life is verbal abuse.[102] In another work he in fact describes an extended insult-*cum*-rock throwing match which he witnessed in his youth between a group of Shiites sailing on a canal in southern Iraq and a group of Sunnis on the shore.[103] Similarly, in Bahā' al-Dīn's case, his neglect to adhere strictly to *taqiyyah* at al-'Urḍī's lesson in Aleppo resulted in his being insulted in public.

II. *TAQIYYAH* AS PERFORMANCE

In his study of the Druze in modern Israel, Layish sees *taqiyyah* as a complex behavioral pattern which involves a sustained and careful act. A Druze tradition attributed to al-Ḥākim states, "Keep me in your hearts but wear what is proper to wear and represent yourselves (*taẓāharū*), to the best of your ability, as wholly belonging to that religion [Christianity or Islam]."[104] A manual of the Druze faith requires Druze fathers to teach their sons how to adapt to the environment.[105] Layish's main focus is the application of family law in modern Israel, and he finds that the Druze have long paid lip-service to the Ḥanafī school as regards family and inheritance law, while nevertheless following, in many cases, contradictory or distinctly Druze practices.[106] He concludes, "*Taqiyya* is a dynamic, not a static, doctrine; adaptation and assimilation to the environment are not one-time acts but continuous processes determined by changing circumstances of place and time."[107]

As members of an Islamic sect which has often been viewed as heretical by the Sunni majority, Shiites possess a stigma, or a particular discrediting attribute which is seen by non-Shiites to bar their full acceptance as members of society.[108] They run risks of rejection, unfavorable treatment, or harm from their Sunni interlocutors. The stigma of Shiism, unlike many physical disabilities, for example, is relatively easy to conceal upon interaction with Sunnis; the Shiite is, in Goffman's terms, *discreditable* rather than *discredited*.[109] The Shiite therefore develops a routine or collection of behaviors whose purpose is to conceal his discrediting attribute, i.e., his adherence to Shiism, and it is these behaviors which are termed *taqiyyah*. *Taqiyyah* is in this sense identical to the general sociological term "passing," the strategy of managing undisclosed discrediting information about the self that a stigmatized individual adopts in trying to blend in with "normals."[110] Phenomena similar to *taqiyyah* have been treated by anthropologists under the rubric of ethnicity[111] and by sociologists under the rubrics of impression management, identity management, or identity negotiation.[112] A key feature of these analyses is their use of the dramatic concept of a role. Persons adopting a certain identity are acting out a role, and all their actions and the information they give out must be consistent with the requirements of that role. *Taqiyyah* is in essence a method used to alter or conceal part of one's identity, and may be treated using similar concepts.

The need for *taqiyyah* only arises during social interactions, and occurs as a response to a specific social situation in which the performer senses fear or compulsion before a potentially hostile audience. *Taqiyyah* may therefore be viewed as a dramaturgical discipline governing the behavior of the performer in the presence of this audience.[113] Since its purpose is the control of social information, the performance of *taqiyyah* is a complex process which depends not only on the intentions of the performer but also on societal expectations, audience, interactional situations, and feedback. For example, since Shiism is a tribal stigma held to run in families, a performer of *taqiyyah* will find it necessary to control information about his family connections as part of the performance, even though they may be of no immediate relevance to the interaction itself. Alluding to the interconnectedness of such information, a *ḥadīth* from al-Kulaynī's compilation warns, "Beware the consequences of slip-ups" (*iḥdharū 'awāqiba 'l-'atharāt*).[114] While this statement may be taken simply as a moralistic imperative to consider the consequences of one's sins, al-Kulaynī seems to have included it in his section on *taqiyyah* in part to imply that *taqiyyah* is not a single statement or action during a time of duress, but rather a careful and sustained performance which might involve many disparate acts. These occasional acts are interrelated in a complex narrative which makes up the individual's social identity, and a contradictory statement or act may betray an intended portrayal built up in the course of previous statements or acts. The questions which face the performer of *taqiyyah* are those which face the stigmatized individual trying to hide his stigma; in Goffman's words, "To display or not to display; to tell or not to tell; to let on or not to let on; to lie or not to lie; and in each case, to whom, how, when, and where."[115]

That *taqiyyah* involves a sustained act is clear. Khomeini observes that Shiites in Sunni regions are afflicted with *taqiyyah* "night and day" (*laylan nahāran*).[116] Al-Shahīd al-Awwal, the scholar mentioned above who was executed in Damascus, spent many years studying and teaching in a predominantly Sunni environment. Ibn al-Labbān (d. 749/1349), a Damascene Sunni teacher of al-Shahīd al-Awwal to whom he was particularly close, makes the following remarks about him: "He was an accomplished scholar in law, syntax, and recitation of the Qur'ān. He was my fellow for a lengthy period, and I never heard from him anything contrary to the Sunnis."[117] Even though their relationship lasted for a long time (*muddah madīdah*), probably a number of years, Ibn al-Labbān saw no evidence whatsoever that his student was a Shiite. This was clearly a sustained performance on al-Shahīd al-Awwal's part. Similarly, Bahā' al-Dīn's observer in Jerusalem, Raḍiyy al-Dīn Ibn Abī 'l-Luṭf al-Maqdisī, remarks that although Bahā' al-Dīn stayed there for some time, no one could attribute any fault to him. This remark, together with the anecdotal evidence showing Bahā' al-Dīn using *taqiyyah* on many separate occasions during his travels, also supports the suggestion that practical *taqiyyah* should be seen as a performance more than a collection of disparate acts.

III. THE PERFORMER OF *TAQIYYAH*: *AL-MUTTAQĪ, ṢĀḤIB AL-TAQIYYAH*

The use of *taqiyyah* involves a performer, termed *al-muttaqī* or *ṣāḥib al-taqiyyah* "one who exercises caution."[118] Al-Jazā'irī sees performers of *taqiyyah* as falling into two main categories, commoners (*'awāmm*) and scholars (*khawāṣṣ*), and implies that scholars are generally better informed about *taqiyyah* and therefore more successful performers.[119] Khomeini gives four categories of performers: 1) the Prophet and the Imams, 2) Shiite legal scholars and religious leaders (*ru'asā' al-madhhab*), 3) Shiite rulers and officials, and 4) common people such as merchants.[120] He holds that if the performer of *taqiyyah* is looked upon as a leader or someone of importance by the the common people, certain types of *taqiyyah* which would be allowed for an ordinary person would be forbidden to him. For example, for a religious leader to drink alcohol out of *taqiyyah* would weaken the religion or violate its sanctity and would therefore be forbidden, while a commoner's doing so would not have the same effect and so would be permissible.[121] Khomeini also reports that

Shiite commoners (*al-'āmmah*) wrongly resort to ruses rather than exercising *taqiyyah*, avoiding prayer in public places such as the mosque or the market so that they might perform it in the correct manner in private, and thus needlessly cause themselves harm.[122] He reports, for example, that in recent times when the Sunnis stand at 'Arafah on the eighth day of the pilgrimage (it should be the ninth) because they sighted the new moon a day before the Shiites, ignorant Shiites (*juhhāl al-shī'ah*) try to make it up the next day rather than simply following along with the majority.[123] Bahā' al-Dīn's status as a scholar and his familiarity with the doctrine and legal stipulations of *taqiyyah*, as well as its more popular manifestations, presumably made him a better performer than a commoner. Because of his background, he also must have had considerable information at his disposal concerning social life, customs, and intersectarian relations in the regions through which he was traveling which were then under Ottoman rule. On the other hand, his interest in scholarship and desire to debate religious issues with Sunnis might get him into more difficult situations than a commoner would generally face, such as his altercation with al-'Urḍī in Aleppo.

The performance of *taqiyyah* is governed to a great extent by the individual judgment of the believer. While there are few detailed discussions of the exact circumstances which require performance of *taqiyyah* in legal sources, a *ḥadīth* attributed to Muḥammad al-Bāqir, the fifth Imam, gives the principle that the individual believer must use his own judgment in deciding when to do so: "*Taqiyyah* is for every necessity, and he who is compelled to use it knows best when [the need to use] it befalls him" (*at-taqiyyatu fī kulli ḍarūratin wa-ṣāḥibuhā a'lamu bihā ḥīna tanzilu bih*).[124] Al-Ḥurr al-'Āmilī emphasizes the fact that the performance of *taqiyyah* is dependent on the personal judgement of the performer, holding, "the one who is present sees what he who is absent does not" (*wa'l-ḥāḍiru yarā mā lā yarāhu 'l-ghā'ib*).[125] He stresses that the evaluation of possible harm is subjective and must be left up to the individual: "The fear of harm is an emotional state and has many causes of which, in most instances, only the one affected can be aware" (*wa-khawfu 'ḍ-ḍarari wijdāniyyun wa-asbābuhā kathīratun lā yaṭṭali'u 'alayhā ghayru ṣāḥibuhā ghāliban*).[126] Nevertheless, a performer is often part of a group, Goffman's "team," who cooperate with him in order to effect a particular performance and who are privy to discrediting information which the audience does not possess.[127] This social fact is not usually stressed in the legal sources, which focus on the obligations of individuals, there being no specific term for this group other than vague references to fellow sectarians such as *ikhwān*, "brothers," or *mu'minūn*, "believers." In the case of Bahā' al-Dīn, it is clear that the "brother" who is mentioned in his *ijāzah*, as well as the Persian merchants with whom he traveled, were fully aware of his actual identity and actively cooperated in concealing it while at the same time trying to pass as Sunnis themselves.

IV. THE AUDIENCE OF *TAQIYYAH: AL-MUTTAQĀ MINHU*

As a performance, *taqiyyah* involves an interlocutor or audience, termed *al-muttaqā minhu*, "he before whom one exercises caution."[128] Al-Ḥurr al-'Āmilī states that the audience may be either Sunni scholars (*'ulamā' al-'āmmah*) or illegitimate rulers (*salāṭīn al-jawr wa-ḥukkām aḍ-ḍalālah*).[129] It is not clear whether by this last statement he means to include illegitimate Shiite rulers as well as Sunni rulers, but the rest of his discussion shows that he deems *taqiyyah* to be used primarily for a Sunni audience, common people included, whom he terms *al-mukhālifūn* "(our) opponents."[130] In a more comprehensive list, Khomeini holds that the audience may consist of (1) non-Muslims (*kuffār*), whether rulers (*salāṭīn*) or common people (*ra'iyyah*); (2) Sunni rulers and government officials (*salāṭīn al-'āmmah wa-umarā'uhum*); (3) Sunni judges (*quḍāt*) and legal scholars (*fuqahā'*); (4) Sunni commoners (*'awāmm*); or (5) Shiites, whether rulers (*salāṭīn*) or commoners (*'awāmm*).[131] The possible audiences for *taqiyyah* are presented here not merely out of legal thoroughness but also because of the principle that the performance of *taqiyyah* must be adjusted according to the audience in question. Al-Ḥurr al-'Āmilī states this principle succinctly when he remarks that a certain use of *taqiyyah* is advisable "because the criterion is he from whom one fears harm" (*li'anna 'l-mu'tabara huwa man yukhāfu minhu 'ḍ-ḍarar*).[132] As an example of how audience affects the performance of *taqiyyah*, he remarks that whereas Shiites in many regions might successfully claim to be Shāfi'īs, this would be of no avail in areas of North Africa with entirely Mālikī populations, where, he reports, they kill whoever claims to be a Shāfi'ī on the mere grounds of that *madhhab*'s affinity with Shiism.[133]

While the original *taqiyyah*, that of 'Ammār b. Yāsir, was directed at a pagan audience, Shiite *taqiyyah* has been traditionally discussed and practiced with the audience of the Sunni majority in mind. Most *ḥadīth*s refer implicitly to the Sunnis (*al-mukhālifūn*) though they do not limit the application of *taqiyyah* to them.[134] Khomeini states in another passage that during the modern period, the Shiites' need to use *taqiyyah* is mostly limited to Sunni audiences,[135] so that, one assumes, the relevant categories with respect to practical *taqiyyah* are Sunni rulers, government officials, judges, legal scholars, and commoners. Khomeini therefore sees the term *dār al-taqiyyah*, "the Abode of Caution," as applying in the contemporary era almost exclusively to territory under Sunni rule, although he clearly envisions the possibilty of the *dār al-taqiyyah* referring to an area under Christian rule, for example.[136] One *ḥadīth* attributed to Muḥammad al-Bāqir emphasizes political rule as the crucial factor in deciding whether or not to use *taqiyyah*: "Go along with them outwardly but oppose them inwardly when the rule belongs to childish fools." (*khāliṭūhum bi 'l-barrāniyyah, wa khālifūhum bi 'l-juwwāniyyah, idhā kānat il-imratu ṣibyāniyyah*).[137] The modern Iraqi Shiite author al-Muẓaffar holds that Shiites have needed to use *taqiyyah* most with respect to Sunni governments, particularly "the enemies of the family of the Prophet," which include, according to him, the Umayyads, the Abbasids, and the Ottomans.[138]

In Bahā' al-Dīn's case, the audience were obviously Sunnis in general, and the accounts suggest a division of the audience into three sub-categories similar to those found in Khomeini's list: government officials, scholars, and commoners. Bahā' al-Dīn was in an area under Sunni Ottoman rule, a situation he shared with other Shiites traveling in the region for trade or to perform the pilgrimage, but at that particular time, the Ottomans were at war with his patrons, the Shiite Safavids. The danger which faced Bahā' al-Dīn was not only that he be accused of heresy, but also, perhaps, that he be accused of spying for the Safavids. These two threats were in fact closely related. While Sunni scholars could accuse him of heresy, they could only have him executed by recourse to the government, and Muslim sectarians were most often repressed if they were perceived to threaten the state.[139] The example of the martyrdom of al-Shahīd al-Thānī a generation earlier would alone have convinced a

Shiite scholar to keep a low profile. The Ottomans might have considered Bahā' al-Dīn a Safavid government agent, in which case he would not have been allowed to wander around as he pleased, and his presence would be interpreted as a threat to security, especially if, as al-'Urḍī mentions, the Shiites of Jabal 'Āmil flocked to him in droves. Bahā' al-Dīn was obviously worried about this. It is also likely that he feared Ottoman officials would have access to discrediting or incriminating information about him from their spies in the Safavid Empire. Bahā' al-Dīn's concern with avoiding contact with government officials is seen in his extreme disturbance at being stopped at the border at Amid for so long, and his repeated requests for *kitmān* or "concealment." Al-'Urḍī's report of the changed dedication of a treatise on *tafsīr* points to Bahā' al-Dīn's need to hide his connections with the Safavid government and his worries about being stopped by Ottoman officials (*umarā' al-dawlah*). It also shows, however, that Bahā' al-Dīn had a contingency plan in the event he were actually apprehended. He would claim that he had fled from the Safavid Shah and intended to petition the Ottoman Sultan. The treatise on *tafsīr* al-'Urḍī claims was dedicated to the Sultan Murād III would serve as evidence that this was so, for it was common practice for scholars to write a work dedicated to a ruler when seeking refuge at his court or employment in his administration. It was, in effect, Bahā' al-Dīn's Sunni passport.[140] Similarly, the *ijāzah* Bahā' al-Dīn received in Jerusalem may have been intended to serve less as an indication of his scholarly credentials in a general sense than as additional proof that he was a Sunni in the event he were stopped.[141]

The image of Bahā' al-Dīn as a cunning hero who always managed to stay just out of the reach of inimical Ottoman officials lives on in the folklore of Shiite southern Lebanon.[142] According to a modern 'Āmilī folk tale ascribing supernatural powers to Bahā' al-Dīn, Ottoman soldiers tried to arrest him many times, without success. Whenever they had him cornered, he would disappear, for he was endowed with the ability to become invisible at will. Finally, the Ottoman soldiers tricked him into contracting a temporary *mut'ah* marriage, for they knew that Bahā' al-Dīn would not be able to become invisible when in a state of ritual impurity. Bahā' al-Dīn fell for the trap, and was successfully captured after consummating the marriage. As the soldiers carried him down the street, however,

Bahā' al-Dīn noticed that a woman was about to pour out some water from a window above. Quickly performing the declaration of intention (*niyyah*) in preparation for a major ablution (*ghusl*), he regained his ritual purity when the water landed on him, turned invisible, and escaped once again.[143]

When al- Urḍī endeavors to excuse himself for insulting Bahā' al-Dīn, he claims that it was not appropriate to say such things in the presence of the common people (*al-'a wāmm*). His argument, which provokes the remark "This is an excuse more heinous than the fault itself" (*hādhā 'udhrun aqbaḥu min adh-dhanb*) on the part of Muḥsin al-Amīn,[144] defines two remaining groups of Sunnis before whom Bahā' al-Dīn must perform *taqiyyah*: scholars and commoners. Al-'Urḍī implies that the commoners will either be quick to take offense and judge Bahā' al-Dīn a heretic, or else likely to be led astray by his remarks, whereas scholars like himself can be more understanding and tolerant of differences of opinion. Bahā' al-Dīn clearly had many contacts with Sunni scholars during his journey, and while one assumes that they had more authority to denounce him as a heretic, they were also the men Bahā' al-Dīn sought out as colleagues with whom he could have learned discussions and exchanges. The anecdotes make it clear that personal, private connections between scholars allowed Bahā' al-Dīn to reveal more than he could in a public situation. This distinction between public and private settings is seen in a number of the anecdotes of the journey. Raḍiyy al-Dīn al-Maqdisī relates how he gradually won Bahā' al-Dīn's confidence and studied with him, and the banquets held for Bahā' al-Dīn in Aleppo and Damascus provided the opportunities where he could speak more freely, though he apparently even in these settings did not reveal outright that he was a Shiite. This may be contrasted with the example of al-Shahīd al-Thānī, who was probably passing as a Shāfi'ī student of law in Cairo in 942-43/1535-37, yet records a private conversation he had with one of his Shāfi'ī teachers, Abū 'l-Ḥasan al-Bakrī, which clearly reveals that al-Bakrī was aware of his Shiite identity.[145] The banquet in Aleppo is of particular significance, for it appears that here Bahā' al-Dīn was manipulating the setting, by having al-'Urḍī as a guest at a private gathering surrounded by Bahā' al-Dīn's friends and patrons, in order to induce him to apologize for his behavior in the more public lesson.

V. THE SUBSTANCE OF *TAQIYYAH: AL-MUTTAQĀ FĪHI*

The bulk of secondary literature on *taqiyyah* implies that it allows one to do two things: deny one's faith or violate individual points of law to follow majority practice, as in performing prayer or ritual ablutions. The substance of *taqiyyah* is generally seen as being limited to these areas.[146] In Shiite legal literature as well, *taqiyyah* of the *iḍṭirāriyyah* variety is considered with regard to its effect upon specific legal obligations. It is viewed as a type of special dispensation (*rukhṣah, ḍarūrah, 'udhr*) which changes the effect of a legal ruling for a given situation without altering its essence.[147] It rests on the assumptions that some extremely important legal obligations, such as the duty to preserve life, override lesser obligations, such as the duty to pray in a specific manner, and that the intention (*niyyah*) or inner state (*bāṭin*) of the believer is generally a truer indication of his faith than his outer actions.

The actual substance of *taqiyyah, i.e.*, the specific information which is being concealed or controlled or the acts which are being performed or omitted, is termed by Khomeini *al-muttaqā fīhi*, "that concerning which caution is exercised."[148] Al-Ḥurr al-'Āmilī, though he does not use this specific term, sees *taqiyyah* as applying to two main categories of activity, ritual obligations (*'amal*) and, the domain of jurists in particular, issuing legal opinions (*fatwā*).[149] According to Khomeini, the substance of *taqiyyah* may include (1) committing a forbidden act (*fi'l muḥarram*); (2) omitting an obligatory duty (*tark wājib*); (3) omitting a necessary part of or prerequisite for a duty (*tark sharṭ aw juz'*) or committing an act which in reality invalidates or prevents the fulfillment of a duty (*fi'l māni' aw qāṭi'*); or (4) acting in accordance with an extra-legal circumstance (*mawḍū' khārijī*) in the manner the audience of the *taqiyyah* performance deems necessary.[150] In practice, Khomeini observes that since the main audience for *taqiyyah* are Sunnis, categories one and two above, which concern absolute or essential obligations (*taklīfāt*), are generally irrelevant because Sunni interlocutors would not pressure Shiites to drink wine or give up performing the ritual prayer, for example.[151] Most actual instances which require *taqiyyah* involve circumstantial obligations (*waḍ'iyyāt*), encompassed in the last two categories above, with which, Khomeini reports, Shiites are afflicted continually.[152] Similarly, al-Ḥurr al-ʿĀmilī remarks that *taqiyyah* is most often applied to particular acts (*juzʾiyyāt*) falling under the legal categories of *makrūh* "reprehensible" and *mustaḥabb* "commendable," rather than essential or general obligations (*kulliyyāt*).[153] Examples of such obligations are performing the prayer in the Sunni manner or breaking the fast when the Sunnis declare that the month of Ramaḍān has ended. The bulk of concrete examples in Khomeini's treatise deal with ritual prayer and ablutions, fasting and breaking the fast, and the rites of the pilgrimage to Mecca. These are the most public ritual obligations, concerning which the average Shiite believer may be most exposed to criticism or danger from the Sunni majority. Of special concern is the pilgrimage, because it represents, for many Shiite participants—and especially Iranians since the sixteenth century—their first and often only experience in a majority Sunni setting. Furthermore, the pilgrimage rituals force them to fulfill their religious obligations in close proximity with Sunnis, and the participants' conscience of the pilgrimage's sanctity renders criticism on ritual matters all the more likely and infractions all the more serious. Bahāʾ al-Dīn was also, of course, performing the pilgrimage, whatever other motives were behind his trip, and it is probable that any Shiite believer of his day would have paid some attention to the topic of *taqiyyah* when about to undertake this pious journey from Iran into Sunni-controlled areas.

Khomeini and other scholars in the Shiite legal tradition discuss some of the exceptions to *taqiyyah*. These include, according to him, the greatest forbidden things (*ʿaẓāʾim al-muḥarramāt*) such as the destruction of the Kaʿbah, the tomb of the Prophet, or other holy sites (*mashāhid musharrafah*) or criticism of Islam, the Qurʾān, or *tafsīr* in a way which would lead to the corruption of the faith and the spread of atheism.[154] He also considers *taqiyyah* forbidden if the ruler tries to change fundamental principles of Islam, such as the laws concerning prayer, pilgrimage, divorce, or inheritance.[155] A number of *ḥadīth*s state that one may not drink wine, give up *mutʿat al-ḥajj*—performing the *ʿumrah* immediately before performing the regular pilgrimage—or perform *al-masḥ ʿalā ʾl-khuffayn*—wiping the shoes in ritual ablution for prayer instead of washing the feet in certain circumstances[156]—out of *taqiyyah*, but Khomeini holds that these cannot be taken literally, it being better to perform prayer without performing ablutions properly than not to pray at all, or better to perform the pilgrimage without an additional *'umrah* than not to perform the pilgrimage at all, and permissible to drink wine if in great danger, although one should be able to avoid drinking wine through some other excuse.[157] Other *ḥadīths* suggest that 'Alī told his followers that they could insult him if need be but not deny him, but Khomeini holds that one is allowed to deny the Imam, holding that the *ḥadīth* in question "sounds like a lie."[158] One cannot kill anyone out of *taqiyyah*, for such an act would contradict *taqiyyah*'s original purpose, to protect lives.[159] Al-Muẓaffar adds that one must not use *taqiyyah* if it results in the spreading of falsehood and injustice.[160]

Since Shiite legal literature focuses on the legal status of individual acts, it tends to treat cases atomistically despite the fact that they may be part of on-going processes, as is clearly the case with the use of *taqiyyah* by Shiites living within predominantly Sunni societies. As Khomeini notes above, such Shiites are afflicted with *taqiyyah* "night and day." Al-Ḥurr al-'Āmilī stresses that certain points concerning the workings of *taqiyyah* are only fully clear to some one who has lived among Sunnis for a considerable period of time and practiced it among them (*man 'āshara l-mukhālifīna wa-'amila bi't-taqiyyati fīmā baynahum*).[161] When Raḍiyy al-Dīn al-Maqdisī, the Sunni native of Jerusalem who recorded Bahā' al-Dīn's stay in the city, observes, "All the while he stayed there, no one could attribute any fault to him," he reveals the importance of *taqiyyah* as a sustained performance and not a single act. This aspect of *taqiyyah*, although not completely lost in the legal literature, is not stressed because of the particular constraints and concerns of that genre.

In addition, the legal literature is not as a rule interested in actions devoid of intrinsic legal significance unless they impinge upon some legal obligation. For example, the fact that, say, one's neighbor breaks the Ramaḍān fast a day early has in itself no legal value, for his actions do not affect the original obligation to break the fast at the end of the month. If the Sunnis in a particular region break the fast a day early, however, Khomeini holds that one should break the fast along with them.[162] Here, he has considered an extra-legal circumstance (*mawḍū' khārijī*)—i.e., the fact that the Sunnis broke the fast—only because it impinges upon a specific religious obligation of the Shiites. In actuality, there are many extra-legal circumstances, in the form of information, customs, actions, etc., which do not impinge directly on religious obligations[163] but nevertheless impinge on social identity, and therefore may form part of the performance of *taqiyyah*. Several *ḥadīth*s contained in *al-Kāfī* and attributed to Muḥammad al-Bāqir point to such an extended view of *taqiyyah*, indicating that *taqiyyah* is to be applied to anything in which coercion or necessity is involved. They read, "*Taqiyyah* is to be used in every necessity" (*at-taqiyyatu fī kulli ḍarūrah*)[164] and "*Taqiyyah* is to be applied to everything to which man is compelled" (*at-taqiyyatu fī kulli shay'in yuḍṭarru ilayhi 'bnu ādam*).[165] In line with these *ḥadīth*s, Goldziher states of the Shiite believer, "In a region ruled by his enemies he must *speak and act* (italics mine) as though he were of their number in order not to draw down peril and persecution on his comrades."[166] Such aspects are not treated in detail in the legal literature, and it is only from actual performances such as that of Bahā' al-Dīn that one may gain a better understanding of the role they play in practical *taqiyyah*. The following discussion focuses on the substance of *taqiyyah* in Bahā' al-Dīn's performance.

1. *TAQIYYAH* AND DOCUMENTS

In modern times, a plethora of documents exists as an aid to establishing an individual's identity, including such things as passports, driver's licenses, and identification cards. These documents may also include other information intended to render attempts to conceal a particular identity more difficult, such as photographs, fingerprints, social security numbers, etc.[167] In the pre-modern Middle East, some such documents, such as special seals or insignia identifying official embassies and letters of introduction from rulers or other political figures, certainly existed, and it is likely that the Ottomans kept detailed files on important figures in the Safavid Empire. It is not known whether Bahā' al-Dīn carried any such official documents, or what documentation was required of him before he could leave Iran or enter the Ottoman Empire. While it would appear in keeping with his dervish disguise that he not carry any such official documents, there is evidence that other, less official documents served as additional props for his performance.

A. BAHĀ' AL-DĪN'S TREATISE ON *TAFSĪR*

It has been mentioned above that the Aleppan scholar al-'Urḍī claims that Bahā' al-Dīn replaced the introduction to a treatise on *tafsīr* which he had dedicated to the Safavid Shah with a dedication to the Ottoman Sultan. Al-'Urḍī's report about a treatise which was originally dedicated to Shah 'Abbās I in particular is impossible, since Bahā' al-Dīn was traveling in 991-93/1583-85 and Shah 'Abbās did not assume the throne until 996/1587, but there is additional evidence to support the gist of al-'Urḍī's story. Bahā' al-Dīn seems to have taken a particular interest in *tafsīr* during this period. He lectured on *tafsīr* to a private audience in Damascus, and the *ijāzah* he received in Jerusalem included two famous Sunni *tafsīr* works, *al-Kashshāf* by al-Zamakhsharī (d. 538/1144) and *Anwār al-tanzīl* by al-Bayḍāwī (d. ca. 716/1316). This was a field in which communication across sectarian boundaries was relatively easy, and in which Bahā' al-Dīn could impress his peers without inciting them against him, as happened when he began the debate on *ḥadīth* with al-'Urḍī's father in Aleppo. Bahā' al-Dīn wrote several works of Koranic commentary himself, including *al-'Urwah al-wuthqā fī tafsīr al-qur'ān* and *'Ayn al-ḥayāt*.[168] His anthology *al-Kashkūl* cites many Sunni commentaries on Koranic verses and includes a short biography of al-Qāḍī al-Bayḍāwī in which Bahā' al-Dīn writes, ". . . and the most famous of his works in our time is his Koranic exegesis entitled *Anwār al-tanzīl*."[169] Bahā' al-Dīn wrote a *ḥāshiyah* (gloss or marginal commentary) on al-Bayḍāwī's exegesis,[170] and his student Ḥusayn b. Ḥaydar al-Karakī states that it is the best available commentary on that work.[171] Bahā' al-Dīn's interest in al-Bayḍāwī should be contrasted, however, with Mīrzā Makhdūm's report that one of the heinous crimes of the Safavids was their destruction of al-Bayḍāwī's tomb in Tabriz along with the tombs of other great Sunni scholars.[172] Bahā' al-Dīn also wrote glosses on *al-Kashshāf*, but they are not known to be extant.[173]

A short treatise on *tafsīr* that is included in *al-Kashkūl* and based primarily on a section of *al-Kashshāf* appears to resemble the treatise to which al-'Urdī referred in the passage cited above, and may have served as something like Sunni credentials for Bahā' al-Dīn during his travels. The treatise appears on pp. 480-91, vol. 1 of the Qum edition, and deals with the interpretation of verse 23 of *sūrat al-baqarah*: "And if you are in doubt as to what We have revealed to Our servant, then produce a *sūrah* like unto it." (*wa-'in kuntum fī raybin mimmā nazzalnā 'alā 'abdinā fa-'tū bi-sūratin mithlih*). He wrote the treatise while in Mecca, as indicated by a statement in the introduction, "I wished to achieve my desire and record this discussion in the courtyard of the Sacred House of God, asking Him not to let me slip from the true path."[174] He states later on in the treatise that he was inspired with a particular interpretation at the Ka'bah: "I was inspired with the correct analysis of this passage in the courtyard of the Sacred House of God."[175] In the treatise Bahā' al-Dīn avoids any indication of his Shiism. He gives a blessing of the Prophet's Companions twice in the introduction, something unusual for a Shiite author, once at the very beginning of the treatise, and once in the invocation for the Sultan.[176] The works he cites include al-Zamakhsharī's *Kashshāf*, al-Taftazānī's (d. 791/1390) commentary on *al-Kashshāf*, al-Taftazānī's shorter commentary on *Talkhīṣ al-miftāḥ* by al-Khaṭīb al-Qazwīnī (d. 739/1338), *Futūḥ al-ghayb* by al-Ḥasan b. Muḥammad al-Ṭībī (d. 743/1342), *Ḥawāshī al-Kashshāf* by Quṭb al-Dīn al-Shīrāzī (d. 710/1311), and *Mafātīḥ al-ghayb* by Fakhr al-Dīn al-Rāzī (d. 606/1210), all works by authors well known as Sunnis.

The treatise begins with a flowery introduction, quite long considering the total length of the treatise, including an elaborate dedication to an unnamed ruler. This ruler may, indeed, have been the Ottoman Sultan, yet the Sultan's name seems to have been removed. Many of the honorific titles given might conceivably apply to the Safavid Shah as well as the Ottoman Sultan, such as "The Recipient of Kisses of the Mouths of Kings and Sultans" (*muqabbal afwāh al-akāsirah wa 's-salāṭīn*), "The Greatest Sultan" (*as-sulṭān al-a'ẓam*), "Master of the Necks of the Sultans of the Nations" (*māliku riqābi salāṭīni 'l-umam*), etc., but one in particular, "Protector of the Stronghold of the Splendid Faith" (*ḥāmī ḥawzati 'l-millati 'z-zahrā'*),[177] which refers to the Ottoman Sultan's role as the protector of Islamic territory and the Ḥijāz in particular against infidel attack, makes it unlikely that the dedication could be directed to anyone else, especially in conjunction with Bahā' al-Dīn's indication that he was writing in Mecca itself. If written to the Shah, this epithet would have been an embarrassing reminder that the Safavids did not control the Shiite shrines of Iraq, let alone the Ḥijāz, and the parallel epithet most often applied to the Shah would have been *murawwij al-madhhab*, "Propagator of the Sect." It appears that the name of the Sultan, which must have been Sulṭān Murad III, who reigned from 982/1574 until 1003/1595, has been edited out, because the long list of honorifics leads into an equally flowery and drawn out benediction, *khallada 'Llāhu salṭanatah* ... "may God preserve his rule ..." without any intervening name at the juncture where one would expect it.[178] It appears, as al-'Urḍī claims, that Bahā' al-Dīn wrote this work on *tafsīr* and dedicated it to the Ottoman Sultan as a preventive measure, to protect himself by announcing his respect for and submission to the authority of the Sultan in case he were stopped by Ottoman officials. It could also serve as an indication of his scholarly merit which Sunni scholars could appreciate. The dedication had to be altered when back in Safavid territory, and Bahā' al-Dīn presumably edited out the Sultan's name for fear of offending the Shah. The later Safavid scholar, Mīrzā 'Abd Allāh al-Iṣfahānī (d. ca. 1130/1719) discusses another sixteenth-century work with two different dedications in various manuscript copies and remarks that such changes in the preface (*khuṭbah*) or introduction (*dībājah*) to works were quite common.[179]

B. THE *IJĀZAH* ISSUED TO BAHĀ' AL-DĪN IN JERUSALEM

As mentioned above, Bahā' al-Dīn received an *ijāzah* from the Shāfi'ī *muftī* of Jerusalem, Muḥammad Ibn Abī 'l-Luṭf al-Maqdisī, during his stay there in Jumādā I 992/11 May-9 June 1584. In the *ijāzah*, Bahā' al-Dīn assumed a false identity, claiming to be a Sunni. In fact, it is not clear, at first glance, that the recipient actually was Bahā' al-Dīn. One modern scholar mentions that an *ijāzah* issued by Muḥammad Ibn Abī 'l-Luṭf al-Maqdisī to Bahā' al-Dīn and dated A.H. 992 is included in the *ijāzah* section of al-Majlisī's *Biḥār al-anwār*, but does not note the problematic nature of the *ijāzah*, explain its significance, or indicate what led him to this conclusion.[180]

The *ijāzah* is indeed preserved in Muḥammad Bāqir al-Majlisī's (d. 1111/1699) monumental work *Biḥār al-anwār al-jāmi' ah li-durar akhbār al-a'immah al-aṭhār*.[181] Among a large collection of *ijāzah* documents given or received by Shiite scholars of the four previous centuries, this *ijāzah* stands out in particular, since a caption above it, probably written by Mīrzā 'Abd Allāh al-Iṣfahānī, a student of al-Majlisī and compiler of part of *Biḥār al-anwār*, states that it was granted by one Sunni scholar to two other Sunni scholars: "By al-Shaykh Muḥammad al-Shāfi'ī to al-Shaykh Bahā' al-Dīn Muḥammad and al-Shaykh Burhān al-Dīn, the two sons of al-Shaykh 'Izz al-Dīn Abū al-Maḥāmid. All of these are Sunni scholars, and the latter two were descendants of Abū Ḥāmid al-Ghazālī."[182] Their names are given in the text of the *ijāzah* as follows: "... Mawlānā Abū al-Faḍā'il Bahā' al-Dīn Muḥammad and Mawlānā Abū al-Ḥaqq Burhān al-Dīn, the two sons of the virtuous, learned Master, 'Izz al-Millah wa 'l-Dīn Abū al-Maḥāmid, who traces his ancestry to Ḥujjat al-Islām Abū Ḥāmid."[183] The date given in the colophon of the *ijāzah* is Jumādā I 992/11 May-9 June 1584, and a passage in the *ijāzah* indicates that it was written in Jerusalem. Muḥammad Ibn Abī 'l-Luṭf states, "When they came to visit Jerusalem and arrived at the springs of this most sanctified place, and the humble servant had the opportunity to meet them and to benefit from the beacons of their blessings ..."[184] At the outset, it seems odd that an *ijāzah* involving only Sunni scholars should be included in this Shiite work. It is possible to show, however, that this *ijāzah* was actually given by a Sunni scholar to two Shiite scholars, one of whom was Bahā' al-Dīn.

Muḥammad b. Muḥammad b. Muḥammad b. Abī 'l-Luṭf al-Maqdisī, the scholar who granted this *ijāzah*, was born in Jerusalem in 940 or 941/1533-35. The Ibn Abī 'l-Luṭf family produced a number of prominent scholars who held the posts of both Shāfi'ī and Ḥanafī *muftī* in Jerusalem for most of the sixteenth and seventeenth centuries. Muḥammad studied in Cairo and Damascus and took over the post of Shāfi'ī *muftī* upon his father's death in Rajab 971/February-March 1564, holding it until his own death in late Ṣafar 993/February 1585.[185] The *ijāzah* was given in Jerusalem in 992/1584, less than a year before he died.

Though there is no question as to the identity of the scholar who issued the *ijāzah*, it is not immediately clear who the recipients were. On the surface level, the Bahā' al-Dīn al-Muḥammad of the *ijāzah* matches the name Bahā' al-Dīn Muḥammad al-'Āmilī. The *ijāzah* gives the patronymic (*kunyah*) Abū al-Faḍā'il, which also matches that of al-'Āmilī.[186] More importantly, convincing evidence that the Shaykh Bahā' al-Dīn Muḥammad mentioned in the *ijāzah* is in fact Bahā' al-Dīn al-

'Āmilī is provided by a Shiite scholar writing in 1182/1768, almost two hundred years later. In his biographical work *Lu'lu'at al-baḥrayn*, Yūsuf b. Aḥmad al-Baḥrānī (d. 1186/1772-73) includes a lengthy *ijāzah* to his two sons in which he mentions his chains of transmission (*isnād*s) going back to the authors of certain famous books. Ibn Abī al-Luṭf al-Maqdisī issued his *ijāzah* for four works: al-Bukhārī's *Ṣaḥīḥ*, Muslim's *Ṣaḥīḥ*, al-Bayḍāwī's *Anwār al-tanzīl*, and al-Zamakhsharī's *al-Kashshāf*. Al-Baḥrānī's *ijāzah* happens to include these same four works, and for each of them, his *isnād* goes back through Bahā' al-Dīn al-'Āmilī to Muḥammad b. Muḥammad b. Muḥammad B. Abī 'l-Luṭf, without any other scholars intervening.[187] Bahā' al-Dīn must have received the *ijāzah* in question and transmitted its contents to Shiite students once he had returned to Iran. The *isnād* goes back in the following order:

> Yūsuf b. Aḥmad al-Baḥrānī (d. 1186/1772-73)
> from Muḥammad b. Yūsuf b. Kunbār al-Baḥrānī (d. ?),
> from Muḥammad b. Mājid al-Baḥrānī (d. ?),
> from Muḥammad Bāqir al-Majlisī (d. 1111/1699),
> from Muḥammad Taqī al-Majlisī (d. 1070/1659-60),
> from al-Shaykh al-Bahā'ī (d. 1030/1621),
> from Muḥammad Ibn Abī 'l-Luṭf al-Maqdisī (d. 993/1585).

According to al-Baḥrānī's statement, Muḥammad Bāqir al-Majlisī transmitted the authority for these books from his father, Muḥammad Taqī, who was a student of Bahā' al-Dīn. This would explain how al-Majlisī gained possession of a copy of the *ijāzah*, and how it ended up in *Biḥār al-anwār*.

Other information shows that Bahā' al-Dīn was in the right place at the right time to receive the *ijāzah*. As mentioned above, the *ijāzah* was given in Jerusalem in Jumādā I 992/11 May-9 June 1584, and Bahā' al-Dīn's statement that he read al-Zarkashī's *Mujallī al-afrāḥ* in Jerusalem in 992/1584 proves that he was in Jerusalem that very year. The exchange of poems between Bahā' al-Dīn and 'Umar Ibn Abī 'l-Luṭf al-Maqdisī and the account of Raḍiyy al-Dīn Ibn Abī 'l-Luṭf al-Maqdisī show that Bahā' al-Dīn spent a considerable amount of time in Jerusalem and was acquainted with members of the Ibn Abī 'l-Luṭf family.[188] This evidence, coupled with al-Baḥrānī's statement, strongly supports the view that

Bahā' al-Dīn was indeed the recipient of the *ijāzah*.

One may only guess who the other recipient of the *ijāzah*, posing as Bahā' al-Dīn's brother and fellow Sunni scholar, could have been. One candidate is Bahā' al-Dīn's real brother, 'Abd al-Ṣamad b. Ḥusayn. The facts that Bahā' al-Dīn is mentioned first in the *ijāzah* and that he read while his partner listened seem to indicate that Bahā' al-Dīn was the senior of the two. 'Abd al-Ṣamad was born on 3 Ṣafar 966/15 November 1558[189] and lived until 1020/1612-13,[190] so that he could have been present to receive the *ijāzah*. He was about thirteen years younger than Bahā' al-Dīn and would have been twenty-six years old when the *ijāzah* was granted in 992/1584. The name in the *ijāzah*, Abū al-Ḥaqq Burhān al-Dīn, however, bears no resemblance to 'Abd al-Ṣamad Abū Turāb, although the name of the father mentioned in the *ijāzah*, 'Izz al-Dīn Abū al-Maḥāmid, matches in part that of Bahā' al-Dīn's father, 'Izz al-Dīn Ḥusayn.[191]

Another scholar who may have been Bahā' al-Dīn's companion is one of his students, Ḥusayn b. Ḥaydar al-Karakī. Although some give his death date as 1076/1665-66, Āghā Buzurg gives the more plausible date 1041/1631-32, though it is not clear what his source for this information is.[192] Ḥusayn accompanied Bahā' al-Dīn on many of his journeys, as is clear from an *ijāzah* which Bahā' al-Dīn issued to him on 7 Jumādā II 1003/17 February 1595 in Baghdad.[193]. Ḥusayn also states "I, the humble servant of God, also have transmissions and *ijāzāt* other than those mentioned from the masters of Mecca, al-Madīnah, Jerusalem, Syria, Egypt, Iraq, and other places which it would take a long time to mention."[194] Thus, Ḥusayn went to Jerusalem at some point during his lifetime, and since it appears that he accompanied Bahā' al-Dīn most of the time, it is likely that they went to Jerusalem together. The earliest independent evidence which places them together is a statement, mentioned above, in *Biḥār al-anwār* that Bahā' al-Dīn related a *ḥadīth* to Ḥusayn b. Ḥaydar in Isfahan in 993/1585, not long after Bahā' al-Dīn's return to Iran. It is not certain that Ḥusayn accompanied Bahā' al-Dīn on his journey over the previous two years, but it appears likely. Ḥusayn b. Ḥaydar states elsewhere that he accompanied Bahā' al-Dīn for forty years, both when he was travelling and when he was not: *kuntu fī khidmatihi mundhu arba'īna sanatan fī 'l-ḥaḍari wa 's-safar*.[195] This statement, if literal, would indicate that he was with Bahā' al-Dīn from ca. 990/1582 until his death in 1030/1621, in which case he may well have accompanied him on this trip in Ottoman territories and might possibly be the "brother" mentioned in the *ijāzah*.

It was important for Bahā' al-Dīn, like any serious scholar, whether Shiite or Sunni, working in this tradition based on manuscripts, to establish chains of authority back to the authors of important reference works. *Ijāzah*s gave them the authority to teach and cite these works and served as a guarantee of the integrity of the text they used. Nevertheless, Bahā' al-Dīn probably intended this particular *ijāzah*, like the treatise on *tafsīr* mentioned above, to served as Sunni credentials in case he were stopped by Ottoman officials. It is known that *ijāzah*s occasionally served similar purposes. The Iranian Sunni Mīrzā Makhdūm al-Shīrāzī relates that during the reign of Shah Ṭahmāsb he requested an *ijāzah* from the Shiite scholar 'Abd al-'Ālī b. 'Alī al-Karakī (d. 993/1585) in order to protect himself from his anti-Sunni enemies in Iran, most likely the Qizilbash: "I asked him for an *ijāzah* in order to stave off the harm of the heretical Shiite thugs" (*fa-ṭalabtu minhu 'l-ijāzata daf'an li-ḍarri ajlāfi 'r-rāfiḍah*).[196]

2. *TAQIYYAH* AND DRESS

Frequent mention of Bahā' al-Dīn's clothing begs attention. In the account presented above, the Safavid chronicler Iskandar Beg Munshī states that Bahā' al-Dīn left his post, donned the clothes of a wandering dervish, probably a rough woolen cloak, and set out on his journey. Iskandar Beg tries to impress upon the reader that Bahā' al-Dīn gave up his respected position and worldly goods out of piety and humility, but when taken all together, the references indicate that Bahā' al-Dīn's garb was as much a disguise as a sign of piety. That Bahā' al-Dīn's clothes served as a disguise is especially clear in al- Urḍī's passage, which states that Bahā' al-Dīn "had come in secret, disguised as a dervish" (*qadima mustakhfiyan . . . mughayyiran ṣūratahu bi-ṣūrati rajulin darwīsh*).[197] Bahā' al-Dīn presumably could not have traveled through the Ottoman Empire wearing a large turban and magnificent robe, advertising his status as an important Safavid scholar. Adopting the dress of an itinerant dervish was one way to travel incognito.

Three centuries later, Jamāl al-Dīn al-Afghānī would use mode of dress in a similar fashion to modify his identity. Muḥsin al-Amīn interprets al-Afghānī's adoption of a variety of types of dress as indicative of his personality or psychological make-up.[198] Al-Amīn notes that al-Afghānī is pictured wearing a large black Iranian turban with an *'abā'ah* or large cloak; a *kūfiyyah* (head-scarf) with a wrap-around *'iqāl* (head-band); a white turban with a *ṭarbūsh* (fez) and *jubbah* (robe); or a fez without a turban.[199] It should be noted that the outfit of the large black turban and large cloak is the typical dress of traditional Iranian Shiite scholars, the color black indicating that the wearer of the turban is a *sayyid* or descendant of the Prophet, the outfit with the white turban and fez is the typical garb of Sunni scholars at al-Azhar in Cairo, and the fez alone the garb of upper-class Egyptians and government employees of that period.

3. *TAQIYYAH* AND THE ARABIC NAME: *ISM, NISBAH,* AND *NASAB*

The well-known Egyptian novelist Naguib Mahfouz has found that a name can be troublesome. In his younger years, he was on occasion the victim of discrimination in his native Egypt because of anti-Christian sentiment. This at first seems strange, since Naguib Mahfouz is actually a Muslim. The reason for his problems was that his name looks like a Christian name, since it does not include a name which is exclusively Muslim in Egyptian usage, such as Aḥmad, Muḥammad, Ḥusayn, etc. The same phenomenon is found in Shiite-Sunni relations; certain names are marked for sect. 'Umar, 'Uthmān, and Abū Bakr, the names of the Caliphs the Shiites curse for usurping 'Alī's right to lead the early Muslim community, are almost exclusively Sunni in medieval and modern usage, as is 'Ā'ishah, the name of the Prophet's wife who dared take the battlefield against 'Alī in the struggles over the Caliphate. Shiites often name their sons after one of the Imams—'Alī, Ḥasan, Ḥusayn, Riḍā, etc.—and Fāṭimah is a favorite name for girls, but these names are not as clearly marked as Abū Bakr, 'Umar, and 'Uthmān, since they are all very common Sunni names as well.

Another part of the Arabic name, the *nisbah*, is often a clearer indication of sectarian allegiance. The *nisbah* is a denominal adjective ending in *-ī*, which may be formed from the name of one's tribe or clan (e.g.,

Qurashī, "of the Quraysh tribe"), the school of law one follows (e.g., Ḥanafī), or a profession, but is most often derived from the village, city, or region of a person's origin, birth, or residence.[200] The *nisbah* derived from a place-name often reveals one's sectarian background, because many areas of the Middle East are to a large degree segregated by sect. Jabal 'Āmil has been known as a Shiite region since the eighth/fourteenth century at the latest until the present day, and many Shiite scholars from that region were known by the *nisbah* derived from that place name, al-'Āmilī. Like the *nisbah* Baḥrānī in Bahrain, the nisbah al-'Āmilī seems limited to Shiites in usage. An insulting poem written by the Egyptian scholar Yūsuf b. Zakariyyā al-Maghribī (d. 1019/1612),[201] cursing Bahā' al-Dīn and punning on the word *'āmil*, shows what bad connotations this *nisbah* could have in Sunni circles.

> *inna 'l-yahūdiyya ghadā 'āmilan fi 'n-nāsi bi 'l-jawri wa 'l-bāṭilī*
> *ya malu fi 'd-dīni kamā yashtahī fa-la'natu 'llāhi 'ala 'l-'āmilī*
>
> Now the Jew treats people with injustice and falsehood!
> In matters of religion, he acts as he pleases, so God damn al-'Āmilī![202]

It was therefore necessary for the 'Āmilī scholar to omit the *nisbah* al-'Āmilī and replace it with some other plausible *nisbah* if he wanted to hide his sectarian allegiance. Goffman reports that name-changing is one of the most common methods of information control used to conceal signs that have become symbols of a particular stigma.[203]

The accounts of Bahā' al-Dīn's journey show that he omitted parts of his name in order to hide his connections with Jabal 'Āmil and the Safavid government. The *ijāzah* gives his name as Abū al-Faḍā'il Bahā' al-Dīn Muḥammad; al-Ṭāluwī's report from Raḍiyy al-Dīn Ibn Abī 'l-Luṭf al-Maqdisī gives Bahā' al-Dīn Muḥammad al-Hamdānī al-Ḥārithī al-Qazwīnī; al-Ghazzī gives Muḥammad b. al-Ḥusayn al-Ḥārithī; al-Muḥibbī's account gives al-Bahā' al-Ḥārithī; and al-'Urḍī's account gives al-Munlā Bahā' al-Dīn. Although these versions do not falsify any part of Bahā' al-Dīn's name, they conspicuously omit the name of Bahā' al-Dīn's father, 'Izz al-Dīn Ḥusayn b. 'Abd al-Ṣamad—except al-Ghazzī's account and the *ijāzah*, which presents his name only as 'Izz al-Dīn—and the *nis-*

bah al-ʿĀmilī. Bahāʾ al-Dīn's father had lived and taught in Ottoman lands until about 960/1553, just over thirty years earlier, and had traveled to Cairo, Damascus, Aleppo, and Istanbul. The fact that he was an important religious authority in the Safavid Empire was probably well known. His name could have brought Bahāʾ al-Dīn under suspicion not only of Shiism but also of ties to the Safavid government.

Bahāʾ al-Dīn deliberately concealed his *nisbah* al-ʿĀmilī, but, in most cases, did not replace it with another *nisbah* derived from a locality. He most often gave the *nisbahs* al-Hamdānī and al-Ḥārithī which refer to his ancestor, al-Ḥārith b. Aʿwar of the Yemeni Arab tribe of Hamdān, a companion of ʿAlī b. Abī Ṭālib. One account, that of Raḍiyy al-Dīn as reported by al-Ṭāluwī, adds the *nisbah* al-Qazwīnī, indicating that Bahāʾ al-Dīn resided in Qazvin. Al-Ṭāluwī may have inserted this *nisbah* into Raḍiyy al-Dīn's account simply because Qazvin was then the Safavid capital, and al-Ṭāluwī assumed Bahāʾ al-Dīn lived there. He may have used the *nisbah* al-Ṭūsī as well, since he claimed that he was descendant of al-Ghazālī, and as such probably a native of Ṭūs.

It is well known that Jamāl al-Dīn al-Afghānī also modified his *nisbah*, changing it from al-Asadābādī to al-Afghānī because the former would have indicated his Iranian origin and subjected him to the suspicion that he was a Shiite. Another example of *nisbah* modification is provided by al-Shahīd al-Awwal, the eighth/fourteenth-century Shiite scholar martyred in Damascus. He was born in the village of Jizzīn in Jabal ʿĀmil, and was thus known by the *nisbahs* al-Jizzīnī and al-ʿĀmilī. It appears, however, that he adopted the *nisbah* al-Dimashqī to protect himself in Sunni environments. In Baghdad in 758/1356, at the age of about twenty-four, he received an *ijāzah* from the Shāfiʿī jurist Muḥammad b. Yūsuf al-Qurashī al-Shāfiʿī al-Kirmānī (d. 7861384), in which his name is given as Shams al-Dīn Muḥammad b. Jamāl al-Dīn Makkī b. Shams al-Dīn Muḥammad al-Dimashqī.[204] The *nisbah* al-ʿĀmilī is conspicuously absent, and the *nisbah* al-Dimashqī gives the impression that he was a native of Damascus, a city not known for its Shiite population. His use of this *nisbah* may not have been an outright falsification, for he had probably stayed in Damascus at some time before this, but the impression given is that he was a native of Damascus.

The *nasab*, pedigree or genealogy, is another important part of the

Arabic name.[205] The importance assigned to the *nasab* goes back to pre-Islamic Arabian patrilineal system of tribal organization, and the respect paid to *sayyids* or descendants of the Prophet is only one example of the importance assigned to genealogy in the Islamic period. Entire works (*kutub al-ansāb*) were devoted to recording the genealogies of the descendants of the Prophet and the Imams, and the professional genealogist (*nassābah*) was highly respected. The "Marshall of the Nobility" (*naqīb al-ashrāf*), an official entrusted with keeping records of the genealogies of *sayyids,* was found in many governments in Islamic history.[206] The *nasab* was the closest thing in the pre-modern Middle East to the modern identity card or Social Security number; to know someone's genealogy was to know exactly who he was. Many aspects of Islamic family law, including, for example the *'iddah* or prescribed term a divorced woman must wait before marrying again, are based on the need to be able to determine the *nasab* of a child accurately. Another indication of this function of the genealogy is found, oddly enough, in certain points of the Twelver Shiite doctrine of the Imamate. According to the Shiite jurist al-Shaykh al-Ṭūsī (d. 460/1067), the way to determine whether someone might be the Hidden Imam is to inquire about his genealogy. If his genealogy is known, he cannot be the Imam, because one may not determine the identity of the Imam during the period of occultation, but if his genealogy cannot be determined, then he might be the Imam.[207]

In modern Egypt, for example, the *ism thulāthī*, "tripartite name," that is, one's *nasab* going back two generations, consisting of one's given name, one's father's name, and one's grandfather's name, is used on all official documents and is considered a fairly reliable indication of one's religious background. In June 1992, the leftist columnist and Secretary General of the Coalition Party in Egypt, Rif'at al-Sa'īd, who happens to be a Muslim, reported that a reader angry about his portrayal of Islamic activists wrote in asking him to give his *ism thulāthī*. This query carried the obvious implication that Rif'at al-Sa'īd's perceived "anti-Islamic" views could only be expected from a Christian inimical to Muslims, and that he was not a good Muslim.[208]

In the *ijāzah* discussed above, Bahā' al-Dīn went a step beyond *nisbah* modification, falsifying his genealogy to claim descent from the famous Sunni scholar al-Ghazālī (d. 505/1111). Claiming descent from a prominent Sunni scholar would not only gain respect from a Sunni interlocutor but also serve as a strong indication that one was actually a Sunni. Similarly, Jamāl al-Dīn al-Afghānī claimed to be a descendant of the famous Sunni scholar al-Tirmidhī (d. 279/892-93), the author of one of the six *ḥadīth* compilations used as standard references by Sunnis.[209] By adopting a false *nasab* in this manner, the performer of *taqiyyah* is engaging in full impersonation rather than simply claiming membership in a social category other than his own.[210] The motives for singling out al-Ghazālī as an ancestor seem to have been primarily geographical. It was known that al-Ghazālī originally came from Ṭūs, near Mashhad in Iran. He died and was buried there, and his tomb was well known. It is clear that Bahā' al-Dīn and his companion would not have been able to hide the fact that they had come from Iran, especially if they were traveling with Persian merchants, and it would seem plausible to scholars outside Iran that descendants of al-Ghazālī still remained in that area. Although he was born in Lebanon, Bahā' al-Dīn may have had some Persian accent, let alone manners. The *ijāzah*'s use of the term Mawlānā, al-'Urḍī's use of the term Munlā (= Mullā) as well as Raḍiyy al-Dīn Ibn Abī 'l-Luṭf al-Maqdisī's statement that Bahā' al-Dīn was one of the great Persian masters tend to indicate that Bahā' al-Dīn was fairly easily identifiable as Iranian. Having spent time in Mashhad itself, Bahā' al-Dīn may have been familiar with local lore about al-Ghazālī, besides knowing of his scholarly achievements. The image of al-Ghazālī was strong in Iran. Thus Bahā' al-Dīn's choice seems to have been dictated not only by the sort of interlocutors he faced, but also by his residence in Iran and his personal experience. Similarly, Jamāl al-Dīn al-Afghānī could not have hidden his Persian accent and pretended that he was a native Arab. Claiming to be an Afghānī would seem more plausible. He drew on his past experiences in creating his Sunni image, for he had spent several years in Afghanistan and knew something about the region. His claim of descent from al-Tirmidhī seems also to be due to geographical considerations, for al-Tirmidhī's native village, Tirmidh, lay near Balkh in Transoxania, and it would seem plausible that he had descendants in the region of Afghanistan.

The picture which emerges is that Shiite performers of *taqiyyah* occasionally found it expedient to alter their names or assume modified identities when living or traveling in Sunni environments. The exact modifications had to be adjusted, depending, primarily, on the place of origin of the performer of *taqiyyah* and the place where the dissimulator needed to perform it. This adjustment may have had a great deal to do with accent or other sorts of mundane behavior. Studying in Baghdad, al-Shahīd al-Awwal adopted the *nisbah* al-Dimashqī. This claim would be relatively easy to support in Baghdad—to an Iraqi, al-Shahīd al-Awwal's dialect of Arabic would have sounded very much like that of a Damascene—but this claim would hardly have worked in Damascus itself. The *nisbah* one chose as an alternative therefore depended as much on the location where it was to be used as on the actual place of origin of the performer. It is well known that Jamāl al-Dīn al-Afghānī adopted the *nisbah* al-Afghānī for use in Egypt; it is less well known that he had earlier adopted the *nisbahs* Rūmī and Istanbūlī for use in Afghanistan during the period 1863-68.[211]

4. *TAQIYYAH* AND *MADHHAB*.

If a Shiite is to pretend to be a Sunni he must also claim adherence to one of the Sunni legal schools or *madhhabs*, particularly if he is a scholar. While the *ijāzah* does not give Bahā' al-Dīn's *madhhab* explicitly, the claim to be descended from the Shāfi'ī jurist al-Ghazālī, together with the fact that he received the *ijāzah* from the Shāfi'ī *muftī* of Jerusalem, suggests that he probably was claiming membership in the Shāfi'ī school of law. This would have been plausible, for it was known that, at least prior to the Safavids, many Sunni Iranian scholars were Shāfi'īs. It is also generally held by Shiite jurists that Shāfi'ī law is the closest to their own,[212] so that claiming to be a Shāfi'ī would be the easiest path to follow for someone trained in Shiite law. Mawlānā 'Abd Allāh al-Shushtarī, an Iranian Shiite scholar contemporary to Bahā' al-Dīn, unsuccessfully claimed to be a Shāfi'ī when he was captured by the Uzbeks in Mashhad in 997/1588-89 and tried as a heretic in Bukhārā.[213] Bahā' al-Dīn would certainly have been aware of previous Shiite claims to adherence to the Shāfi'ī *madhhab* on the part of al-Shahīd al-Awwal and other scholars.[214] In the case of al-Shūshtarī, the choice of the Shāfi'ī *madhhab* may have been to be better able to defend himself from the Ḥanafī scholars associated with the Uzbek government, and the fact that the official *madhhab* of the Ottoman government was also the Ḥanafī school may have influenced Bahā' al-Dīn as well to choose the Shāfi'ī *madhhab*. While there are many possible reasons for the choice of the particular Sunni *madhhab* out of *taqiyyah*, geography seems to be a major consideration here also. A statement by Muḥammad 'Abduh that al-Afghānī belonged to the Ḥanafī school of law provokes the remark by Muḥsin al-Amīn, "Of course, because the Ḥanafī school is that most widespread among the Afghanis."[215] One's choice of *madhhab*, like one's choice of *nisbah*, must go along with the rest of the identity one adopts.

5. THE CLAIM OF REVERSE *TAQIYYAH*

Bahā' al-Dīn supposedly claimed to be a Sunni victim of persecution in the Safavid empire who pretended to be a Shiite while in Iran, out of a Sunni version of *taqiyyah*. This is shown by his statement as reported by al-'Urḍī: "I am a Sunni who loves the Companions, but what can I do? Our Sultan is a Shiite who kills the Sunni scholars." This reported confession to being secretly a Sunni seems to be offensive to the Shiite scholar Muḥsin al-Amīn, who omits this sentence when citing al-'Urḍī's text.[216] Al-Amīn apparently finds it disheartening to Shiites that a scholar of Bahā' al-Dīn's stature would go to such lengths in endeavoring to present himself as a Sunni, and feels either that this statement is a slander against Bahā' al-Dīn or else should be withheld from public view. Perhaps he believes this information to be a lie concocted by al-'Urḍī, but his choice to omit this phrase is one indication that, in the eyes of some Shiite scholars, Bahā' al-Dīn's use of *taqiyyah* had exceeded proper bounds. The advantages of such a claim were clear. If confronted with any evidence that he was actually a Shiite concerning his past in Iran, Bahā' al-Dīn would have an automatic excuse. This claim of reverse *taqiyyah* is what Goffmann terms a protective, defensive, or corrective practice used to compensate for discrediting occurrences commonly encountered.[217] The disadvantage, however, was that it would make him suspect in the eyes of Shiites, and Muḥsin al-Amīn seems to resent this statement because it provides Sunnis with strong evidence that Bahā' al-Dīn was actually one of their own.

Several scholars in Ottoman lands were so convinced Bahā' al-Dīn was a Sunni that they went out of their way to prove that this was actually the case. Al-ʿUrḍī seems to have had great respect for Bahāʾ al-Dīn, and was concerned to present him in a positive light. He gives three possible interpretations of Bahāʾ al-Dīn's behavior: (1) that he had always been a Sunni, but pretended to be a Shiite out of *taqiyyah*, which, al-ʿUrḍī stresses, is an accepted Sunni practice, as indicated by the Koranic verse 16:106; (2) that he had been a Shiite in his younger years but later repented and adopted Sunnism; or (3) that, despite the fact that he meant well and was even an inspiration to Sunni scholars, he was actually a Shiite, and therefore damned.[218] With regard to this last interpretation, al-ʿUrḍī states, "Perhaps—God forbid—he was like a candle which lights the path but is itself consumed in the lantern."[219] Several other scholars present Bahāʾ al-Dīn as a Sunni who pretended to adopt Shiism while in Iran. The Damascene scholar al-Muḥibbī states,

> News of him reached the Sultan of Isfahan, Shah Abbās, who sent for him to be the leader of the scholars. Bahāʾ al-Dīn assumed this post and became famous and respected. Nevertheless, he did not share the heretical beliefs of the Shah, as is clear from his wide reputation for having sound faith, but was zealous in his love for the descendants of the Prophet (*āl al-bayt*).[220]

Influenced by these accounts, Buṭrus al-Bustānī (d. 1301/1883) was convinced that Bahāʾ al-Dīn was a Sunni. "He was a Sunni, but was extreme in his love, respect, and reverence for the descendants of the Prophet. It appears that he feigned Shiism while residing in Persia."[221] Niʿmat Allāh al-Jazāʾirī relates that a certain Shaykh ʿUmar, a seventeenth-century Sunni scholar from Baṣrah, held that Bahāʾ al-Dīn was a Sunni but hid his belief from the Shiite Shah (*illā annahū kāna yattaqī min sulṭāni 'r-rāfiḍah*).[222] Similarly, Yūsuf al-Baḥrānī mentions that he met a Sunni scholar who claimed that Bahāʾ al-Dīn was a Sunni and who related a number of accounts, probably some of those presented above, to prove this.[223] These Sunni scholars interpreted Bahāʾ al-Dīn's behavior as being the reverse of the Shiite *taqiyyah*, accepting Sunni *taqiyyah* modeled on the Shiite version as a normal reaction to sectarian pressure in Iran. They concluded that he was dissimulating while in Iran, pretending to be a Shiite, and that he could only profess his true belief while safe in Ottoman territory. Al-ʿUrḍī accepted Bahāʾ al-Dīn's *taqiyyah* as legitimate from a Sunni scholar, and the above-mentioned Shaykh ʿUmar saw nothing strange in using the verb *yattaqī* ("to dissimulate") to describe the behavior of a man he believed to be Sunni. In fact, the crypto-Sunnis of Safavid Iran developed the practice of dissimulation in order to survive.[224] Well into the sixteenth century, important families which produced both scholars and government officials were secretly Sunnis, as the events of Shah Ismāʿīl II's reign make clear. When the Safavid government took steps to enforce adherence to Shiism within the Empire, Sunnis became a persecuted minority, and it was natural for them to adopt *taqiyyah*.

There is no question that Bahāʾ al-Dīn was a Shiite by background, practice, and conviction. The time he spent in Ottoman territory was only a small fraction of his career. Those scholars who claimed Bahāʾ al-Dīn was a Sunni could only do so because they were not familiar with his accomplishments in Iran and his legal and other works, many of which showed his Shiite heritage and beliefs. Bahāʾ al-Dīn's most popular works in Ottoman territories were his poetry and manuals on mathematics and astronomy, which did not reveal a Shiite bias.[225] As seen above, Bahāʾ al-Dīn also relied on *tafsīr* as a field in which he could demonstrate his accomplishments without incriminating himself or provoking controversy. Al-Baḥrānī's response to the Sunni scholar who claimed that Bahāʾ al-Dīn was a Sunni was to show him Bahāʾ al-Dīn's work *Miftāḥ al-falāḥ* ("The Key to Salvation"), a guide to daily religious devotions for the Shiite believer.[226] The Sunni scholar was shocked upon reading it.[227] To judge by the results, Bahāʾ al-Dīn was a master of practical *taqiyyah*, in that he succeeded in gaining the acceptance of nearly everyone. It is a tribute to his ability to get along with scholars of different backgrounds as well as to his scholarly and literary merit that he was able to gain such wide acceptance in Sunni circles. Bahāʾ al-Dīn adopted the philosophy expressed in one of the lines of his poem *Wasīlat al-fawz*,

> *ukhāliṭu abnāʾa 'z-zamāni bi-muqtaḍā*
> *uqūlihim kay lā yafūhū bi-inkāri*
>
> I associate with my contemporaries according to
> their understandings, lest they reject me.[228]

While *taqiyyah* is an Islamic religious doctrine and a legal concept, it is also a complex pattern of behavior which allows Twelver Shiites and other sectarian groups to reduce the risks entailed by participation in societies dominated by a Sunni majority. The sketch presented above of Bahā' al-Dīn's behavior in the course of his journey through Ottoman territory in 991-93/1583-85 gives a more detailed understanding of practical *taqiyyah* than that evident in legal analyses. His performance of *taqiyyah* involved a complex modification of his identity and included not only the verbal denial of his sectarian allegiance and, presumably, performance of ablutions and prayer in the Sunni manner, but also the adoption of a disguise, the suppression of parts of his name and other personal information, and the adoption of a false genealogy. Two documents, his treatise on *tafsīr* dedicated, in all probability, to the Ottoman Sultan Murad III and the *ijāzah* he received from a scholar in Jerusalem, served as important additional supports for his modified identity. Moreover, his claim to be a victim of anti-Sunni persecution in Iran and therefore obligated to feign Shiism through *taqiyyah* would serve to counteract any evidence which might incriminate him as a Shiite.

Although it is unlikely that other Shiite scholars or laymen will outdo Bahā' al-Dīn's folkloric fame as the Invisible Man, it is nevertheless likely that many of them have taken similar measures to protect themselves while living in Sunni environments. To borrow the words of Goffman, Bahā' al-Dīn's performance of *taqiyyah* represents an "application of the arts of impression management, the arts, basic in social life, through which the individual exerts strategic control over the image of himself and his products that others glean from him."[229] *Taqiyyah* is a dramaturgical discipline, a collection of performative strategies, similar to those adopted by stigmatized groups in other societies but tempered in its formal details by the special characteristics of the Islamic societies in which it has been used. This tradition has played an important part not only in guiding the behavior of adventurous scholars such as Bahā' al-Dīn, but also in shaping sectarian relations and the everyday lives of Muslim sectarians in many areas of the Islamic world.

Notes

The first version of this study was completed for a graduate seminar in Islamic History at the University of Pennsylvania in 1988. I would like to thank Professor Adel Allouche for his thorough and insightful comments on drafts of the work. A revised version is included in my Ph.D. dissertation (University of Pennsylvania, 1991) and was presented as the paper "*Taqiyyah*: the Case of Bahā' al-Dīn al-'Āmilī" at the Middle East Studies Association conference in Washington D.C., November 1991. I would also like to thank Professors Hossein Modarressi Tabataba'i, Etan Kohlberg, and Andrew Newman for their thoughtful critiques of the study in its present form. Of course, any errors herein are the sole responsibility of the author. This research was supported in part by the University Research Committee of Emory University.

1. *Introduction to Islamic Theology and Law*, trans. Andras and Ruth Hamori (Princeton: Princeton University Press, 1981), 163.
2. This was the case, for example, in the trial of the Shiite scholar Muḥammad b. Makkī mentioned below.
3. Bernard Lewis, "Some Observations on the Significance of Heresy in the History of Islam," *Studia Islamica* 1(1953): 59.
4. *Fayṣal al-tafriqah bayn al-islām wa al-zandaqah* (Cairo: Maṭba'at al-sa'ādah, 1907), 15.
5. Ibn Qāḍī Shuhbah, *Tārīkh Ibn Qāḍī Shuhbah*, vol. 1, ed. 'Adnān Darwīsh (Damascus: al-Ma'had al-'ilmī al-faransī, 1977),134-35; Muḥsin al-Amīn, *A'yān al-Shī'ah*, 10 vols. (Beirut: Dār al-ta'āruf li 'l-maṭbū'āt, 1983), 10: 60-61. The execution of al-Shahīd al-Awwal was not an isolated incident, and seems to have been the result of a continual concern of the Mamlūks to control Shiite groups around Damascus and especially near the Mediterranean coast in the area which is now Lebanon. Mamlūk military expeditions were sent against the Shiites and Druze of Kisrāwān in 691/1292, 699/1300, and 704/1305. Ḥasan b. Muḥammad al-Sakākīnī, a Shiite and the son of a Damascene scholar of considerable repute, was sentenced to death as a heretic and beheaded in the Sūq al-Khayl on 11 Jumādā I 744/1 October 1343. [Ibn Ḥajar al-'Asqalānī, *al-Durar al-kāminah fī a'yān al-mi'ah al-thāminah*, 4 vols. (Ḥaydarābād: Maṭba'at majlis al-ma'ārif al-'uthmāniyyah, 1930), 2: 34.] In 756/1355, an Iraqi Shiite was arrested at the Umayyad mosque in Damascus and executed. In 768/1367, a Shiite named Maḥmūd

b. Ibrāhīm al-Shīrāzī was executed. On 25 Jumādā II 764/12 April 1363, the Mamlūk viceroy Sayf al-Dīn Qushtamūr issued a decree against the Shiites of Beirut, Ṣaydā, and the surrounding area. See Urbain Vermeulen, "The Rescript Against the Shī'ites and Rāfiḍites of Beirut, Ṣaida and District (764 A.H./1363 A.D.)," *Orientalia Lovanensia Periodica* 4(1973): 169-75; Henri Laoust, *Les schismes dans l'islam,* 259; *idem.*, *Essai sur les doctrines sociales et politiques de Takī-d-Dīn Aḥmad b. Taimiya*, 60. It seems that the Mamlūks were particularly worried that the Shiites would ally with Mongol or Christian powers. In fact, Ibn Taymiyyah accuses the Shiites of doing just that, and cites this as proof that the Shiites are inimical to Islam and the Muslim community. [*Kitāb minhāj al-sunnah al-nabawiyyah fī naqḍ kalām al-shī'ah wa al-qadariyyah*, 4 vols. (Beirut: Dār al-kutub al-'ilmiyyah, 1973), 1: 5.] While it is clear that political motives and fears for security entered into many of these executions and other actions, there is no doubt that these individuals were executed as Shiite heretics and were charged and tried within a framework provided and justified by the religious legal establishment.

6. On *taqiyyah* in general, see Ignaz Goldziher, "Das Prinzip der *takijja* im Islam," *Gesammelte Schriften*, 5 vols., ed. Joseph Desomogyi (Hildesheim: Georg Olms Verlagsbuchhandlung, 1970), 5: 59-72; R. Strothmann, "Takiyya" *Encyclopaedia of Islam*, 1st ed. reprint, 9 vols. (Leiden: E.J. Brill, 1993), 8: 628-29; Egbert Meyer, "Anlass und Anwendungsbereich der taqiyya," *Der Islam* 57 (1980): 246-80; Muḥammad Ḥusayn Ṭabāṭabā'ī, *Shi'ite Islam,* trans. Seyyed Hossein Nasr (Albany: State University of New York Press, 1975), 223-25; Etan Kohlberg, "Some Imāmī-Shī'ī Views on Taqiyya," *Journal of the American Oriental Society* 95(1975): 395-402; Mahmoud M. Ayoub, *The Qur'ān and Its Interpreters, Volume II: The House of 'Imrān*, 77-81.

7. Goldziher, "Das Prinzip der *takijja* im Islam," 59-60.

8. Goldziher, *Introduction to Islamic Theology and Law*, 180-81; Kohlberg, "Some Imāmī-Shī'ī Views on Taqiyya," 396-97.

9. Goldziher, "Das Prinzip der *takijja* im Islam," 59-60, 63; Kohlberg, "Some Imāmī-Shī'ī Views on Taqiyya," 399; Ṭabāṭabā'ī, *Shi'ite Islam*, 223.

10. *Risālah fī al-taqiyyah*, in *al-Rasā'il,* 2 vols. (Qum: Mu'assasat Ismā'īliyān, Rabī' I, 1385), 2: 173-210. He completed the work on 27 Sha'bān 1373/1 May 1954. Meyer discusses some aspects of Khomeini's treatise in "Anlass und Anwendungsbereich der taqiyya," 250-58.

11. See, for example, Erving Goffman, *Stigma: Notes on the Management of Spoiled Identity* (New York: Simon and Schuster, 1986); Edward E. Jones, et al., *Social Stigma: The Psychology of Marked Relationships* (New York:

W.H. Freeman and Co., 1984); Jeffrey Richards, *Sex, Dissidence and Damnation: Minority Groups in the Middle Ages* (London: Routledge, 1990); Richard T. Schaefer, *Racial and Ethnic Groups*, 5th ed. (New York: Harper Collins, 1993).

12. Aharon Layish, "*Taqiyya* among the Druzes," *Asian and African Studies* 19 (1985), 245-81; L.P. Harvey, "Crypto-Islam in Sixteenth-Century Spain," in *Actas: Primer congreso de estudios árabes e islámicos* (Madrid, 1964), 163-81.

13. On Bahā' al-Dīn al-'Āmilī in general, see the following: Iskandar Beg Munshī, *Tārīkh-i 'ālam-ārā-yi 'Abbāsī*, 2 vols. (Tehran: Chāp-i gulshan, 1971), 1: 155-57, 2: 967-68; Najm al-Dīn al-Ghazzī, *al-Kawākib al-sā'irah,* 3 vols. (Beirut: al-Maṭba'ah al-amīrkāniyyah, 1945-58), 3: 70-71; al-Sayyid 'Alī Khān Ibn Ma'ṣūm al-Madanī, *Sulāfat al-'aṣr fī maḥāsin al-shu'arā' bi-kull miṣr* (Cairo: al-Khanjī, 1905), 289-302; Muḥammad b. al-Ḥasan al-Ḥurr al-'Āmilī, *Amal al-āmil fī 'ulamā' Jabal 'Āmil*, 2 vols. (Baghdad: Maktabat al-andalus, 1965-66), 1: 155-60; Muḥammad al-Muḥibbī, *Khulāṣat al-athar fī a'yān al-qarn al-ḥādī 'ashar*, 4 vols. (Beirut: Dār ṣādir, 1970), 3: 440-55; Mīrzā 'Abd Allāh Afandī al-Iṣfahānī, *Riyāḍ al-'ulamā'*, 5: 88-97; Yūsuf al-Baḥrānī, *Lu'lu'at al-Baḥrayn*, ed. Muḥammad Ṣādiq Baḥr al-'Ulūm (Najaf: Maṭba'at al-nu'mān, 1966), 16-23; Muḥammad Bāqir al-Khwānsārī, *Rawḍāt al-jannāt fī aḥwāl al-'ulamā' wa al-sādāt*, 8 vols. (Tehran: al-maṭba'ah al-islāmiyyah, 1970), 7: 56-84; Ḥusayn al-Nūrī al-Ṭabarsī, *Mustadrak al-wasā'il,* 3 vols. (Tehran, 1903-4), 3: 417-20; Muḥammad b. Sulaymān Tunkābunī, *Qiṣaṣ al-'ulamā'* (Tehran, n.d.), 233-48; Sa'īd Nafīsī, *Aḥvāl va-ash'ār-i fārsī-yi Shaykh-i Bahā'ī* (Tehran, 1937); Carl Brockelmann, *Geschichte der arabischen Litteratur*, 2 vols. + 3 suppls. (Leiden: E.J. Brill, 1937-49), GII: 414-15; SII: 595-97; Muḥsin al-Amīn, *A'yān al-shī'ah,* 10 vols. (Beirut: Dār al-ta'āruf li 'l-maṭbū'āt, 1984), 9: 234-49; Jan Rypka, *Iranische Literaturgeschichte* (Leipzig: Otto Harrassowitz, 1959), 426-28; 'Abd al-Ḥusayn Aḥmad al-Amīnī al-Najafī, *al-Ghadīr fī al-kitāb wa al-sunnah wa al-adab*, 3d. ed., 11 vols. (Beirut: Dār al-kitāb al-'arabī, 1967), 11: 244-84; Āghā Buzurg al-'Ṭihrānī, *'Ṭabaqāt a'lām al-shī'ah. al-Rawḍah al-naḍirah fī 'ulamā' al-mi'ah al-ḥādiyah 'asharah* (Beirut: Mu'assasat fiqh al-shī'ah, 1990), 85-87; Muḥammad al-Tūnjī, *Bahā' al-Dīn al-'Āmilī: adīban—shā'iran—'āliman* (Damascus: Manshūrāt al-mustashāriyyah al-thaqāfiyyah li 'l-jumhūriyyah al-islāmiyyah al-īrāniyyah, 1985); Andrew Newman, "Towards a Reconsideration of the 'Isfahan School of Philosophy': Shaykh Bahā'ī and the Role of the Safawid 'Ulamā'," *Studia Iranica*, 15 (1986), 165-98; 'Alī Muruwwah, *al-Tashayyu' bayn Jabal 'Āmil wa-Īrān* (London: Riad El-Rayyes Books, 1987), 60-82; C.E. Bosworth, *Bahā' al-Dīn al-'Āmilī and His Literary Anthologies* (Manchester, England: University of Manchester,

1989); Etan Kohlberg, art. "Bahā' al-Dīn 'Āmelī," *Encyclopaedia Iranica* (1989); Ja'far al-Muhājir, *al-Hijrah al-'āmiliyyah ilā Īrān fī al-'aṣr al-ṣafawī: asbābuhā al-tārīkhiyyah wa-natā'ijuhā al-thaqāfiyyah wa al-siyāsiyyah* (Beirut: Dār al-rawḍah, 1989), 153-80; *idem*, *Sittat fuqahā' abṭāl* (Beirut: al-Majlis al-islāmī al-shī'ī al-a'lā, 1994), 187-297; Devin J. Stewart, "Review of C.E. Bosworth, *Bahā' al-Dīn al-'Āmilī and His Literary Anthologies*," *Studia Iranica* 19(1990): 275-82; *idem*, "A Biographical Notice on Bahā' al-Dīn al-'Āmilī (d. 1030/1621)," *Journal of the American Oriental Society* 111(1991): 563-71; *idem*, "The First *Shaykh al-Islām* of the Safavid Capital Qazvin," *Journal of the American Oriental Society* (forthcoming).

14. 'Alī b. Aḥmad Ibn Ma'ṣūm al-Madanī, *Sulāfat al-'aṣr fī maḥāsin al-shu'arā' bi-kull miṣr* (Cairo, 1905), 290.

15. Āghā Buzurg al-'Ṭihrānī, '*Ṭabaqāt a'lām al-shī'ah. al-Rawḍah al-naḍirah fī* 'ulamā' *al-mi'ah al-ḥādiyah 'asharah*, 87; Muḥsin al-Amīn, *A'yān al-shī'ah*, 9: 239-40.

16. E.G. Browne, *A Literary History of Persia*, 4 vols. (Cambridge: Cambridge University Press, 1951), 2: 528.

17. *Qiṣaṣ al-'ulamā'*, 238.

18. Nafīsī, *Aḥvāl va-ash'ār*, 34-35; Newman, "Towards a Reconsideration of the 'Isfahan School of Philosophy'," 172, 187; Ja'far al-Muhājir, *al-Hijrah al-'āmiliyyah*, 161-62. Newman suggests that Bahā' al-Dīn made a second journey through Ottoman territory in 1015-19/1606-10, but this cannot be the case, for the contemporary chronicle *Tārīkh-i 'abbāsī* places Bahā' al-Dīn at the Safavid court in Iran in 1017/1608 and 1018/1609. See Jalāl al-Dīn Munajjim Yazdī, *Tārīkh-i 'abbāsī* (Tehran: Intishārāt-i vaḥīd, 1987), 347, 360.

19. Mīrzā Makhdūm al-Sharīfī al-Shīrāzī, al-Nawāqiḍ fī al-radd 'alā al-rawāfiḍ, MS, Princeton, Princeton University Library, Garrett Collection 2629, fol. 102a. Though Mīrzā Makhdūm's report may be somewhat biased, it is indicative of the intensity of the conflict between Sunnis and Shiites during this period. Nevertheless, it is perfectly likely that Ḥusayn b. Ḥasan al-Karakī, who was strongly supported by the Qizilbash because of his extremism, actually espoused this opinion.

20. Mīrzā Makhdūm, al-Nawāqiḍ, fol. 131b.

21. See R. M. Savory, "The Principle Offices of the Ṣafawid State During the Reign of Ismā'īl I (907-30/1501-24)," *Bulletin of the School of Oriental and African Studies* 23 (1960): 91-105, esp. 103-5.

22. Mīrzā Makhdūm, al-Nawāqiḍ, fols. 131b-132a.

23. Devin J. Stewart, "A Biographical Notice," 570-71.

24. Mīrzā Makhdūm, al-Nawāqiḍ, fol. 98.

25. Mīrzā Makhdūm, al-Nawāqiḍ, fol. 99a.

26. Bahā' al-Dīn al-'Āmilī, *al-Wajīzah*, ed. Muḥammad al-Mishkāt (Tehran: Maṭba'at al-majlis al-shūrī, 1937), 8.

27. Stewart, "A Biographical Notice," 567-68.

28. Other accounts appear in Newman, "Towards a Reconsideration," 172-75; Bosworth, *Bahā' al-Dīn al-'Āmilī and His Literary Anthologies*, 29-41; Ja'far al-Muhājir, *Sittat fuqahā' abṭāl*, 207-35. I have discussed Bosworth's treatment of the trip in my review of his work.

29. *Tārīkh-i 'ālam-ārā-yi 'abbāsī*, 1: 156-57.

30. Al-Muhājir cites this statement from an autograph notes on a manuscript of the Majmū'ah of Bahā' al-Dīn's great grandfather Shams al-Dīn Muḥammad b. 'Alī al-Juba'ī (d. 886/1481-82) preserved in the collection of Madrasat al-Sayyid Burūjirdī in Najaf. See Ja'far al-Muhājir, *al-Hijrah al-'āmiliyyah*, 154, 178 n. 29; *idem*, *Sittat fuqahā' abṭāl*, 209.

31. Bahā' al-Dīn al-'Āmilī, *al-Risālah fī taḍārīs al-arḍ*, printed with Mūsā b. Muḥammd Qāḍī-zādah, *al-Sharḥ al-Chaghmīnī* (Tehran, 1893-94), 22.

32. Savory translates this phrase, *ba'd az istis'ād-i 'uẓmā*, literally "after reaching the greatest happiness," as "on his return" (to Iran after performing the pilgrimage understood). [*Tārīkh-i 'ālam-ārā-yi 'abbāsī*, 2 vols., trans R.M. Savory (Boulder, Colorado: Westview Press, 1978), 1: 248.] This would imply that Bahā' al-Dīn returned to Iran before traveling in these other lands, which was not the case. Iskandar Beg clearly means by this phrase that Bahā' al-Dīn fulfilled his hope of performing the pilgrimage, and implies that he traveled to the other areas mentioned immediately afterwards.

33. *Tārīkh-i 'ālam-ārā-yi 'abbāsī*, 1: 156-57.

34. Ja'far al-Muhājir thinks that Bahā' al-Dīn went on the pilgrimage through Iraq, but the mention of Iraq in *al-Kashkūl* which al-Muhājir cites probably refers to a trip Bahā' al-Dīn made there in 1003/1595. See al-Muhājir, *Sittat fuqahā' abṭāl*, 253; al-Majlisī, *Biḥār al-anwār*, 110: 6, 12.

35. Bahā' al-Dīn al-'Āmilī, *al-Kashkūl*, 2 vols., ed. Muḥammad Ṣādiq Nāṣirī (Qum: Dār al-'ilm, 1958-59), 1: 355.

36. In the text, *rāfiḍī shī'ī*. The origins of the term *rāfiḍī* (pl. *rawāfiḍ*, collective pl. *rāfiḍah*) are disputed and have been discussed in detail by Etan Kohlberg in "The Term Rāfiḍa in Imāmī Shī'ī Usage," *Journal of the American Oriental Society* 99(1979): 39-47; idem, "Rāfiḍa" EI2, 8: 386-89. The term literally denotes a warrior who deserted his commander, and was first

applied to followers of Ja'far al-Ṣādiq after they disassociated themselves from him by Mughīrah b. Sa'īd al-Bajalī. Another tradition holds that it originally applied to the Shiites who renounced Zayd b. Zayn al-'Ābidīn upon his refusal to curse Abū Bakr and 'Umar. The term in this context would therefore refer to non-Zaydī Shiites, which is closer to the general Sunni usage throughout the pre-modern period. See Ibn Manẓūr, *Lisān al-'arab*, 15 vols. (Beirut: Dār ṣādir and Dār bayrūt, 1968), 7: 157. Al-Ash'arī interprets the term as referring to all Shiites on the ground that they reject (*yarfuḍūn*) Abū Bakr and 'Umar in his *Maqālāt al-islāmiyyīn wa-ikhtilāf al-muṣallīn*, 2 vols., ed. Muḥammad Muḥyī al-Dīn 'Abd al-Ḥamīd (Cairo: Maktabat al-nahḍah al-miṣriyyah, 1969), 88-89. From the fourth/tenth century on, the term *rāfiḍī* was used as a blanket insult for Shiites and Twelver Shiites in particular. This equation of the rāfiḍah with Twelvers in the Safavid period is made explicitly clear by the seventeenth-century Iraqi scholar Ni'mat Allāh al-Jazā'irī in *Zahr al-rabī'* (Beirut: Mu'assasat al-balāgh, 1990), 336. A rendition in English might be "Companion-hater!" or simply "Shiite heretic!"

37. The term Munlā is a variant of Mullā, which derives from Mawlā and is an honorific meaning "Master." Both are used in Arabic sources of this period to designate a scholar from Iran.

38. As Newman has pointed out, this cannot have been the case, for Shah 'Abbās had not yet assumed the throne. The reigning Shah would have been Muḥammad Khudābandah. Newman, "Towards a Reconsideration," 173 n. 26.

39. Abū al-Wafā' al-'Urḍī, *Ma'ādin al-dhahab fī 'l-a'yān al-musharrafah bihim Ḥalab*, ed. Muḥammad al-Tūnjī (Damascus: Dār al-milāḥ li 'l-ṭibā'ah wa al-nashr, 1987), 288-89. An incomplete version of this passage is cited by al-Muḥibbī in *Khulāṣat al-athar*, 3: 443-44. Newman and Ja'far al-Muhājir, following al-Muḥibbī's order of presentation, take the account to refer to Bahā' al-Dīn's sojourn there on his way from Damascus toward Iran. [Newman, "Towards a Reconsideration," 173; al-Muhājir, *Sittat fuqahā' abṭāl*, 230-32.] This is unlikely for several reasons. The account mentions Bahā' al-Dīn's arrival from Iran as well as his intention to perform the pilgrimage should he be able. The droves of Shiites from Jabal 'Āmil would be likely to come to Aleppo to see him upon hearing of his arrival from Iran, rather than upon hearing of his arrival there from Damascus, itself much closer to Jabal 'Āmil than Aleppo.

40. *al-Durr al-manthūr*, 2: 202. The author of *al-Durr al-manthūr* believes that they met in Karak Nūḥ in A.H. 983, citing as evidence a short document, referred to as a *ṣaḥīfah*, which was written by Bahā' al-Dīn for al-Ḥasan in 983 A.H. Bahā' al-Dīn may have written this document to send to al-Ḥasan

with his father, who performed the pilgrimage in that year, for other evidence indicates that Bahā' al-Dīn remained in Iran. [See Stewart, "A Biographical Notice," 567-68.] This does not preclude that Bahā' al-Dīn met al-Ḥasan in Karak Nūḥ in A.H. 991—the author of *al-Durr al-manthūr* may have mistakenly joined two distinct pieces of information.

41. On the Syrian pilgrimage caravan in this period, see Muhammad Adnan Bakhit, *The Ottoman Province of Damascus in the Sixteenth Century* (Beirut: Librairie du Liban, 1982), 107-115; Akram Ḥasan al-'Ulabī, *Dimashq bayn 'aṣr al-mamālīk wa 'l-'uthmāniyyīn* (Damascus: al-Sharikah al-muttaḥidah li't-tawzī', 1982), 145-55.

42. al-'Ulabī, *Dimashq bayn 'aṣr al-mamālīk wa 'l-'uthmāniyyīn*, 151. This appears to be slightly later than the departure date in earlier centuries. Ibn Kathīr reports that the pilgrimage caravan of A.H. 726, for example, departed Damascus on the tenth of Shawwāl. *al-Bidāyah wa al-nihāyah* (Cairo, n. d.), 14: 124.

43. *al-Kashkūl*, 1: 481. This treatise will be discussed in greater detail below.

44. Lane reports that in the early nineteenth century, the pilgrims generally returned to Cairo towards the end of the month of Ṣafar. Edward W. Lane, *Manners and Customs of the Modern Egyptians* (London: East-West Publications, 1989), 428.

45. *al-Kashkūl*, 1: 34, 38-39.

46. Darwīsh Muḥammad al-Ṭāluwī, Sāniḥāt dumā al-qaṣr fī muṭāraḥāt banī al-'aṣr, MS, Princeton, Princeton University Library, Garrett Collection, 4250 (1), fols. 123-25. Al-Ṭāluwī obtained this information from an unnamed Egyptian scholar during his own stay in Egypt six years later, in 998/1589-90.

47. Al-'Urḍī, *Ma'ādin al-dhahab*, 289.

48. 'Alī b. Muḥammad al-'Āmilī, *al-Durr al-manthūr min al-ma'thūr wa ghayr al-ma'thūr*, 2 vols. (Qum: Mar'ashī Library, 1978), 2: 163-65. For biographies of both Muḥammad and his father Abū al-Ḥasan, see Muḥyī al-Dīn 'Abd al-Qādir b. 'Abd Allāh al-'Aydarūsī, *al-Nūr al-sāfir 'an akhbār al-qarn al-'āshir*, ed. Muḥammad Rashīd al-Ṣaffār (Baghdad: al-Maktabah al-'arabiyyah, 1934), 414-32.

49. Al-Ṭāluwī, Sāniḥāt dumā al-qaṣr, fols. 124a-125b. Also cited in Shihāb al-Dīn al-Khafājī, *Rayḥānat al-alibbā*, 1: 210-11.

50. Ni'mat Allāh al-Jazā'irī, *al-Anwār al-nu'māniyyah*, 4 vols. (Tabriz, 1954-9), 1: 93-94. Another version of this story, related in *Rawḍāt al-jannāt*, 7: 71, has this discussion taking place in Syria, and Bahā' al-Dīn claiming to be a Shāfi'ī in particular.

51. *al-Kashkūl*, 1: 17.

52. *al-Kashkūl*, 1: 63-65. On this scholar see al-Muḥibbī, *Khulāṣat al-athar*, 3: 220-21.

53. *al-Kashkūl*, 1: 65-66.

54. Sāniḥāt dumā al-qaṣr, fols. 80a, 122a-123b. Al-Ṭāluwī heard this account from Raḍiyy al-Dīn when he passed through Jerusalem on his way to Egypt in 998/1589-90. This was the first al-Ṭāluwī had heard of Bahā' al-Dīn. Raḍiyy al-Dīn was the grandson of 'Umar's paternal uncle, Abū 'l-Luṭf Ibn Abī 'l-Luṭf al-Maqdisī. See *Khulāṣat al-athar*, 4: 272-73.

55. Sāniḥāt dumā al-qaṣr, fols. 122a-123b.

56. Muḥammad Bāqir al-Majlisī, *Biḥār al-Anwār*, 110 vols. (Tehran: al-Maktabah al-islāmiyyah, 1956-72), 109: 97-101. It is not immediately clear that this *ijāzah* was actually issued to Bahā' al-Dīn, for he was using an assumed name. This issue will be discussed in detail below.

57. *al-Durr al-manthūr*, 1: 169-70.

58. Sāniḥāt dumā 'l-qaṣr, fol. 123.

59. An edition of the work, the full title of which is *Rawḍāt al-jinān wa jannāt al-janān*, has been published (Tehran: Bungāh-i tarjumah va nashr-i kitāb, 1970).

60. Sāniḥāt dumā 'l-qaṣr, fol. 123.

61. Najm al-Dīn al-Ghazzī, *al-Kawākib al-sā'irah bi-a'yān al-mi'ah al-'āshirah*, 3 vols. (Beirut: al-Maṭba'ah al-amīrkāniyyah, 1945-48), 3: 70.

62. Newman translates this as "a 'ruined' quarter of the city." [Newman, "Towards a Reconsideration," 173.] The *Kharāb* quarter was small section of Damascus inhabited by Shiites and situated to the west of the Tūmā Gate, between a larger Christian section and a Sunni section of the city. [See al-'Ulabī, *Dimashq bayn 'aṣr al-mamālīk wa al-'uthmāniyyīn*, 78.] The word *kharāb* literally means "ruins" or "uncultivated or barren land," and it and related words such as *khirbah* have been used to designate actual ruins. [See, e.g. EI 2 s. v. "Khirbat al-Baydā" (H. Gaube), "Khirbat al-Mafjar" (E. Baer), and "Khirbat al-Minya" (E. Baer).] These same terms, however, are also found as names of intact, inhabited city quarters which were formerly destroyed by fire, flood, etc., but had since been reconstructed. There were several such quarters in mediaeval Baghdad, among them one named *Kharābāt Ẓafar*. See George Makdisi, "The Topography of Eleventh Century Bagdād: Materials and Notes," *Arabica* 6 (1959): 288, 288 n. 6.

63. al-Muḥibbī, *Khulāṣat al-athar*, 3: 443.

64. Ḥasan al-Būrīnī, *Tarājim al-aʿyān min abnāʾ al-zamān*, 2 vols., ed. Ṣalāḥ al-Dīn al-Munajjid (Damascus: Maṭbūʿāt al-majmaʿ al-ʿilmī al-ʿarabī, 1963), 1: 165-69.

65. al-Būrīnī, *Tarājim al-aʿyān*, 1: 165-69.

66. Jaʿfar al-Muhājir holds that Bahāʾ al-Dīn went to Istanbul at this point, basing this conclusion on the fact that Bahāʾ al-Dīn cites a poem by the chief muftī Ebū s-Suʿūd Effendi (d. 9821574) and a brief description of Istanbul giving the number of its mosques, public baths, etc. in *al-Kashkūl*. [al-Muhājir, *Sittat fuqahāʾ abṭāl*, 234-35.] The description of Istanbul is indeed dated A.H. 991, but Bahāʾ al-Dīn states specifically that he is citing the report of someone else. No other documentation supports the claim that he traveled to Istanbul, and all other indications imply that he followed the trade route Damascus-Aleppo-Amid-Van-Tabriz on the return trip.

67. Bahāʾ al-Dīn al-ʿĀmilī, *al-Kashkūl*, 1: 25.

68. Saʿīd Nafīsī, *Aḥvāl va ashʿār-i fārsī-yi Shaykh-i Bahāʾī* , 34, 127 n. 1. Nafīsī found this *ghazal* on several autograph folios of Bahāʾ al-Dīn he had in his possession.

69. Saʿīd Nafīsī, *Aḥvāl va ashʿār*, 126-27.

70. Bahāʾ al-Dīn al-ʿĀmilī, *al-Kashkūl*, 1: 93.

71. al-Majlisī, *Biḥār al-anwār*, 42: 3. I thank Professor Adel Allouche for bringing this reference to my attention.

72. Stewart, "A Biographical Notice," 570-71.

73. See *The Presentation of Self in Everyday Life* (New York: Anchor Books, 1959); *idem*, *Stigma*.

74. Gustave E. von Grunebaum, *Medieval Islam: A Study in Cultural Orientation*, 2nd ed. (Chicago: University of Chicago Press, 1954), 190-91.

75. Kohlberg, "Some Imāmī-Shīʿī Views on Taqiyyah."

76. Kohlberg, "Some Imāmī-Shīʿī Views on Taqiyyah," 395.

77. Muḥsin al-Amīn, *Aʿyān al-shīʿah*, 4: 207.

78. Muḥammad b. Yaʿqūb al-Kulaynī, *al-Kāfī*, 10 vols. (Tehran: Chāp-khānah-yi ḥaydarī, 1961), 2: 217-21.

79. Khomeini, *Risālah fī al-taqiyyah*, 185.

80. Khomeini, *Risālah fī al-taqiyyah*, 174-75.

81. al-Kulaynī, *al-Kāfī*, 2: 218.

82. al-Kulaynī, *al-Kāfī*, 2: 224.

83. al-Kulaynī, *al-Kāfī*, 2: 219.

84. *The Sociology of Georg Simmel*, trans. and ed. Kurt H. Wolff (Glencoe, Illinois: The Free Press, 1950), 345-76.

85. Khomeini, *Risālah fī al-taqiyyah*, 175.

86. Khomeini, *Risālah fī al-taqiyyah*, 185.

87. Modern scholars, however, see in *kitmān* a principle relevant to revolutionary Islamic movements aiming to overthrow existing systems and establish rule based on Islamic law. Muḥammad Fawzī, *Mafhūm al-taqiyyah fī al-islām* (Beirut: Mu'assasat al-wafā', 1984), 101-5.

88. Khomeini, *Risālah fī al-taqiyyah*, 174-75, 195-98, 200; Muḥammad Riḍā Muẓaffar, *'Aqā'id al-imāmiyyah*, 2nd ed. (Cairo: Maṭba'at nūr al-amal, 1961), 72.

89. al-Kulaynī, *al-Kāfī*, 2: 219.

90. al-Kulaynī, *al-Kāfī*, 2: 219.

91. Khomeini, *Risālah fī al-taqiyyah*, 203.

92. Khomeini, *Risālah fī al-taqiyyah*, 174-75.

93. Muḥammad b. al-Ḥasan al-Ḥurr al-'Āmilī, *al-Fawā'id al-ṭūsiyyah* (Qum al-Maṭba'ah al-'ilmiyyah, 1983), 469-70.

94. Ni'mat Allāh al-Jazā'irī, *Zahr al-rabī'* (Beirut: Mu'assasat al-balāgh, 1990), 335.

95. al-Kulaynī, *al-Kāfī*, 2: 221.

96. al-Kulaynī, *al-Kāfī*, 2: 219.

97. Goffman, *Stigma*, 4.

98. Khomeini, *Risālah fī al-taqiyyah*, 174, 176.

99. Goldziher, "Das Prinzip der *takijja* im Islam," 65-66.

100. Khomeini, *Risālah fī al-taqiyyah*, 177.

101. al-Ḥurr al-'Āmilī, *al-Fawā'id al-ṭūsiyyah*, 470.

102. al-Jazā'irī, *Zahr al-rabī'*, 335.

103. al-Jazā'irī, *al-Anwār al-nu'māniyyah,* 4: 306. For an English translation of this episode, see Devin J. Stewart, "The Humor of the Scholars: The Autobiography of Ni'mat Allāh al-Jazā'irī (d. 1112/1701)," *Iranian Studies* 22(1989): 60-61.

104. Layish, "*Taqiyya* among the Druzes," 251.

105. Layish, "*Taqiyya* among the Druzes," 252.

106. Layish, "*Taqiyya* among the Druzes," 257-71.

107. Layish, "*Taqiyya* among the Druzes," 261. Layish also mentions other types of *taqiyyah* practiced by the Druze without exploring them in detail. He states that the Druze most often pretend to be Muslims, and are often considered a Muslim sect, though in his view they adhere to a quite distinct religion; that some Druze converted to Christianity in the Levant in the 1830s to avoid conscription into the Egyptian army; that some became Muslims to avoid conscription into the Israeli army but re-adopted the Druze religion when they were conscripted nevertheless [p. 274]. Some Druze in Israel pretend to adopt Judaism and take Hebrew names for economic reasons, and later change their name back to the original [p. 274].

108. Goffman *Presentation of Self*, 141; idem, *Stigma*, 54.

109. Goffman, *Stigma*, 4, 41-42.

110. Goffman, *Stigma,* 42, 73-91.

111. See Fredrik Barth, ed., *Ethnic Groups and Boundaries: The Social Organization of Cultural Difference* (Boston: Little, Brown & Co., 1969), especially Harald Eidhein, "When Ethnic Identity is a Social Stigma," pp. 39-57.

112. See e.g., Peter J. Burke, "Identity Processes and Social Stress," *American Sociological Review* 56 (1991): 836-49; Alice E. Moses, *Identity Management in Lesbian Women* (New York: Praeger Publishers, 1978); William B. Swann Jr., "Identity Negotiation: Where Two Roads Meet," *Journal of Personality and Social Psychology* 53 (1987): 1038-51.

113. See Goffman, *Presentation of Self*, 216-18.

114. al-Kulaynī, *al-Kāfī*, 2: 221.

115. Goffman, *Stigma*, 42.

116. Khomeini, *Risālah fī al-taqiyyah*, 191.

117. Muḥammad al-Jazarī, *Ghāyat al-nihāyah fī ṭabaqāt al-qurrā'*, 2 vols., ed. G. Bergstrasser (Cairo: Maṭba'at al-sa'ādah, 1932-35), 2: 265.

118. Khomeini, *Risālah fī al-taqiyyah*, 175; *al-Kāfī*, 2: 219.

119. al-Jazā'irī, *Zahr al-rabī'*, 335.

120. Khomeini, *Risālah fī al-taqiyyah*, 175.

121. Khomeini, *Risālah fī al-taqiyyah*, 178.

122. Khomeini, *Risālah fī al-taqiyyah*, 202-6.

123. Khomeini, *Risālah fī al-taqiyyah*, 196.

124. al-Kulaynī, *al-Kāfī*, 2: 219.

125. al-Ḥurr al-ʿĀmilī, *al-Fawāʾid al-ṭūsiyyah*, 470.

126. al-Ḥurr al-ʿĀmilī, *al-Fawāʾid al-ṭūsiyyah*, 468.

127. Goffman, *Presentation of Self*, 77-105.

128. Khomeini, *Risālah fī al-taqiyyah*, 175.

129. al-Ḥurr al-ʿĀmilī, *al-Fawāʾid al-ṭūsiyyah*, 467.

130. al-Ḥurr al-ʿĀmilī, *al-Fawāʾid al-ṭūsiyyah*, 468-69. Al-Jazāʾirī uses the same term in the course of his discussion of *taqiyyah*. *Zahr al-rabīʿ*, 335.

131. Khomeini, *Risālah fī al-taqiyyah*, 175.

132. al-Ḥurr al-ʿĀmilī, *al-Fawāʾid al-ṭūsiyyah*, 469.

133. al-Ḥurr al-ʿĀmilī, *al-Fawāʾid al-ṭūsiyyah*, 470.

134. Khomeini, *Risālah fī al-taqiyyah*, 177.

135. Khomeini, *Risālah fī al-taqiyyah*, 190-91.

136. Khomeini, *Risālah fī al-taqiyyah*, 190-91. This term was used as early as the fourth/tenth century. See Kohlberg, "Some Imāmī-Shīʿī Views on *Taqiyyah*," 397.

137. al-Kulaynī, *al-Kāfī*, 2: 220.

138. Muẓaffar, *ʿAqāʾid al-imāmiyyah*, 74.

139. Bernard Lewis, "The Significance of Heresy," 61.

140. The treatise will be discussed in greater detail below.

141. The *ijāzah* will also be discussed in greater detail below.

142. Jaʿfar al-Muhājir discusses the existence of many such stories and legends concerning Bahāʾ al-Dīn in Iran and Lebanon. *al-Hijrah al-ʿāmiliyyah*, 167-69.

143. I am indebted to my colleague Dr. Mahmoud Ayoub, Professor of Islamic Studies at Temple University and a native of Jubāʿ in southern Lebanon, for telling me this story. Jaʿfar al-Muhājir does not relate this story, but mentions that in some stories, Bahāʾ al-Dīn possesses a special eye ointment which allowed him to become invisible (*kuḥl al-istikhfāʾ*). *al-Hijrah al-ʿāmiliyyah*, 169.

144. Muḥsin al-Amīn, *Aʿyān al-shīʿah,* 9: 241.

145. *al-Durr al-manthūr*, 2: 164-65; Devin J. Stewart, "Twelver Shīʿī Jurisprudence," 178-82, 305-7.

146. Goldziher, "Das Prinzip der *takijja* im Islam," 59-60, 63; Kohlberg, "Some Imāmī-Shīʿī Views on Taqiyya," 399; Ṭabāṭabāʾī, *Shiʿite Islam*, 223.

147. Khomeini, *Risālah fī al-taqiyyah*, 174.

148. Khomeini, *Risālah fī al-taqiyyah*, 175.

149. al-Ḥurr al-ʿĀmilī, *al-Fawāʾid al-ṭūsiyyah*, 470.

150. Khomeini, *Risālah fī al-taqiyyah*, 175.

151. Khomeini, *Risālah fī al-taqiyyah*, 190-91.

152. Khomeini, *Risālah fī al-taqiyyah*, 191.

153. al-Ḥurr al-ʿĀmilī, *al-Fawāʾid al-ṭūsiyyah*, 468.

154. Khomeini, *Risālah fī al-taqiyyah*, 177.

155. Khomeini, *Risālah fī al-taqiyyah*, 178.

156. See Charles Pellat, "*al-Masḥ ʿalā ʾl-khuffayn*," EI2, 6: 709-10.

157. Khomeini, *Risālah fī al-taqiyyah*, 178-80, 190.

158. Khomeini, *Risālah fī al-taqiyyah*, 181-84.

159. al-Kulaynī, *al-Kāfī*, 2: 220.

160. Muḥammad Riḍā al-Muẓaffar, *ʿAqāʾid al-imāmiyyah*, 73.

161. al-Ḥurr al-ʿĀmilī, *al-Fawāʾid al-ṭūsiyyah*, 469.

162. Khomeini, *Risālah fī al-taqiyyah*, 175.

163. Khomeini, *Risālah fī al-taqiyyah*, 188. He defines such an entity as "a circumstance which has no effect whatsoever on the plane of legislation" *(al-mawḍūʿ alladhī lam yakun lahu atharun fī ʿālami ʾt-tashrīʿi muṭlaqan)*.

164. al-Kulaynī, *al-Kāfī*, 2: 219.

165. al-Kulaynī, *al-Kāfī*, 2: 220.

166. Goldziher, *Introduction to Islamic Theology and Law*, 181.

167. Goffman, *Stigma*, 56-62.

168. Brockelmann, *GAL*, SII: 597.

169. Bahāʾ al-Dīn al-ʿĀmilī, *al-Kashkūl*, 1: 56.

170. Printed on margins of *Anwār al-tanzīl* (Tehran, 1855).

171. An *ijāzah* written by Ḥusayn b. Ḥaydar al-Karakī cited in al-Khwānsārī, *Rawḍāt al-jannāt*, 7: 59.

172. Mīrzā Makhdūm, al-Nawāqiḍ, fol. 127a.

173. al-Muḥibbī, *Khulāṣat al-athar*, 3: 441; al-Baḥrānī, *Luʾluʾat al-baḥrayn*, 21.

174. Bahāʾ al-Dīn al-ʿĀmilī, *al-Kashkūl*, 1: 481.

175. Bahāʾ al-Dīn al-ʿĀmilī, *al-Kashkūl*, 1: 488.

176. Bahā' al-Dīn al-'Āmilī, *al-Kashkūl*, 1: 480, 482.

177. Bahā' al-Dīn al-'Āmilī, *al-Kashkūl*, 1: 481.

178. Bahā' al-Dīn al-'Āmilī, *al-Kashkūl*, 1: 481-82.

179. al-Iṣfahānī, *Riyāḍ al-'ulamā'*, 2: 67.

180. al-Amīnī al-Najafī, *al-Ghadīr*, 11: 250-51.

181. al-Majlisī, *Biḥār al-anwār*. The *kitāb al-ijāzāt* is contained in vols. 105-10.

182. The *ijāzah* is printed in *Biḥār al-anwār*, 109: 97-101, and the caption appears on p. 97. A facsimile of the handwritten copy is included in the back half of the same volume, pp. 112-15.

183. al-Majlisī, *Biḥār al-anwār*, 109: 97. "Ḥujjat al-Islām" is the well-known sobriquet of the famous scholar Abū Ḥāmid Muḥammad b. Muḥammad al-Ghazālī (d. 505/1111).

184. al-Majlisī, *Biḥār al-anwār*, 109: 98.

185. Najm al-Dīn al-Ghazzī, *al-Kawākib al-sā'irah,* 3: 11-12; 'Abd al-Ḥayy Ibn al-'Imād al-Ḥanbalī, *Shadharāt al-dhahab fī akhbār man dhahab*, 8 vols. (Cairo: Maktabat al-qudsī, 1351), 8: 466. On his father, see *Shadharāt al-dhahab*, 8: 431.

186. al-Iṣfahānī, *Riyāḍ al-'ulamā'*, 2: 110.

187. al-Baḥrānī, *Lu'lu'at al-baḥrayn,* 434-37. Al-Baḥrānī also mentions that he transmits authority for al-Fīrūzābādī's (d. 476/1083) *Qāmūs* through Bahā' al-Dīn from Muḥammad Ibn Abī 'l-Luṭf al-Maqdisī [al-Baḥrānī, *Lu'lu'at al-baḥrayn*, 428]. This would imply that Bahā' al-Dīn received a second *ijāzah* from the same scholar which is not included in *Biḥār al-anwār.*

188. Bahā' al-Dīn al-'Āmilī, *al-Kashkūl*, 1: 63-66.

189. al-Iṣfahānī, *Riyāḍ al-'ulamā'*, 2: 230

190. al-Baḥrānī, *Lu'lu'at al-baḥrayn*, 21.

191. I have been unable to find a *kunyah* recorded for Ḥusayn in the biographical sources.

192. al-Amīnī al-Najafī, *al-Ghadīr*, 11: 254; Āghā Buzurg al-Ṭihrānī, '*Ṭabaqāt a'lām al-shī'ah. al-Rawḍah al-naḍirah fī 'ulamā' al-mi'ah al-ḥādiyah 'asharah* (Beirut: Mu'assasat fiqh al-shī'ah, 1990), 181. A.H. 1076 is actually the death date of Shihāb al-Dīn Ḥusayn b. Ḥaydar al-Karakī, author of *Hidāyat al-abrār*. He was born ca. 1012/1603-4 and was perhaps a grandson of Bahā' al-Dīn's student. See al-Iṣfahānī, *Riyāḍ al-'ulamā'*, 2: 75-78.

193. al-Majlisī, *Biḥār al-anwār*, 110: 6, 12

194. al-Majlisī, *Biḥār al-anwār*, 110: 12

195. al-Khwānsārī, *Rawḍāt al-jannāt*, 7: 58. Al-Khwānsārī is here citing an *ijāzah* written by Ḥusayn, but does not give the source.

196. Mīrzā Makhdūm, al-Nawāqiḍ, fol. 102 b.

197. Muḥsin al-Amīn, *A'yān al-shī'ah,* 9: 241.

198. Muḥsin al-Amīn, *A'yān al-shī'ah,* 4: 208.

199. Muḥsin al-Amīn, *A'yān al-shī'ah,* 4: 208.

200. See EI 2, s. v. "Ism."

201. For a biography of this scholar, see Shihāb al-Dīn Aḥmad al-Khafājī, *Rayḥānat al-alibbā wa-zahrat al-ḥayāt al-dunyā*, 2 vols., ed. 'Abd al-Fattāḥ Muḥammad al-Ḥilw (Cairo: 'Īṣā al-Bābī al-Ḥalabī, 1967), 2: 32-37; al-Muḥibbī, *Khulāṣat al-athar*, 4: 501-3.

202. al-Khafājī, *Rayḥānat al-alibbā*, 2: 33. This poem puns on the *nisbah al-'Āmilī* and the active participle *'āmil*, one who acts or performs something, especially religious duties. The fourth hemistich may also be construed as "God damn whoever does this!"

203. Goffmann, *Stigma*, 58-59.

204. al-Majlisī, *Biḥār al-anwār*, 107: 183-84.

205. See EI 2, s. v. "Ism."

206. See, for example, Louis Massignon, "Cadis et Naqībs bagdadiens," *Wiener Zeitschrift fĬr die Kunde des Morgenlandes*, 51 (1948): 106-15.

207. Muḥammad b. al-Ḥasan al-Ṭūsī, *'Uddat al-uṣūl*, 246.

208. Lecture at the American University in Cairo, June 1992.

209. Muḥsin al-Amīn, *A'yān al-shī'ah,* 4: 207. On al-Tirmidhī, see EI1, s. v. "al-Tirmidhī" (A.J. Wensinck).

210. On impersonation, see Goffman, *Presentation of Self*, 60; *idem*, *Stigma*, 63.

211. Homa Pakdaman, *Djamal-ed-Din Assad Abadi dit Afghani* (Paris: G.P. Maisonneuve et Larose, 1969), 36-44.

212. al-Ḥurr al-'Āmilī, *al-Fawā'id al-ṭūsiyyah*, 467.

213. Iskandar Beg Munshī, *Tārīkh-i 'ālam-ārā-yi 'Abbāsī*, 155; Savory, *History of Shah 'Abbās*, 2 45-46. Savory's translation of the passage in question is flawed since it states that al-Shūshtarī claimed to be a descendant of the Prophet in addition to a Shāfi'ī. The original text reads *bi-shi'ār-i ahl-i bayt taqiyyah kardah khod-rā shāfi'ī bāz nemūd*, "Performing *taqiyyah,* according to the proud custom of the descendants of the Prophet, he showed himself to be a Shāfi'ī."

214. See "Conformance to Consensus: Shiite Participation in the Shāfi'ī Legal Guild," in Devin J. Stewart, Twelver Shiite Jurisprudence and Its Struggle with Sunni Consensus, Ph.D. diss., University of Pennsylvania, 1991, pp. 151-201.

215. Muḥsin al-Amīn, *A'yān al-shī'ah,* 4: 207.

216. Muḥsin al-Amīn, *A'yān al-shī'ah,* 9: 241

217. Goffmann, *Presentation of Self,* 13, 229-33.

218. al-'Urḍī, *Ma'ādin al-dhahab*, 287.

219. al-'Urḍī, *Ma'ādin al-dhahab*, fol. 287.

220. al-Muḥibbī, *Khulāṣat al-athar*, 3: 441.

221. Buṭrus al-Bustānī, *Dā'irat al-ma'ārif,* 11 vols. (Beirut, 1876-1900), 11: 463.

222. al-Khwānsārī, *Rawḍāt al-jannāt*, 7: 66.

223. al-Baḥrānī, *Lu'lu'at al-baḥrayn*, 19.

224. Martin B. Dickson, 'Shah Tahmasp and the Uzbeks, Ph. D. dissertation, Princeton University, 1958, 192-93.

225. See, e.g., Sāniḥāt dumā al-qaṣr, fol. 124b, where al-Ṭāluwī reports that "He has excellent works . . . especially in the mathematical sciences."

226. Bahā' al-Dīn al-'Āmilī, *Miftāḥ al-falāḥ* (Beirut: Mu'assasat al-a'lamī li'l-maṭbū'āt, 1970).

227. al-Baḥrānī, *Lu'lu'at al-baḥrayn*, 19.

228. Line 11 of the *qaṣīdah. Al-Kashkūl* (Cairo, 1872), 404. Bahā' al-Dīn seems to allude in this line to a *ḥadīth* which expresses a similar view with regard to prophets: "We, the assemblage of the prophets, have been commanded to address the people according to the capacity of their understanding" (*innā ma'āshira 'l-anbiyā' umirnā 'an nukallima n-nāsa 'alā qadri 'uqūlihim*). Cited in Muḥammad Ḥusayn Ṭabāṭabā'ī, *al-Mīzān fī tafsīr al-qur'ān*, 5th ed., 20 vols. (Beirut: Mu'assasat al-a'lamī li l-maṭbū'āt, 1983), 10: 294.

229. Goffman, *Stigma*, 128.

The Valorization of the Human Body in Muslim Sunni Law

BABER JOHANSEN

I. The Hanafite school of law is the oldest and numerically the most important of the Muslim Sunni law schools. It became the dominant law school in the eastern regions of the Muslim world from the ninth century onwards and in the western regions of the Muslim world under the Ottoman Empire. I will discuss the Muslim jurists' valorization of the human body in light of the discussions of the Hanafite Transoxanian jurists of the tenth to the twelfth centuries concerning the different forms of circulation of persons and goods in the spheres of social exchange and commercial exchange. In commercial exchange, commodities are exchanged for commodities. In social exchange, goods or monetary values are considerations for non-commodities, or non-commodities are reciprocally given and taken. Whereas the Hanafite jurists call the first form of exchange *tijāra*, trade,[1] they did not develop a generic terminological classification for the second kind of exchange. I will call it the symbolic or social exchange.[2]

Between the two forms of exchange there are four main differences:

1. Firstly, commercial exchange is open and *accessible to everyone* whose rational capacities qualify him for the calculation of profit and loss; everybody has access to the bazaar. As the eleventh-century Transoxanian jurist Sara<u>kh</u>sī explains:

> The Muslim and the non-Muslim under Muslim rule, the subject of a non-Muslim government and he who comes from non-Muslim territory with a guarantee of security, the free person and the slave who has been authorized to trade and also the slave who has the permission to redeem his freedom, they are all equal in the contract of tenancy because this contract belongs to the contracts of commercial exchange and in these contracts all are equal.[3]

By contrast, admission to social exchange is selective. It depends on the individual's or the family's standing in the five major social hierarchies, which are determined by religion, gender, kinship, generation and the relation of free persons to slaves.

2. Secondly, the partners to commercial exchange are *equal* with regard to the offer and acceptance of their respective goods, the right to the appropriation of the things exchanged and the protection of their goods and rights by the political authorities. Neither political power nor social prestige should give a privilege to any of the parties concerning these exchange relations. The contract of sale is the model for this equality in the commercial sphere[4]. It represents a transactional justice[5] which depends on a common value measure of the things exchanged[6] and the idea of reciprocation in arithmetical terms.

By contrast, social exchange is open only to those who are accepted as equals by their partners. It is selective and valorizes the partners according to their standing in the five major social hierarchies. The marriage contract is the model for this kind of selective and classificatory exchange. The principles which regulate the access to the marriage contract and to the realm of social exchange remind us of Aristotle's proportional justice in which "equality must be equal for equals"[7] and "justice is equality...but not for all persons, only for those that are equal. Inequality also is thought to be just; and so it is, but not for all, only for the unequal. We make bad mistakes if we neglect this 'for whom' when we are deciding what is just."[8] Under Muslim law, the criteria for admission to social exchange serve to underline a principle of proportional justice that would have satisfied Aristotle: social relations, i.e. relations concerning the association of new members with the household or the establishment of kinship relations through marriage, are conditional on the equal ranking of the exchange partners.

3. The third difference between the commercial and social exchange is that the first one is based on a precise calculation of the value relation between the commodities exchanged, whereas in the second no common measure exists between the goods or the money given as a consideration for the social relationship acquired. The jurists, therefore, uphold the idea that commercial exchange is based on the precise calculation of the value relation that exists between the countervalues exchanged[9] whereas social exchange is based on generosity and toleration.[10] This is largely due to the fact that the value of the social good acquired cannot be measured exactly in commercial terms.

4. Fourthly, commercial exchange presupposes the complete and voluntary consent (*riḍā tāmm*) of the partners to a contract.[11] If one or both of the parties act under duress, i.e. under the influence of force and fear, or in complete or partial ignorance of the objects exchanged, the voluntary consent is non-existent and the contract is either not valid or has to be authorized retroactively by the partner who acted under duress.[12] The contracts have to be interpreted in light of the parties' intentions (*nīya*)[13] and purposes (*maqṣūd*).[14] They cannot be interpreted in a formalistic way.[15]

Things are different in the contracts concerning social exchange; contracts concerning social exchange and associations with or dissociation from households and families are nearly always contracts which indicate social ranking. The marriage contract, for example, is a contract of selection and classification. It classifies people into those whom one can marry and those whom one cannot. This implies a high social risk of rupture and conflict, because the refusal of a demand in marriage, let alone the withdrawal of an acceptance in marriage, indicates negative ranking and classification.[16] Marriage presupposes, therefore, as the jurists say, a period of negotiation and betrothal before the actual exchange of marriage declarations takes place.[17] This is not a legal obligation: it is a conventional practice. But once it comes to the conclusion of the contract, the subject matter is much too explosive and the risk of frustration and strife too important to leave to the parties the same range of maneuvering that they enjoy in commercial exchange. In the marriage contract the formula once spoken is binding and produces its legal effects. According to the Hanafite doctrine, but not to that of other Muslim Sunni law schools, if the parties to a marriage contract act under duress, under the influence of force and fear, their declarations are valid and produce their legal effects. Contrary to commercial contracts, duress does not annul the binding force of the contracts of social exchange.[18] These contracts follow the principle of a strict formalism which leaves very little place for intent, purpose, and knowledge of the parties concerned.[19] Social exchange is a very serious business in which room for maneuvering is restricted to the utmost in order to avoid the disruptive effects of frustrated hopes and expectations and of negative classification.

II. According to the Hanafite jurists, a free person can never become the object of commercial exchange as one can never, legally, lose her or his freedom. "Man," writes the illustrious eleventh-century Transoxanian jurist Sarakhsī, "is created as an owner and not as a property."[20] The dignity (*karāma*) and the right to inviolability (*ḥurma*) of the free human body prevent its circulation by the means of commercial exchange or its gratuitious appropriation.[21] The circulation of a good or a person as a commodity or as an appropriated good implies, according to the jurists, its "profanation" (*ibtiḏāl*), a term which is defined by the jurists through its opposition to protection, conservation and chastity (*ṣaun* or *ṣiyāna*), and to *ḥurma*, inviolability and sacred status. It implies the idea of use and abuse by everybody. Profanation is a characteristic of commodities and of appropriated goods that circulate freely from one hand to another and are thus usable by everybody. It contradicts the religious status of the free human body which neither in its entirety nor in its parts may be transformed into a commodity or a freely circulated good.[22] With regard to his body, the free person is an owner who cannot sell his property. And this has, in the twentieth century and with regard to organ transplants, given rise to long and sometimes bitter discussions, much as in the U.S.A. and in Europe.

The human body of the free person is circulated and valorized according to the norms of social exchange. But different criteria dominate different spheres of social exchange: the sphere of sexual desire, of sexual appropriation of the other person's body, follows other criteria than the sphere of violence, homicide and grievous bodily harm. Only enslaved persons follow, in both fields, the criteria of commercial exchange.

III. Sexual desire of the other person's body leads to different legal results in the different spheres of exchange. Every adult person's body, according to Muslim law, is compartmentalized into zones of shame (*'aura*) which are gender specific and—in the case of women—change with slavery or freedom. They have different legal signification for members of the same or the opposite sex, for relatives or strangers, for free persons or slaves. In the man's body the shame zone covers the part between the navel and the knees[23] whereas the free woman's body as a whole, face and hands (and according to others, feet and forearms) excepted, is a zone of shame.[24] These shame zones must be hidden from the sight of strangers. Milder rules apply to the exchange of looks between persons of like sex[25] or between persons of different sex who are forbidden to intermarry for reasons of kinship or any other marriage impediment.[26] Women may licitly touch the parts of other women's bodies that they are allowed to see and so may men who are related to women through kinship or other marriage impediments (e.g. their mothers, sisters, aunts, etc.), provided that they can do so without concupiscence.[27] But they are forbidden to touch adult free women to whom they are not related through kinship or other marriage impediments[28] or to look at them with desire or concupiscence.

Only if a man intends to marry a woman may he look at her with avidity.[29] Only through marriage do free men and women acquire the right to show each other their body with its shame zones uncovered. The illicit look at a woman's sex establishes an impediment to marriage with her mother and daughter not only for the man who commits the transgression but also for his near male relatives. It stands, as the jurists say, for illicit sexual intercourse and is considered as such.[30] To allow one's body to be seen is a way to give oneself to the person who looks. In the relationship between free men and women this right can be acquired only through marriage and it is a right that both parties acquire.[31] The lustful look on the other person's uncovered shame zones is conceived of as a form of appropriation of that body, and is, for that reason, allowed only between wives and their husbands or between male slave-owners and their female slaves.[32]

The consensual agreement of a man and a woman to enter into a sexual relationship does not render this relationship licit. There is no personal autonomy with regard to one's sexual desires. The zones of shame are imposed upon the human body and access to them is only to be had by the prescribed legal procedure. The penal law punishes sexual intercourse between a man and a woman who are not married to each other unless the man owns the woman as his slave.[33] There are, then, only two ways for the man to the licit appropriation of the woman's body: the marriage of the free woman or the ownership of the slave-woman.

But being admitted to marriage presupposes that the bridegroom of a free woman qualifies as equal to the woman's male relatives in terms of genealogy, religious reputation and the historical depth of his family's adherence to Islam, as well as in terms of social prestige, profession, wealth and power.[34] Through reference to genealogy a hierarchy of ethnic groups is established: the highest ranking group are the prophet's tribe, the Quraish; they are followed by the Arabs and below these follow the non-Arab Muslims. It is important to see that the equality between Quraish and the Arabs is measured in terms of collectivities, i.e. tribes and clans, whereas the non-Arab Muslims are compared as individuals.[35]

The Hanafite doctrine on the equality of ranking (*kafāʾa*) thus links the status of the individual man to his being included into or excluded from the systems of kinship of the dominant ethnic categories. The equality measured in these terms is a legal claim of the bride's agnatic relatives who are entitled to repeal the shame (*al-ʿār as̲h̲-s̲h̲ayn*) that stems from an unworthy alliance.[36] Therefore, the agnatic relatives of the elder generation can marry off their family's boys and girls who have not yet come of age and who have had no licit sexual experience, against their will, to partners that the agnatic relatives choose, so that *de facto* the married minors become objects of, not parties to, the contract.[37] The ranking of the male lineages and individuals in these terms constitutes the framework for the bride's valorization, i.e. for the criteria through which her bride price is determined. The bride price or the nuptial payment (*mahr*) which the bridegroom pays as a necessary effect of the valid marriage contract[38] and which is considered to be the payment for the "ownership of the woman's sex"[39] is determined by a comparison of the bride's qualities with those of the women of her father's lineage—her aunts, sisters, cousins, etc.—and with the nuptial payments which they received. The qualities in question are age, beauty, wealth, reason, religious reputation and chastity. The amount of the bride's nuptial payment is thus largely determined through the social ranking and prestige of the male lineage to which she belongs. It is before this background that her individual qualities are taken into account.[40]

The jurists insist that the property of the marriage bond which the husband acquires cannot become an object of commercial exchange. They teach: "What becomes property through marriage is no commodity,"[41] and "the female sex is no object of trade (*wa'l-buḍ' laisa bi-māl*)."[42] They define marriage as: "A reciprocal contract in which a commodity is exchanged against a non-commodity."[43] And they are categorical in stating: "Marriage does not belong to commercial exchange, because commercial exchange is an exchange of commodities and marriage is an exchange of (legitimate access to) sex for a commodity (*wa'n-nikāḥu laisa mina't-tijārati li'anna't-tijārata mu'āwaḍatu'l-māli bi'l-māl wa'n-nikāḥu mu'āwaḍatu'l-buḍ'i bi'l-māl*)"[44] They explain why a non-Muslim whose wife converts to Islam has his marriage dissolved without any monetary compensation whereas the non-Muslim slave owner whose slave converts to Islam is entitled to sell his slave to a Muslim and appropriate the price as his property: "The property of marriage is not an object of trade whose value is guaranteed by the law. It can, therefore, be licitly annulled if the husband refuses to accept Islam. By contrast, the property of a slave is a protected commodity respected by the law because of the contract of protection. It is not licit to gratuitously annul this property...through the slave's emancipation."[45]

Marital relations do not follow the profit motive and, consequently, cannot form part of commercial transactions or of the protection granted by the law to the commodity value.[46]

The property of marriage (*milk an-nikāḥ*) is a social property. Among free persons it can only be acquired through contract, not through inheritance, as would be the case with patrimonial values. The social property of marriage establishes an unequal, hierarchical relationship between the husband and his wife, whose body becomes his exclusive property as far as sexual intercourse and all lustful exchanges are concerned. But it is a personal relationship in which the partners are not exchangeable. The husband can neither sell his wife nor marry her to somebody else. He does not have the power to profane his wife through abusing her. He enters into a social relationship with her in which both parties are to enjoy rights and duties even if the power of repudiation, of disciplinary measures and of the control of his wife's sexual activity is unilaterally placed in the hands of the husband. That this is not an equal relationship is freely admitted by the religious tradition which speaks metaphorically of marriage as a form of slavery for the wife.[47] According to Kāsānī, the nuptial payment serves to compensate the humiliation which the woman suffers through marriage.[48] For the same reason, the wife has to pay a price if she wants a consensual divorce from her husband. This price is considered to be the price of her liberation which annuls the husband's property rights over her body.[49] Ideally, it should correspond to the nuptial payment made by the husband.

As regards her social distance from men, the criteria for the valorization of her body, and her sexual life in marriage, the free woman is clearly characterized by the jurists as a person whose integration into the existing hierarchies of kinship, gender, ownerhip and religion entitles her to participate actively in social exchange. As far as social distance is concerned, the concept of the zones of shame that determine the right to look at her and to touch her creates a large social distance between her and all men who are not related to her through kinship (including fosterage, *rada*' and other impediments to marriage) and marriage. This large gendered social distance is a right and a duty of the free woman. The valorization of her body as defined by the nuptial gift is clearly determined by her integration into the agnatic lineage. The relative prestige of the male ethnic group, the tribe, the clan determines the prestige of its female members. Only in comparison to the women of her agnatic clan is the bride's ranking established through her individual qualities. If, however, she resides far from her clan, the jurists look for women of the urban or tribal society in which she lives as appropriate objects of comparison and ranking. The ranking criteria of the social hierarchies among ethnic groups and lineages and of the women within these lineages are then translated into monetary values established by the jurists according to the customary practices of the various urban and regional societies.

Finally, the free woman can have a licit sexual life in marriage only. Marriage is an unequal relationship between her and her husband: he has the right to forbid her to leave the house, to punish her if she is not obedient, to marry other women besides her and to repudiate her unilaterally when he sees fit.[50] But the relationship between husband and wife is a personal relationship which constitutes the framework of an unequal exchange between the partners. The woman is never entirely the object of the man's disposition. She keeps the right to own property to which her husband has no access.[51] She can replace her services with those of servants. In her sexual relationships with her husband, she does not have the right to withhold herself from him, but she is not a passive object either. She is, morally (but not necessarily legally), entitled to claim sexual intercourse with her husband as her right (*muṭālabat al-waṭ'*).[52] She is entitled to refuse her husband the right to perform coitus interruptus if she sees it as conflicting with her legal and moral right to conceive children through marital sexual intercourse.[53] The jurists construe this unequal exchange relationship as grounded on unity of purpose and interest: "The marriage contract" teaches the eleventh-century Transoxanian jurist Sarakhsī, "establishes between husband and wife a unity with regard to the purpose of marriage (*wa-hādhā li'anna bi'aqdi'n-nikāḥi yathbutu 'l-ittiḥādu bainahumā fīmā huwa'l-maqṣūdu mina'n-nikāḥ*)."[54] This unity of purpose obliges the woman to serve the husband within the house, whereas it does not oblige her to help him in his commercial business.[55] Her obligations are restricted to the house, to sexual life and to child rearing. It goes without saying that the husband cannot sell her nor rent her nor marry her to third persons. Social exchange protects its partners against these forms of profanation. Its inequalities unfold in personal relationships concerning the association with or the dissociation from a family or a household.

As far as the establishment of gendered social distance is concerned, slave women are under the double obligation to hide their shame zones and to expose their bodies to the public. The jurists report that the Caliph 'Umar (ruled from 634-644) forbade slave women to veil and to dress like free women in the *jilbāb* which hides the body completely. The caliph's female slaves are said to have served his guests unveiled, "their heads uncovered and their bodies all shaking (*kāshifāt ar-ru'us* muḍṭarabāt *al-badan*)."[56] The seductive role of the slave woman is supported by the tradition. Brunschvig states that under the law "[t]he Muslim slave-woman is not under as strict an obligation to 'hide her nakedness' (*satr al-ʿaura*) at the ritual prayer as the free woman."[57] And according to the Hanafite school of law, men who are unrelated through marriage or kinship or ownership to female slaves may still look at their bodies as if they were free women related to them through close family ties. The jurists justify this rule through the fact that the slave women are sent out of the house in their working clothes in order to serve the needs of their masters; that they serve the guests of their masters and that, for this reason, they may be touched and looked at, except their back and their belly.[58] "With regard to strangers," teaches the twelfth-century Transoxanian jurist Marg͟hīnānī, "their status outside of the house is like the status of the woman in the house for those of her male kin who cannot marry her."[59]

Gendered social distance is, in the case of the slave woman, reduced to a general familiarity that puts her in everybody's reach and touch. When the ownership of the slave's body is circulated by commercial exchange, this familiarity is changed into the probing look of inspection. As an object of transaction the female slave's body is profaned in many ways. Recently, Yūsuf Rāġib has described the mechanisms of the slave markets on which, in all important cities of the Middle East, slaves were offered, naked or half-naked, to buyers who carefully and shamelessly examined their bodies and who often bought them with the option of returning them if a more careful checking of their bodies, to be effected in their own homes, would result in the discovery of redhibitory bodily vices.[60] Not all of these practices would have met with the approval of the jurists. But the Hanafite jurists take it for granted that a man who buys a female slave is entitled to look at her, to uncover her legs, her arms, her breast (*ṣadr*), and to touch her carefully "to examine the softness of her skin."[61] Whether he is allowed to look lustfully at her body is a matter of discussion. But it is clear that at the point where the female slave is turned into the object of a commercial transaction, her right to gendered social distance is reduced to the barest minimum.

Through the act of sale, slaves—male and female—are transformed into commodities while at the same time remaining human beings. This poses major problems for the jurists' classifications. A commodity's value (*māliyya*) is, as they say, defined by the commodity's genus (*jins*), its species (*naủ*), its quality (*ṣifa*) and its legal measure (*qadr*) if it is a fungible good.[62] Whereas, in the case of slaves who are goods *in specie*, the species and the quality are largely identified with ethnic affiliation,[63] but the question of the genus of the slaves raises many problems. Are slaves to be defined as a genus different from free persons?[64] Do they form one genus or different genera? If they are a commodity genus how is their value to be established?

In Muslim law, the question of the definition of genera of commodities pervades the whole field of commercial exchange: the unequal exchange that is characteristic of usury (*ribā*), which is forbidden under Muslim law, is defined in terms of an exchange of identical genera against each other in unequal quantities or at different times.[65] The licitness of contracts that include a time horizon separating payment and delivery, such as the salam, the contract of forward-buying, is constantly discussed in terms of genera relations. In general, in any conceivable commercial exchange, the question of the genera and the species of the commodities that are to be exchanged determines whether or not the transaction is licit.

By which criteria is a genus defined? The Hanafite jurists make it abundantly clear that all commodities have a commodity character and an exchange value (*māliyya*) and that, therefore, this common characteristic cannot define their individual genera[66] and mark them off against each other. The individual genus of commodities is rather defined by the material from which they are produced,[67] their 'origin' (*aṣl*) as the jurists say.[68] The name (ism) that they carry,[69] the form (*hai'a*) that they take,[70] and the method by which they are produced (*ṣanʿa, minhāj*)[71] if it "imposes a change in name and use"[72] are equally important criteria for the determination of commodity genera and of their delimitation against each other. One of the most important tests of an authentic difference between commodity genera is the question whether a specific commodity can be retransformed into its original state. If it can be so retransformed then it is not an independent commodity genus, otherwise it is.[73] The material origin of the commodity is, therefore, one aspect only of genus determination. Also, the formation of an independent commodity genus is not only dependent on its production and the criteria derived from it, like form, method of production, transformation and retransformation. It depends also on the demand side and the use assigned to the particular genus of commodities by the buyers. The idea of the commodity's licit use (*intifāʿ*),[74] as defining the range of licit 'purposes' (*maqāṣid, agh̲rāḍ*) assigned to it by the buyer,[75] is an essential criterion for the differentiation between commodity genera. In many cases, it is more important than the material 'origin' and the form of the commodity for the determination of the genus.

The apparatus of classificatory criteria outlined above is applied to the slaves in order to determine their value and their genus. While following their argument we should keep in mind that, due to the jurists' casuistic method of reasoning, in juridical parliance, as Schacht says, "differences between two genera are often not greater or more essential than those between several species within the same genus."[76] The fact has not escaped the attention of the Hanafite jurists. ʿAynī, writing in the fourteenth century, underlines on several occasions that the jurists' use of genus (jins) corresponds to the use of species[77] and Nāṣir ad-Dīn al-Muṭarrizī in his thirteenth-century dictionary of legal terms ascribes to the jurists their own way of defining genus and species.[78] But even if we accept this reservation, the Hanafite discussion clearly shows that for the jurists the importance of the gender criterion outweighs that of the difference between free male persons and male slaves. According to Hanafite doctrine, male slaves and free men are one genus because they may be used for the same purposes. As Sarak̲h̲sī puts it:

> The free and the slave are one genus. As far as his origin is concerned, the human being is free. Slavery intervenes as an accident. The emancipation annihilates this accidental slavery. So slavery does not bring about a change in the genus, neither through a difference in the (material) origin nor the form nor the purpose, because this (difference) does not exist between free males and slave males (*faʾinnaʾl-ādamiyya biʿtibāriʾl-asli ḥurr. T̲h̲umma yaʿtariḍuʾr-riqqu fīh. Waʾl-iʿtāqu itlāfu li-d̲h̲ālikaʾr-riqqiʾ-l-ʿārid. fa-la yūjibu tabdīlaʾl-jinsi immā biʾk̲h̲tilāfiʾl-aṣli awiʾl-haiʾati au al-maqṣūd wa-d̲h̲ālika la yūjadu bainaʾl-aḥrāri waʾl-ʿabīd*).[79]

Male human beings, slave and free, have the same human origin, the same form and they are used for the same purposes. There is no genus-differentiation between them. The male slave is temporarily in the accidental state of slavery, but attributes change in the course of time and their changing sequence does not bring about a change in the genus of the human being.[80] Some jurists refer mainly to the fact that male humans, slave or free, are put to the same use by other persons;[81] other jurists refer to the identity of form and function between free and slave males in order to justify their belonging to the same genus.[82] Some stress their common human origin (see note 79). Many refer to the fact that slaves may be emancipated and return to their original status of free persons.[83] According to the jurists, only Abū Yūsuf upheld the idea that the attribute of being a slave suffices to constitute slaves as a genus of their own.[84] All in all, the Hanafite jurists quite convincingly use the apparatus of classificatory categories that they developed for the commodity exchange in order to uphold the doctrine that free and slave males belong to the same genus. As far as the constitution of the genus is concerned, the common human character is of higher importance than the difference between slaves and free persons.[85]

The same reasoning does not hold true when it comes to female slaves. According to the Hanafite doctrine, male and female slaves are not two species of one genus but form two different genera. They ascribe to female slaves a genus that is different from that of male slaves. This genus is determined by their functions. Zufar Abū Hudhail, one of the students of Abū Ḥanīfa and one of the most prominent Hanafite jurists of the eighth century, had upheld the position that "all of Adam's children are one genus and this holds true for their males and their females."[86] Against this doctrine the dominant opinion of the Hanafite school of law is formulated by the eleventh-century Transoxanian jurist Sarakhsī as follows:

> The male and the female of Adam's children are legally two genera, because the purpose which is assigned to the one cannot be realized by the other. The function assigned to the female slave is concubinage (istifrāsh) and the production of children and a male slave cannot do anything of this. One

> sees, then, that the difference in the functions assigned to them is bigger than the one between wheat and barley or between cloth from Marw and cloth from Herat. In this, male and female slaves differ from all living creatures.[87]

The same jurists who uphold the unity of the male human genus across the limits between slavery and freedom assign a different genus to the female slaves because, they say, the difference of purposes to which they are put is so enormous that, against all requirements of logic[88] and against all analogies to other animals, male and female slaves cannot be conceived of as forming one genus.[89] Where slavery is combined with the gender difference it destroys the unity of the human kind. With regard to human genders, the commercial and social exchange produce, in fact, different genera of human bodies.[90]

The female slaves' genus is constituted through reference to the fact that the appropriation of their persons does not only imply the control over their bodies, their work, their time, the right to sell them, to lease them or to make them work for the owner. All this is also part of the status of the male slave. The control over the slaves' sex life with third persons is also not peculiar to the female sex: the male slave's master can marry him to any woman he wants or he can forbid him to marry. Such an interdiction would amount to forbidding the male slave any legalized form of sex, because the slave, according to the doctrine of the Hanafite school, is not allowed to have concubines. His legalized sex life is restricted to marriage.[91] What constitutes, according to the jurists, the genus of the female slaves, is the peculiar purpose assigned to them by their masters: they are to serve as concubines and as the children's mothers. The ownership of a female slave includes the right to the use of her sexual organs by her master—which the ownership of the male slave, clearly, does not. The masters of male slaves are never entitled to have sexual intercourse with them.[92] The sexual appropriation of the female slave takes two forms: the commercial and the marital appropriation. The first one concerns her relationship with her master and is mediated through the commercial property titles that the owner holds over his slave; the second one concerns her marital relations with other persons. Both spheres follow their own rules; both are controlled by the slave's owner. In both spheres the predominance of the commercial over social exchange is seen in the annihilation of the role of the woman's agnatic relatives in favor of the slave's owner, in the reduction of the rights and the role of the female slave's husband and in the mutual exclusion of rights and claims that stem from the spheres of the commercial and social exchange. The last one finds its clearest expression in the incompatibility of the commercial ownership (*milk al-māl*) of a person with the ownership of the marriage (*milk an-nikāḥ*) concerning the same woman, but it is also effective in a number of other legal norms.

The commercial appropriation follows the procedure prescribed by the sale contract. The female slave is sold as a commodity on a market. If one compares this bargain to the marriage of the free woman the following are the most striking differences: the slave's family is not represented in the sale. No agnatic relative takes the role of a guardian (*walī*). Rather, it is the owner who offers her for sale. The agnatic relatives play no role in determining whether the partner is their equal. The prospective buyer just has to have enough money to pay the price. The price replaces the nuptial payment (*mahr*) but its amount is not determined by any reference to the status and prestige of the woman's agnatic relatives. In the sale contract, the slave's ethnic origins and affiliations play a role in determining her quality[93] but her agnatic relatives do not. Individual beauty, strength, and capacities determine the price as factors secondary to ethnic affiliation.

Contrary to the marriage contract which, according to the Hanafite doctrine, does not grant the husband the right of options for the wife's redhibitory vices,[94] the buyer of a slave has, much as any other buyer under the contract of sale, the option to inspect and check the slave whom he bought for some days in order to find out whether she or he had any hidden fault. A fault that justifies the buyer's return of the commodity to the seller is called a redhibitory vice (*'aib)*[95] Under Hanafite law it is defined as "a deficiency in the exchange value" (*nuqṣān al-māliyya*)[96] or "a deficiency in the price" (*nuqṣān aṯh-ṯhaman*)[97] or "in the value" (*qīma*)[98]. Whether a given quality is a redhibitory vice (*'aib*), has to be decided, according to the jurists, by reference to "the merchants' customary practice". I quote Saraḵhsī:

> The source of the cognition of redhibitory vices is the merchant's practice...Whatever they consider to be a redhibitory vice is a redhibitory vice. A redhibitory vice is something that diminishes the exchange value (*māliyya*) because the function of the sale is the profit and the profit is realized through the exchange value. Whatever creates a deficiency in the purpose (assigned to the slave) diminishes the exchange value and is a redhibitory vice.[99]

The juridical commentaries of the period under discussion contain lengthy lists of such redhibitory vices of slaves.[100] These redhibitory vices are classified into four main categories:[101] those that are easily visible for everybody, those that result as symptoms of interior sicknesses and are comprehensible only to doctors, those that only women are entitled to see and, finally, those that concern the character evaluation (*ʿaib ḥukmī*).

Many of the criteria by which the jurists classify these defects are related to the slave's physical appearance. They are related to the physical defects which render the slave incapable of fulfilling the purpose assigned to him by the buyer or which diminish the aesthetic pleasure of looking at him.[102] They concern the health status of men or women and the woman's capacity to serve as concubines and to bear children. But in the light of the differentiation between different spheres of social behaviour, the redhibitory vices concerning the moral character (*ʿaib ḥukmī*) constitute certainly the most interesting aspect of this discussion. They show that the behavior of slaves is supposed to follow other norms than those of free persons, that the jurists construe moral character defects according to gender and that their criteria for the evaluation of behavior differ, in the realm of commercial exchange, from those in penal law and in religious ethics. Whereas for free persons marriage is a meritorious act, for slaves of both sexes it is considered to constitute a redhibitory vice:[103] the male slave has to pay the nuptial payment and the subsistence of his wife; the female slave cannot be used as a concubine by her owner if she is married. The financial obligation of the male and the nuptial obligation of the female slave are considered to be redhibitory defects. For free adult persons adultery, *zinā*, constitutes a sin as well as a crime. For the female slave it constitutes a redhibitory vice, because she is bought to have children with her master "and her adultery impairs this purpose (*yukhillu bihādha'l-maqṣūd*) for she sullies his bed."[104] For the male slave, on the other hand, illicit sexual intercourse does not constitute a redhibitory vice: it does not interfere with the purpose for which he is bought, i.e. hard work outside of the house. It does not, therefore, reduce his value. Only if he becomes obsessed with sex to the degree that he does not attend his work any more,[105] or that he will undergo repeatedly dangerous bodily punishment as a consequence of his acts,[106] can his sexual behaviour be construed as a redhibitory vice. In the sphere of the redhibitory vices, sins and crimes are reinterpreted. There is no doubt that they may be punished under the penal law—even though the punishment would not be the same as that of free persons.[107] But as far as the slaves' commercial value and its exchange are concerned, the sin and the crime are evaluated only under the aspect of whether or not they diminish the slaves' exchange value through impairing the functions assigned to them by their masters. If they do, they constitute redhibitory vices; if they do not, they are not relevant under the legal ordinances concerning commercial exchange.[108] In the case of illicit sexual intercourse, the effects of crime and sin on the constitution of redhibitory vices are gender specific. The way in which they are discussed by the jurists shows that the norms of commercial exchange interpret sins and crimes under an angle that is clearly different from that of penal law, from religious ethics and from social exchange, i.e. its influence on the diminution of the slave's exchange value and utility.

If the buyer of the slave retains the option to return her or him after inspection, the buyer is entitled to a rescission of the contract during a specified period of time. The same holds true if he finds a redhibitory vice in the slave. If he buys a female slave with the option that after careful inspection he would either buy or return her, he is entitled to take her home with him and in this case she is likely to become the object of his sexual desire. The jurists do not consider this to be a form of adultery which should be punished under the penal law. If the buyer is a man, the jurists interpret the fact that he kisses the female slave whom he brought home and that he looks lustfully at her naked body and her sex as an expression of his will to waive his right of rescission and to consider the sale as binding.[109] They discuss in the same way the fact that he tolerates the slave woman's lustful advances on him.[110] If he has sexual intercourse with the slave woman, this is a manifest desire to buy her.[111] If he allows third persons to have sexual intercourse with her while she is in his possession, this constitutes a redhibitory vice (*ʿaib*) in the slave for which the buyer is responsible. He, therefore, has to waive his option.[112] If she falls pregnant after having been in his hand, her pregnancy is interpreted as synonymous with his renunciation of the right to rescission.[113] In the commercial appropriation of the female slave, the desire of her body and the sexual intercourse resulting from it is not punished: it is established as a legitimate form of sale. The jurists argue that this must be so, because otherwise the prospective buyer would have had sexual intercourse with a woman to whom he was not married and who was not his property—and that would expose him to the punishment of lapidation. As it can be excluded, with reasonable certitude, that he would risk such a danger, one concludes that his sexual appropriation of the slave woman is an expression of his formal consent to her commercial appropriation:

> If he embraces the slave woman lustfully and if he lustfully looks at her sex, this is a consent to the contract of sale because such an act is permitted only towards a woman who is in his property. The fact that he dares to do this, shows that he demonstrates his consent to the contract of sale.[114]

In the logic of the contract of sale, the option for the right of rescission implies the lack of that voluntary consent of both parties which is a legal requirement for a valid commercial contract. The lustful look and sexual intercourse are, by contrast, forms of appropriation which express the buyer's consent with the contract of sale and his waiver of the right of rescission. Sexual desire is, in this way, integrated into the sale contract and interpreted as a form of consent to its legal consequences.[115]

Once the contract has been definitively concluded and its legal effects come into being, the owner of the slave can dispose of her or him as of any other commodity: he or she can sell them, pawn them, lease them for all kinds of gainful employment, or order them to perform all kinds of work in and out of the house for the owner and his family and friends. As far as the female slave is concerned, the male owner may have sexual intercourse with her, either in order to beget children (*istifrāsh*) or in order to satisfy his desires (*li-qaḍā'i' sh-shahwa*).[116] It goes without saying that the female slave owner is not entitled to have sexual intercourse with her male slaves[117] because only female slaves may be sexually appropriated and only by male owners. The children stemming from the intercourse between a male owner and a female slave are slaves and may in turn be sold, pawned, rented or employed by their procreator and owner. But there is one thing that the slave-owner cannot do: he cannot marry his female slave. The jurists are very explicit about the fact that the commercial property excludes the nuptial property of the slave. The twelfth-century author Kāsānī explains why owners of slaves are not allowed to marry them:

> Marriage consists of a number of legal claims that both partners share in joint ownership (sharika), such as the woman's right to require sexual intercourse from her husband and the husband's claim that his wife enables him to do so. The existence of the ownership of property rights (of the owner over the slave) excludes the joint ownership. And if there is no joint ownership in the fruits of marriage, marriage has no function (la yufīdu'n-nikāḥ) and is not admissible, because it is not admissible that the claims stemming from marriage are exerted against the master by his female slave or against the free woman by her (male) slave. This is so because the ownership of property rights (exerted by the master over his slave) require that the authority (wilāya) be that of the owner and that the owned person be submitted to this authority. The ownership of the marriage requires that the authority be given to the slave over the owner. This leads to a situation in which one and the same person is at one and the same time exerting authority and being submitted to authority concerning the same thing. This is impossible. ... When the ownership of property rights on a slave (milk al-yamīn) interferes with marriage, the marriage will be annulled. Such is the case when one person of the married couple acquires the ownership of his partner or of a part of his.[118]

A husband or a wife can acquire the commercial property of their marriage partners if these are slaves, but if they do, their marriage is annulled.[119] By contrast, the owner of a female slave can never marry her as long as he keeps the commercial ownership title to the property of her person. He has to abandon his commercial property rights in order to acquire what the jurists call the "nuptial property" (*milk an-nikāḥ*). In the same line of reasoning, the slave owner cannot, according to the Hanafite jurists, establish filiation (nasab) with his children from the union with a female slave, unless he waives his ownership rights to them. In stark contrast to other Sunni law schools, the Hanafites do not admit the establishment of filiation (*nasab*) through the mere birth of the child as the fruit of such a union unless the owner explicitly acknowledges the children as his offspring.[120] His acknowledgement of the filiation implies the loss of the commercial property rights concerning the slave mother and her children, and therefore, according to the Hanafite jurists, his explicit recognition of the filiation is necessary.[121] It is the owner's free decision whether he wants to become the master or the father of his children. If he opts for the fatherly relationship, his children are free, they are filiated to him and carry his name, their mother becomes a "children's mother" (*umm walad*), i.e. she remains a slave as long as the master lives and is set free at his death only. But she can no longer be sold. She and her children cease to be commodities, *res in commercio*. Through the owner's option for the fatherly role, the female slave and her children may, therefore, be reintegrated into the social hierarchies of kinship and agnatic lines which determine social exchange. For the slave woman and her children the commercial appropriation thus opens a perspective of reintegration into the social hierarchies.[122]

The marriage of the female slave does not open the same perspective on emancipation and freedom. Her husband cannot set her free, her children do not acquire the status of free persons though carrying the name and filiation of their father. Her owner replaces her agnatic relatives in the role of the marriage guardian and, incidentally, enjoys more power in this role than her agnatic relatives would. He also assigns the husband a secondary rank as far as the authority over the married woman and her children is concerned. Here, as in the commercial appropriation of the slave woman, many of the claims stemming from the commercial and social exchange are mutually exclusive. Marriage is at the core of social exchange among free persons: a meritorius act closely related to the existing hierarchies of kinship and gender relations and, in fact, the most important basis for their reproduction. For the slaves of both sexes, marriage constitutes a redhibitory vice. They are, therefore, not entitled to marry unless their owner gives them the explicit permission to do so.[123] Their master can impose marriage and marriage partners on both the male and the female slaves, minor or adult, against their will.[124] According to the jurists, the master enjoys this competence as a result of his commercial ownership (*milk raqaba*) of the slaves[125] in order to protect his slaves against the vice of adultery, whose punishment could result in a diminution of their exchange value (*māliyya*): the owner acts in order to protect his property's value against possible damage.[126] It is obvious that under these circumstances, the slaves who are married are objects rather than subjects of the contract. Because they are not equivalent to free persons, male slaves are entitled to two wives only.[127]

Because the marriage of male and female slaves has different legal consequences, the categories of persons who are legally qualified to marry them off to their husbands and wives differ. As the slave's marriage entails expenses for the slave's owner, i.e. the nuptial payment and the subsistence which the slave owes to his wife or wives, only the master is entitled to conclude the marriage contract for him or to give him permission to do so or retroactively authorize a marriage concluded by the slave.[128] By contrast, the master profits from the enslaved woman's marriage: the nuptial payment falls to him[129] and, under certain conditions, he is liberated from the obligation to pay her subsistence.[130] Because of the financial advantages to be derived from this marriage, the female slave's marriage contract is supposed to fall under the category of "gainful contracts" (*ʿuqūd al-iktisāb*),[131] i.e. contracts in which a patrimonial value (*māl*) is received without a patrimonial consideration.[132] Therefore, not only the ascendant agnates of the owner and their appointed guardians (*waṣī*) but also his business partners in an unlimited trade association (*mufāwaḍa*) are entitled to take his place in giving his female slaves into marriage.[133] Their relationship with the owner is based on trust and on the unrestricted usefulness (*nafʿ maḥḍ*) of their action for him. Therefore, it enables them to act in his place in "gainful contracts."[134] Such is not the case of partners in a commenda (*muḍāraba*) or a limited trade association (*ʿinān*) because their competences concern commercial exchange only "and the marriage does not belong to commercial exchange,"[135] or, as Sara<u>kh</u>sī puts it, "marrying off a slave is not a feature of trade, nor is it one which the merchants customarily practice. We know of no place in any country having a market devoted to marrying off slaves."[136]

After the marriage contract is concluded, the master keeps control over the female slave's labour. He is not obliged to let her establish a common household with her husband, because, the jurists say, the owner's right to her service is above the husband's right.[137] The husband's right to sexual intercourse with his slave wife is reduced to a hit and run formula. According to the jurists the owner tells him: "When you get hold of her, make love with her (*matā ẓafarta bihā waṭiʾtahā*)"[138] or, as Sara<u>kh</u>sī puts it: "She continues to serve the master in his house as she used to. When the husband finds her alone and in a moment of leisure he satisfies his (sexual) need (*wa-matā wajadaʾz-zauju minhā <u>kh</u>alwatan au farā<u>gh</u>an qaḍā ḥājatahu*)"[139]

Whether it is the slave woman or her master who decides on the licitness of the forms of sexual intercourse with her husband is a matter of debate among the Hanafite jurists. In general, they assume that coitus interruptus is used by a husband who does not want to beget children.[140] A free wife is entitled to refuse her husband this form of sexual intercourse because it may conflict with her legitimate claim to beget children.[141] A concubine is never entitled to refuse her master this form of sexual intercourse because she has no claims against him, neither social nor commercial.[142] In the case of the married female slave, the Hanafites disagree whether it is the female slave who has to give her consent with her husband's practice or whether the permission has to come from her master, because it is his claim to the children of the couple that is put into jeopardy by the coitus interruptus.[143]

This argument refers to another striking difference between the female slave's marriage and the marital life of a free couple: much as in the marriage of a free couple, the children whom the female slave begets in marriage are the legitimate offspring of her husband and carry his name; their filiation (*nasab*) to him is established,[144] but they are the property (*milk*) of her master.[145] The filiation (*nasab*) of the children cannot be combined with an ownership title to their persons; the commercial property of the children excludes the title to their paternity: it has to be abandoned in order to create a relationship between father and children. Parental and commercial authority over the children exclude each other mutually. The two authorities belong to different spheres of the law and may, therefore, be exercized only by two different persons: the father and the owner. Only if the slave's husband is a free man who can prove through witnesses that he married the slave because he was told by her or her guardian that she was a free woman, can his children remain free. In this case, he has to pay their value to the female slave's owner,[146] to buy off his authority over his children. In all other cases, the weak role of the husband as compared to the owner of the female slave, the mutual exclusion of filiation and ownership of the children that result from the marked difference between the commercial and social exchange cause a lack of the husband's coercive authority over his wife and his legitimate children. This lack of the husband's authority combined with the non-existent authority of the female slave's agnatic relatives is one of the factors which prevents the slave's marriage from causing the foundation of a family who would live in a common household and in which husband and wife share that "unity of marital purposes"[147] or that "common ownership of the fruits of marriage"[148] which, according to the jurists, characterizes the free married couple.

The husband's authority, his "ownership of the marriage," is diminished by the owner's authority, which is derived from commercial ownership. Therefore, the Hanafite jurists hold that a female slave who is married by her master may, upon emancipation (*ʿitq*), dissolve the marriage. This is the "option of emancipation" (*khiyār al-ʿitq*), which is open only to female slaves.[149] The jurists underline that, through emancipation, the husband's ownership and authority over the woman increases (*izdiyād al-milk*), the marriage changes its character as far as the woman is concerned and that, for this reason, she should be given an option to dissolve the marriage.[150] The actual exemplification of the rule by the jurists is rather narrow in scope,[151] but the logic of the explanatory figure points to the heart of the matter: through the annihilation of the owner's ownership over the female slave and her children, the husband's authority increases: he can force his wife to live in one household with him, he can forbid her to leave the house or to see other people, he is responsible for the upbringing, the subsistence and the professional formation and activity of his children. As long as they live in his household, he can control their income. He becomes the head of the household in which the family is now organized and the balance of authority between husband, wife, children and the former owner changes. All these changes occur when the owner of the female slave sets her free and leaves the field open for her and her children's integration into the social hierarchies that determine the social ranking and authority among free persons. At that moment, she is entitled to choose whether she wants to continue the marriage under the new conditions.

IV. Social ranking and classification is established not only in the fields of marriage and sexual appropriation but also through the legal consequences of physical violence. The law of retaliation clearly classifies people into those who can use violence against other persons, as a form of retaliation, and those who cannot. Contrary to the ownership of commercial property, the ownership of the human body is not protected in the same way for and against everybody. Retaliation for grievous bodily harm is justice among equals. But the criteria of equality, in the field of retaliation, do not concern the religious and the social standing of the individual nor the social and religious merits of particular families and persons. It is not social stratification that counts but the generic classifications of people according to gender, freedom and health. Families remain important as the group of agnatic male relatives, who form the *'āqila*, responsible for the compensatory payments of unintentional killing or grievous bodily harm, and as the heirs, who receive the payment for unintentional homicide.[152]

Thus far, the individual remains embedded in the kinship structures of social exchange. But, there is no hierarchical ranking among families. All free men have the same "legal value" (*taqawwum*) as far as homicide is concerned. The same holds true for all free women. The ranking takes place between free men, free women, and slaves, who do not have a legally fixed value.[153] In the field of grievous bodily harm, health is introduced as an additional criterion for ranking. According to this classification, women are not the equal of men, crippled limbs are not equivalent to healthy limbs, slaves are not equivalent to free persons. Therefore, in the field of grievous bodily harm, women have no right to retaliation against men, persons with crippled limbs not against those with healthy limbs and slaves neither against free persons nor against each other, because, in this field, they are not considered to be persons but commercial property and commercial property does not enjoy the right of retaliation against other chattel.[154] If they are killed by their owners, no blood money and no talion arises from this act. The master is bound to perform an act of atonement (*kaffāra*).[155]

Conspicuously, the criterion of religious affiliation which is so prominent in the field of sexual relations is absent from the Hanafite law of retaliation. The hierarchical gender roles and the difference between the free and the slave determine the field. The contrast between the strong and healthy on the one hand, and the crippled and paralyzed person on the other hand, is an additional criterion of differentiation.

Concerning grievous bodily harm, the payment of compensation follows the same criteria: a woman's limbs are worth half a man's limbs, the slave's limbs have an exchange value, not a value that is fixed by the law. His exchange value has to be estimated by experts.[156] Compensation for non-intentional homicide follows similar criteria. It is supposed to re-establish a disrupted balance between social groups that has been caused by the loss of the life of one of the group members. The amount of the compensation depends on the generic classification of the persons concerned, i.e. on their gender roles and their status as free persons or slaves. A woman gets half of a man's blood money. The masters of the slaves have a claim for compensation for their exchange value. Neither religious affiliation nor age nor health have any influence on the amount of the blood money that has to be paid.[157] It seems, then, that as far as violence is concerned, the capacity to exert it is decisive for the choice of the criteria for valorization. Gender, health and freedom are the three criteria which determine the classification of persons and the respective prices to be paid for assaults against them.

None of these criteria plays a role in the field of capital punishment for intentional homicide. A twelfth-century jurist, Kāsānī, underlines the equality of all persons in this field:

> It is not required that the killed person be equal to the killer with regard to the perfection of his person, i.e. with

> regard to the integrity of his parts; it is also not required that he be his equal with regard to honor, rank and virtue. One kills the person with healthy limbs for the person whose limbs are cut or paralyzed, the scholar for the ignorant, the man of rank and honor for the commoner, the rational man for the insane, the adult for the minor, the man for the woman, the free for the slave and the Muslim for the non-Muslim.[158]

All subjects of a Muslim government are equal before the Hanafite law as far as the right to retaliation for intentional homicide is concerned. The reason is that life is protected by the Muslim political community's military and political power. The protection of the human life against intentional homicide does not depend on the criteria of the commercial or social exchange, nor on religious virtue nor on the individual's affiliation to a particular family, but on the notion of belonging to the Muslim political community *(dār)* and on the bond (*ʿiṣma*) that ties the subjects to the governments and which guarantees them the authorities' protection of their rights.[159] For that reason, there is no private property of one's life. Suicide is a violation of the bond that ties the subject to the Muslim government. Much as in Greek philosophy,[160] in Hanafite law suicide is an offense against the political commonwealth, against the body politic.[161] Life and death are matters of the political community, not of any social hierarchy. Neither religious affiliation, nor gender, nor the authority of the elder generation or the status of slaves and masters valorizes the body in this field. Hanafite law is the only form of Muslim law that proclaims this form of equality and bases it on the adherence to the body politic. Two exceptions to this principle of equality are conspicuous: the father cannot be killed for homicide against his son, nor the master for homicide against his slave. In both cases, private authority, based on either family and generation or on commercial property, outweighs public authority.

V. It would be tempting to follow in some detail the links between the two spheres of exchange, the social and the commercial one, to the realm of political power and sovereignty. It seems evident to me that the classical theories of the caliphate all link it, via genealogy and religion, gender and freedom, to the sphere of social exchange with its five major hierarchies. It also seems evident to me that this continuity is broken with the upsurge of the Mamluks and that from the thirteenth century onwards we can differentiate between forms of rules whose legitimation is related to the hierarchies of social exchange and those, like the Mamlūks, whose legitimation is not dependent on the hierarchies of social exchange. In these latter regimes one must have been a slave, an object of commercial exchange, in order to pass into the realm of political power. One must come from a non-Muslim origin and not have a family genealogy; in short, one must be clearly separated from the social hierarchies which characterize the society to be governed. For the relationship between government and society, for the legitimacy of a political rule, for the ranking in the political sphere, this change brings about important transformations which characterize the political culture in important parts of the Arab world from the thirteenth century onwards. It seems to me that the rupture between social exchange and the reproduction of the ruling class is a development of utmost importance that makes the thirteenth century the beginning of a new era in the political culture of the Arab world.

VI. The boundaries between the two forms of exchange are, of course, not impervious to the movement of persons and goods. These frequently move from one to the other, changing in these transfers their identity, status and function. The sons of the Mamlūks enter into the hierarchies of social exchange. Poor free women may engage in acts classified as prostitution by the jurists, selling the use of their body to free men and to slaves and thus engage the jurists in complex polemics as to how to interpret the acts, payments and services resulting from these relations.[162] Slaves who in many ways are treated as unprotected and profaned commodities are, legally, also human persons. They are subject to the law. They preserve the capacity to perform legal acts. They have a capacity to enjoy rights, but it is, as the jurists say, "a weak capacity" (*dhimma ḍaʿīfa*).[163] Because slaves are persons enjoying the capacity to perform legal acts, their owner may entitle them to do business for them, in which case they will be equal partners to everybody in the field of commercial exchange but not in marriage and social exchange. Even more importantly, slaves may at any moment regain the field of social exchange through being emancipated or through buying their freedom from their masters. This is the classical example of a marginal case between the commercial and social exchange, discussed at great length by the jurists: the non-commodity of freedom is bought by the slave for a monetary consideration, and for him it is a clear case of social exchange, whereas the owner sells a commodity, i.e. the slave, for another commodity, the payment of the slave, and so for him the exchange remains strictly commercial.[164] Whatever the legal interpretation of such a case, as a result of such an action, which is strongly encouraged by the religious tradition and the law, the slave becomes a free person and enters the field of social exchange, is integrated into its social hierarchies and circulates according to its rule of proportional justice.

Such a conversion from one form of exchange to the other, from one social sphere into the next, leaves its traces on the persons and the goods that perform them and determines their capacity to move in the new field. The liberated slave remains a client (*maulā*),[165] the payment that stems from social exchange follows special rules in the field of commercial exchange.[166] The distinguishing marks that they keep remind us of the transformative difference that separates the social from commercial exchange.

Instead of a conclusion, I should like to offer some ideas on how to continue such research into the twentieth century. If we compare the situation of classical Hanafite law with the situation of Islamic law in most of the Muslim countries of our century, the following seem to be the most important changes and continuities:

1. The differentiation between the spheres of the social and commercial exchange seems to be as vital for twentieth-century societies (and certainly not only Muslim ones) as it was for the societies in which classical Hanafite law developed. But the frontiers, the boundaries, the marginal zones between the two spheres of exchange seem to be less clear than they were eight hundred years ago.

2. Slavery has been abolished in nearly all Muslim countries: there is no longer a commercial exchange of persons.[167]

3. The traditional social hierarchies have weakened: no longer do the older generations enjoy the right to force their children into marriage against their will.[168] For demographic, cultural and economic reasons, the hierarchy of age, the authority of one generation over another, has been

decidedly weakened. Of the five major social hierarchies which characterize social exchange in classical Hanafite law—religion, kinship, gender, generations, and masters versus slaves—the last one has disappeared and the fourth one has been decidedly weakened.

4. In many Muslim countries, the law of retaliation and compensatory payments, which so clearly displayed the gender influence in the field of violence and penal law, has been abolished. Gender roles have lost an important dimension through the formation of a new state, a new penal law and a new economy.

5. Something that has happened unnoticed for most of the observers is the abolition of the formalism of social exchange. Neither in marriage nor in any other field of social exchange do the law codes of Muslim countries keep the binding force of the pronounced formula independently of the intention, the knowledge, the will of the parties concerned. As far as consent and duress are concerned, modern Muslim law has decidedly abolished the formalistic dimension of social exchange and with it one of the procedural aspects that most clearly distinguished the social from commercial exchange.[169]

6. The privileges of access to the female body which slavery granted to the class of well-to-do males disappeared in their old form. With them disappeared, from the realm of the normative structures, a whole dimension of sexual relations in which the satisfaction of sexual desire was not tied to the marriage contract as its only means of realization. The abolition of slavery has not led to the emancipation of desires. Although in literature and in politics women have demanded, and continue to do so, a recognition of their personal autonomy concerning their desires, their love relations and their bodies, most Muslim countries do not admit the right of individual persons to autonomously shape their personal forms of love and sex relations.

7. Of the traditional forms of valorization of the human body, only the nuptial payment and—in a reduced form—the controlling role of the agnatic relatives survives. Both refer to an institution, marriage, which has become a symbol of social hierarchies and social exchange, a symbol of the non-commercial world, and a symbol of a social order of a world that has passed. This symbolical function of the institution weighs heavily on the female body and its legal and social valorization. It sets a limit

to women's efforts to gain access to autonomy and emancipation outside the hierarchies of gender and kinship. It transforms the woman's body itself into a symbol of the permanence of the correct social exchange.

Notes

I am grateful to the Institute for Advanced Study (Princeton, N.J.), for accepting me as a member in the year 1993-94, and to the Deutsche Forschungsgemeinschaft, which funded an extra sabbatical term from April to September 1994. Both institutions have thus granted me the time to work on the project "Commercial exchange and social order in Muslim law," of which this article is a part.

1. Baber Johansen, "Commercial Exchange and Social Order in Hanafite Law," in Christopher Toll and Jakob Skovgaard-Petersen, eds., *Law and the Islamic World. Past and Present* (Copenhagen: The Royal Danish Academy of Sciences and Letters, 1995) pp. 84-85.

2. Y. Linant de Bellefonds, *Traité de Droit Musulman Comparé. Théorie Générale de l'Acte Juridique* (Paris: Mouton, 1965), vol. I, p. 69, calls these forms of exchange "des actes a dominante extrapatrimoniale."

3. Abū Bakr M. b. Abī Sahl as-Sarakhsī, *Kitāb al-Mabsūṭ* (Cairo, 1324 H., offset reprint Beirut: Dār al-ma'rifa, 1398 H./A.D. 1978), vol. XV, p. 134.

4. That the principle of equality (*musāwāt*) dominates commercial exchange is underlined by all jurists. They define equality in terms of

   a) access to commercial exchange (see note 3 above);

   b) the relation between the price and the commodity sold (Abū Bakr b. Mas'ud al-Kāsānī, *Kitāb Badā'i' aṣ-ṣanā'i' fī tartīb ash-sharā'i'* (Cairo, 1910), vol V, pp. 184, 187, 191, cf. pp. 193, 194);

   c) the relations between the partners to the contract, see Sarakhsī, op. cit., vol. XV, p. 134: *wa'l-muslimu wa'dh-dhimmī wa'l-ḥarbī wa'l-musta'minu wa'l-ḥurru wa'l-mamlūku't-tājiru wa'l-mukātabu kulluhum sawā'ūna fī'l-ijārati li'annahā min 'uqūdi' t-tijārati wa-hum fi dhālika sawā'ūn;* see also ibid., vol. XII, p. 126: *li'anna qaḍiyyata'l-mu'āwaḍati't-taswiyatu baina'l - muta'āqidaini fi't-tamlīki wa't-taslīm.* See also Kāsānī, op. cit., vol. V, pp. 237, 238, 243, 249.

   For this reason, the following categories of persons are equal under commercial exchange: 1. men and women (Sarakhsī, op. cit., vol. XII, p. 219; vol. XV, p. 134; vol. XIX, pp. 7, 12); 2. Muslims and non-Muslims (Sarakhsī, op. cit., vol. XIV, p. 168; vol. XII, p. 174; M. b. Ḥasan ash-Shaybānī, *Kitāb al-aṣl*, part I, *Kitāb al-buyūʿ waʾs-salam*, ed. Shafīq Shaḥāta (Cairo 1954), p. 221, no. 20); 3. even slaves with contracts of redemption of their freedom or the permission of their masters to engage in trade (Sarakhsī, op. cit., vol. XV, p. 134) are the equals of free persons in commercial exchange. This equality does not pertain to the dealings of a slave, even if he is permitted to trade, with his master. Everything the slave owns belongs to his master. On the casuistry belonging to this figure, see Kāsānī, op. cit., vol. V, p. 193.

5. For the classical model of transactional justice see *The Ethics* of Aristotle: *The Nicomachean Ethics*, translated by J.A.K. Thomson, revised with notes and appendices by Hugh Tredennick, introduction and Bibliography by Jonathan Barnes (Harmondsworth: Penguin Books, 1976), pp. 179-182, 183-186. The emphasis that is put, in this context, on the difference between transactional and proportional justice can help one to understand the Muslim jurists' differentiation between the commercial and social exchange.

6. This common value measure is expressed by the term *māliyya*, whose use by the jurists oscillates between the meanings of commodity character and exchange value: see Johansen, "Commercial Exchange and Social Order," op. cit.

7. Aristotle, *The Politics*, translated by T.A. Sinclair, revised and re-presented by Trevor J. Saunders (Harmondsworth: Penguin Books, 1992), p. 207, 1282b14.

8. Op. cit., p. 195, 1280a7; cf. *Ethics* 177-179, 1130b32-1132a2.

9. The argument runs as follows: 1. profit is the aim of all commercial exchange; 2. in order to calculate the profit, the *māliyya* or exchange value of the commodities exchanged has to be known. Therefore, the parties to commercial exchange must give precise information on the commodities exchanged in order to enable the other party to calculate the chances of profit, see Sarakhsī, op. cit., vol. XII, pp. 119, 124, 125, 128, 133, 136, 152-153; vol. XIII, pp. 38, 68, 77, 80, 99.

10. Kāsānī, op. cit., p. 48, cf. pp. 49, 54.

11. Sarakhsī, op. cit., vol. XIII, p. 157, cf. pp. 65, 69, 71, 72, 75-76; vol. XXIV, p. 65 (instead of *yaʿtamid* one has to read *yanʿadim*); Kāsānī, op. cit., vol. V, pp. 176-177, 219, 226.

12. Duress (*ikrāh*) destroys voluntary consent (*riḍā*). In a contract of sale, the party under duress can retroactively give his consent to the contract con-

cluded under duress and thus make it valid: see Sarakhsī, op. cit., vol. XXIV, pp. 55-56; Kāsānī, op. cit., vol. V, p. 176.

13. Kāsānī, op. cit., vol. V, p. 133; Sarakhsī, op. cit., vol. XVIII, p. 119; Linant de Bellefonds, op. cit., pp. 69-71.

14. Sarakhsī, op. cit., vol. XII, pp. 121, 140, 154, 187, 189, 190.

15. Sarakhsī, op. cit., vol. XII, p. 140: *fa-ta'thīruhu anna'l-mu'tabara ma huwa'l-maqṣūdu wa-bihi yakhtalifu'l-'aqd lā bi'tibāri'l-lafẓ;* Kāsānī, op. cit., vol. V, p. 133: *wa'l-'ibratu li'l-ma'nā la li'ṣ-ṣūra.*

16. *shayn*, see Kāsānī, op. cit., vol. V, p. 134.

17. Sarakhsī, op. cit., vol. XII p. 109; vol. XIII, p. 156; Linant de Bellefonds, op. cit., vol. II, pp. 29, 39-40.

18. Sarakhsī, op. cit., vol. XXIV, pp. 42-43, 56-57, 59, 62, 63-65, 85; Kāsānī, op. cit., vol. II, p. 310.

19. Linant de Bellefonds, op. cit., vol. I, pp. 75-76, cf. p. 182.

20. Sarakhsī, op. cit., vol. X, p. 53, cf. vol. XV, p. 125.

21. Kāsānī, op. cit., vol. V, p. 145; Sarakhsī, op. cit., vol. XV, p. 125.

22. Kāsānī, op. cit., vol. II, p. 276; vol. V, p. 142, 145; Sarakhsī, op. cit., vol. XII, p. 119; vol. XIII, pp. 96, 156; vol. XXI, pp. 13, 15; cf. vol. XV, pp. 125-126.

23. Ahmad b. M. al-Qudūrī, *al-Kitāb*, printed at the margin of 'Abd al-Ghanī al-Ghanīmī ad-Dimashqi, *al-Lubāb fī sharḥ al-Kitāb* (Cairo: maktabat Muḥammad 'Alī Ṣabīh, 1383 H./1963), vol. IV, p. 163; Sarakhsī, op. cit., vol. X, pp. 146-147; 'Alī b. Abi Bakr al-Marghīnānī, *al-Hidāya sharḥ bidāyat al-mubtadī*, printed at the margin of Muḥammad b. 'Abd al-Wāḥid as-Siwāsī Ibn al-Humām, *Sharḥ Fatḥ al-Qadīr* (Bulāq: al-maṭba'a al kubrā al-amīriyya, 1310 H.), vol. VIII, pp. 100-102; Maḥmūd al-Ūzjandī Qādīkhān, *Fatāwi Qādīkhān,* printed at the margin of *Al-Fatāwi al-'Ālamgīriyya,* second edition (Bulāq: al-maṭba'a al-amīriyya, 1310 H.), vol. III, pp. 407, 408.

24. Sarakhsī, op. cit., vol. X, pp. 145, 152-155; Marghīnānī, op. cit., vol. VIII, pp. 97-98; M. b. M. b. Shihāb Ibn al-Bazzāz al-Kardarī, *Al-Fatāwi al-Bazzāziyya*, printed at the margin of *Al-Fatāwi al-'Ālamgīriyya*, see note 23, vol. VI, pp. 373-374; Mahmūd b. Ahmad al-'Aynī, *an-niyāba fī sharḥ al-hidāya*, second edition (Beirūt: dār al-fikr, 1411 H./1990), vol. XI, pp. 143-146.

25. Sarakhsī, op. cit., vol. X, pp. 147, 157; Marghīnānī, op. cit., vol. VIII, p. 102; Qudūrī, op. cit., vol. IV, p. 163; Qādīkhān, op. cit., vol. III, p. 408; 'Aynī, op. cit., vol. XI, pp. 164-166.

26. Sarakhsī, op. cit., vol. X, pp. 149-151; Marghīnānī, op. cit., vol. VIII, pp. 103-104; Ahmad b. Qaudar Qādizādeh Afandī, *natā'ij al-afkār fī kashf ar-rumūz wa'l-asrār*, printed at the margin of Ibn al-Humām, op. cit., vol. VIII, pp. 103-106; 'Aynī, op. cit., vol. XI, pp. 171-179.

27. Sarakhsī, op. cit., vol. X, pp. 147, 149, 150; Marghīnānī, op. cit., vol. VIII, pp. 102, 106; Qudūrī, op. cit., vol. IV, p. 164; 'Aynī, op. cit., vol. XI, pp. 163-164, 165-166, 174-175, 178-179.

28. Sarakhsī, op. cit., vol. X, p. 154; Marghīnānī, op. cit., vol. VIII, p. 98-99; 'Aynī, op. cit., vol. XI, pp. 147-148; for the qualification of this rule through the criterion of age, see ibid., pp. 148-150.

29. Sarakhsī, op. cit., vol. X, p. 155; Marghīnānī, op. cit., vol. VIII, p. 99; 'Aynī; op. cit., vol. XI, pp. 152-154; Chehata, op. cit., vol. I, pp. 62-63.

30. 'Aynī, op. cit., vol. IV, pp. 530-535; Chehata, op. cit., vol. I, pp. 62-63.

31. Qudūrī, op. cit., vol. IV, p. 164; Sarakhsī, op. cit., vol. X, p. 149; Marghīnānī, op. cit., vol. VIII, p. 103; Qādīzādeh, op. cit., vol. VIII, p. 103; Qādīkhān, op. cit., vol. III, p. 407. Slightly more hesitant to allow the look on the wife's or husband's naked body are the *Fatāwi 'Ālamgīriyya*, vol. V, p. 327, but see the positive opinions ibid. p. 328. See also 'Aynī, op. cit., vol. XI, pp. 166-170, and his prudish efforts to interpret this doctrine and the sharp answer by Qādīzādeh, op. cit., vol. VIII, p. 103.

32. See note 30 and Kāsānī, op. cit., vol. II, p. 331; Marghīnānī, op. cit., vol. II, pp. 367-368; Muhammad b. Maḥmūd al-Bābartī, *Sharḥ al-'Ināya 'ala al-Hidāya*, printed in Ibn al-Humām, vol. II, pp. 367-368.

33. See J. Krcsmàrek, "Beiträge zur Beleuchtung des islamitischen Strafrechts mit Rücksicht auf Theorie und Praxis in der Türkei," *Zeitschrift der Deutschen Morgenländischen Gesellschaft* (1904), vol. LVIII; Baber Johansen, "Eigentum, Familie und Obrigkeit im hanafitischen Strafrecht," *Die Welt des Islams*, N.S. vol. XIX (1979), pp. 1-73.

34. Kāsānī, op. cit., vol. II, pp. 317-321; Marghīnānī, op. cit., vol. II, pp. 393-423; Sarakhsī, op. cit., vol. V, pp. 22-30.

35. Kāsānī, op. cit., vol. II, pp. 319: *quraish ba'ḍuhum akfā' li-ba'ḍin, wa'l-'arabu akfā' li-ba'ḍin ḥayy bi-ḥayy wa-qabīla bi-qabīla wa'l-mawālī ba'ḍuhum akfā' li-ba'ḍin rajulun bi-rajul*; see also Marghīnānī, op. cit., vol. II, pp. 420-421; Sarakhsī, op. cit., vol. V, p. 24, explains the fact that the mawālī are not the equals of the Arabs through the fact that "they lost their genealogies."

36. Kāsānī, op. cit., vol. II, pp. 317-318; Marghīnānī, op. cit., vol. II, p. 419; Sarakhsī, op. cit.,vol. V, pp. 25-26, 27, 131-132. See also Linant de

Bellefonds, op. cit., vol. II, pp. 64, 172.

37. Kāsānī, op. cit., vol. II, p. 238, adduces the guarantee of equal status (*kafāʾa*) as the major justification for the major agnates' right to marry their minor relatives of both sexes without their consent; see also ibid., pp. 240-241 and Linant de Bellefonds, op. cit., vol. II, pp. 64, 172. The father and the grandfather are entitled to marry their minor daughters to men who are not their equals, see Kāsānī, op. cit., vol. II, pp. 245, 318. Other agnates are not entitled to do this. For marriage that is enforced upon minors (*jabr*) see Linant de Bellefonds, op. cit., vol. II, pp. 60-65, 69-73; vol. III, pp. 178, 182-183.

38. Sarakhsī, op. cit., vol. V, pp. 63, 64, 67, 70, 73, 81; Kāsānī, op. cit., vol. II, pp. 274, 275, 287; Marghīnānī, op. cit., vol. II, pp. 434; ʿAynī, op. cit., vol. IV, p. 655, cf. pp. 708-709.

39. Kāsānī, op. cit., vol. II, p. 331, cf. pp. 287-288; cf. Sarakhsī, op. cit., vol. V, p. 64; for the concept of ownership with regard to the woman's body as a consequence of marriage and the *mahr* as consideration for it, see Kāsānī, op. cit., vol. II, p. 331: *wa-minhā milk al-mutʿa wa-huwa ʾkhtiṣāṣuʾz-zauji bi-manafiʿ buḍʿihā wa-sāʾiri aʿḍāʾihā istimtāʿan au milku ʾdh-dhāti waʾn-nafsi fī ḥaqqi ʾt-tamattuʿi ʿalaʾ khtilāfi mashayikhinā fī dhālika liʾanna maqāṣidaʾn-nikāhi la tuḥṣalu bidūnahu*; see also Marghīnānī, op. cit., vol. II, pp. 347-48; Bābartī, op. cit., vol. II, p. 347; Ibn al-Humām, op. cit., vol. II, p. 347.

40. ʿAynī, op. cit., vol. IV, pp. 711-716; cf. Marghīnānī, op. cit., vol. II, pp. 470-471; Kāsānī, op. cit., vol. II, pp. 283, 287; Sarakhsī, op. cit., vol. V, p. 64; ʿĀlim al-ʿAlāʾ, *al-Fatāwi at-Tātarkhāniyya* (Karatshi: idārat al-qurʾān, n.d.), vol. III, pp. 83-84; G.H. Bousquet and L. Bercher, *Le Statut Personnel en droit Musulman Hanéfite* (Paris: Sirey, n.d.), pp. 34-35; Linant de Bellefonds, op. cit., vol. II, pp. 214-215.

41. Sarakhsī, op. cit., vol. XIII, p. 97, cf. pp. 117-118.

42. Kāsānī, op. cit., vol. II, p. 278; cf. Sarakhsī, op. cit., vol. V, p. 78; vol. XIII, pp. 178-179.

43. Kāsānī, op. cit., vol. II, p. 283: *wa-lanā annaʾn-nikāḥa muʿāwaḍatuʾl-māli bimā laisa bi-māl*; cf. Marghīnānī, op. cit., vol. II, p. 462; Bābartī, op. cit., vol. II, p. 462; Ibn al-Humām, op. cit., vol. II, p. 462; ʿAynī, op. cit., vol. IV, pp. 696; Sarakhsī, op. cit., vol. V, p. 68: *annaʾl-mahra innama yastaḥiqqu ʿiwaḍan ʿamma laisa bi-māl.*

44. Kāsānī, op. cit., vol. II, p. 234, see also ibid. p. 245; Sarakhsī, op. cit., vol. V, p. 122.

45. Sarakhsī, op. cit., vol. XIII, p. 133.

46. Sarakhsī, op. cit., vol. XIII, pp. 58, 96-97, 99-100, 117-118.

47. Sara<u>kh</u>sī, op. cit., vol. V, p. 23; Ibn al-Humām, op. cit., vol. II, p. 451; ʿAynī, op. cit., vol. IV, p. 683.

48. Kāsānī, op. cit., vol. II, p. 275; see also Sara<u>kh</u>sī, op. cit., vol. VI, p. 3, and the very explicit statement in vol. XIII, p. 132.

49. Sara<u>kh</u>sī, op. cit., vol. VI, pp. 74, 78, 84-85, 175, 176.

50. Joseph Schacht, *An Introduction to Islamic Law* (Oxford: Oxford University Press), 1964, pp. 163-168; Linant de Bellefonds, op. cit., vol. II, pp. 287-297.

51. Schacht, op. cit., p. 167.

52. Linant de Bellefonds, op. cit., vol. II, pp. 297-299, underlines the lack of sanctions for these claims in the Hanafite school of law.

53. Mar<u>gh</u>īnānī, op. cit., vol. II, p. 494; cf. ʿAynī, op. cit., vol. IV, pp. 757-760.

54. Sara<u>kh</u>sī, op. cit., vol. XV, p. 128.

55. Ibid., vol. XV, p. 128.

56. Sara<u>kh</u>sī, op. cit., vol. X, p. 151.

57. R. Brunschvig, s.v. ʿAbd, in *The Encyclopaedia of Islam*, new edition (Leiden and London: Brill-Luzac, 1960), vol. I, p. 27; what is meant is not so much to cover nakedness as to cover the zone of shame, *satr al-ʿaura*.

58. Sara<u>kh</u>sī, op. cit., vol. X, p. 151; Mar<u>gh</u>īnānī, op. cit., vol. VIII, p. 107.

59. Mar<u>gh</u>īnānī, op. cit., vol. VIII, p. 107.

60. Yusuf Rāgib, "Les Marchés aux Esclaves en Terre d'Islam," in *Mercati e Mercanti nell'Alto Medioevo L'Area Euroasiatica e l'Area Mediterranea* (Spoleto: Presso La Sede del Centro, 1993), pp. 721-766. See also Bernard Lewis, *Race and Slavery in the Middle East. An Historical Enquiry* (Oxford: Oxford University Press, 1990), pp. 12-13, who stresses the importance of the covered space for the slave market.

61. Sara<u>kh</u>sī, op. cit., vol. X, p. 151; cf. Mar<u>gh</u>īnānī, op. cit., vol. VIII, p. 107; Ibn al-Humām, op. cit., vol. VIII, p. 107.

62. Sara<u>kh</u>sī, op. cit., vol. XII, p. 125.

63. Sara<u>kh</u>sī, op. cit., vol. V, p. 68; vol. XIII, p. 38; Kāsānī, op. cit., vol. II, pp. 283-284; ʿAynī, op. cit., vol. IV, pp. 698-699; compare Mar<u>gh</u>īnānī, op. cit., vol. II, p. 462 and Ibn al-Humām, op. cit., vol. II, p. 462.

64. This is sometimes done without much reasoning to justify the statement; see Sara<u>kh</u>sī, op. cit., vol. XIII, p. 83.

65. Nabil A. Saleh, *Unlawful gain and legitimate profit in Islamic Law. Riba,*

gharar and Islamic banking (Cambridge: Cambridge University Press, 1986), pp. 13-18.

66. Sarakhsī, op. cit., vol. XII, pp. 123-124, 152; cf. Kāsānī, op. cit., vol. V, p. 234; vol. VI, p. 142.

67. Saleh, op. cit., pp. 16-18; for examples, see Kāsānī, op. cit., vol. V, p. 189; Sarakhsī, op. cit., vol. XII, p. 177.

68. Sarakhsī, op. cit., vol. XII, pp. 122, 177.

69. Saleh, op. cit., p. 16; Kāsānī, op. cit., vol. V, p. 189; Sarakhsī, op. cit., vol. XII, p. 200.

70. Sarakhsī, op. cit., vol. XII, p. 200.

71. Sarakhsī, op. cit., vol. XII, pp. 122, 175, 182-183; Kāsānī, op. cit., vol. V, p. 140.

72. Ibid., vol. XII, p. 159.

73. Sarakhsī, op. cit., vol. XII, pp. 176-178, 185.

74. Saleh, op. cit., pp. 16-18; Kāsānī, op. cit., vol. V, pp. 140, 141, 142, 143, 144, 189; Marghīnānī, op. cit., vol. V, pp. 102, 107, 198, 202; Bābartī, op. cit., vol. V, p. 107, 198, 202; Ibn al-Humām, op. cit., vol. V, p. 198; Sarakhsī, op. cit., vol. XIII, p. 102.

75. Sarakhsī, op. cit., vol. XII, pp. 176, 177, 178, 181, 187, 195, 200; vol. XIII, pp. 60, 71, 73, 102; Marghīnānī, op. cit., vol. V, p. 155; Bābartī, op. cit., vol. V, p. 155.

76. Schacht, op. cit., p. 205.

77. ʿAynī, op. cit., vol. IV, pp. 696, 699.

78. Maḥmūd Fakhūrī and ʿAbd al-Ḥamīd Mukhtār, eds., *Al-Mughrib fī'l-Muʿrab* (Aleppo: Maktabat Usāma b. Zaid, 1399/1979), p. 174, s.v. *jins*.

79. Sarakhsī, op. cit., vol. XII, pp. 83-84. See Sa'di Jalabī, *ḥāshiya*, printed at the margin of Ibn al-Humām, op. cit., vol. II, p. 465.

80. Sarakhsī, op. cit., vol. V, p. 84.

81. Kāsānī, op. cit., vol. II, pp. 279-280; Marghīnānī, op. cit., vol. II, p. 466; Ibn al-Humām, op. cit., vol. II, p. 465.

82. Ibn al-Humām, op. cit., vol. II, pp. 465-466; Bābartī, op. cit., vol. II, p. 465, defines it through identity of name, quality and function (*maʿnā*); ʿAynī, op. cit., vol. IV, p. 706, refers to form, use, function and name.

83. Sarakhsī, op. cit., vol. V, p. 84; Bābartī, op. cit., vol. II, p. 465; ʿAynī, op. cit., vol. IV, p. 706.

84. Kāsānī, op. cit., vol. II, p. 279; Ibn al-Humām, op. cit., p. 464.

85. It is hard to say whether this doctrine owes some of its arguments to the influence of the cynical and stoical opposition to slavery in classical antiquity which is based on the idea that the human kind is one genus and cannot be divided into masters and slaves: see Bernard Lewis, op. cit., p. 4.

86. Sarakhsī, op. cit., vol. XIII, p. 12.

87. Sarakhsī, op. cit., vol. XIII, pp. 12-13, cf. vol. XV, p. 37.

88. Ibn al-Humām, op. cit., vol. V, p. 206, underlines that logically they should be one genus only.

89. Kāsānī, op. cit., vol. V, p. 140; Marghīnānī, op. cit, vol. V, pp. 206-207; Bābartī, op. cit., vol. II, p. 465; vol. V, p. 206; Ibn al Humam, op. cit., vol. V, pp. 206-207; Sa'di Jalabī, op. cit., vol. II, p. 464.

90. One wonders, in fact, how much of this construction is a reaction to the current practice of slave-dealers to sell young boys as girls and young girls as boys, a practice that should stir the moral fears of the jurists: see Y. Rāġib, op. cit., pp. 759-760, nn. 270 and 271. But it seems more convincing and more fruitful to understand this as a reference to the principal gender differences among slaves as outlined below.

91. Sarakhsī, op. cit., vol. V, p. 129; Kāsānī, op. cit., vol. II, p. 234; *Tātarkhāniyya*, op. cit., vol. III, p. 155.

92. Sarakhsī, op. cit., vol. V, pp. 113-114; Kāsānī, op. cit., pp. 234, 237-238.

93. See above, note 63, for the importance of the ethnic affiliation for determining species and quality of the slave.

94. Sarakhsī, op. cit., vol. V, pp.94-98; Linant de Bellefonds, op. cit., vol. II, pp. 184-185, 187.

95. Black's *Law Dictionary*, Sixth Edition (St. Paul: West Publishing, 1990), p. 1279, s.v. *redhibitory defect or vice*.

96. Sarakhsī, op. cit., vol. XIII, pp. 51, 99, 106; vol. XV, pp. 99, 106, 109, 111; Marghīnānī, op. cit., vol. V, p. 153, identifies the "deficiency of the exchange value" with the "deficiency of the price"; Bābartī, op. cit., vol. V, p. 153.

97. Kāsānī, op. cit., vol. V, pp. 274, 275; Qudūrī, op. cit., in Marghīnānī, op. cit., vol. V, p. 153; Bābartī, op. cit., vol. V, p. 153.

98. Qādīkhān, *Fatāwī*, printed at the margin of *Fatāwī 'Ālamgīriyya*, vol. II, p. 194.

99. Sarakhsī, op. cit., vol. XIII, p. 106; see also ibid., pp. 51, 99, 103; Kāsānī,

op. cit., vol. V, pp. 274, 275; Qādīkhān, op. cit., vol. II, p. 201; Marghīnānī, op. cit., vol. V, p. 153; Bābartī, op. cit., vol. V, p. 153; Ibn al-Humām, op. cit., vol. V, p. 153.

100. E.g. Sarakhsī, op. cit., vol. XIII, pp. 105-115.

101. Sarakhsī, op. cit., vol. XIII, pp. 110-111; cf. Qādīkhān, op. cit., vol. II, pp. 194-195.

102. For the aesthetic criteria see Qādīkhān, op. cit., vol. II, p. 196; Ibn al-Humām, op. cit., vol. V, p. 153.

103. Sarakhsī, op. cit., vol. XIII, pp. 51, 95, 113, 114, 117; Qādīkhān, op. cit., vol. I, pp. 195-196; Marghīnānī, op. cit., vol. II, p. 487; Bābartī, op. cit., vol. II, p. 487; Ibn al-Humām, op. cit., vol. II, p. 487.

104. Sarakhsī, op. cit., vol. XIII, p. 107; Marghīnānī, op. cit., vol. V, p. 155; Bābartī, op. cit., vol. II, pp. 155; Qādīkhān, op. cit., vol. II, p. 195.

105. Sarakhsī, op. cit., vol. XIII, pp. 106-107; Marghīnānī, op. cit., vol. V, pp. 155-56; Bābartī, op. cit., vol. V, pp. 155-56; Ibn al-Humām, op. cit., vol. V, pp. 155-156; Qādīkhān, op. cit., vol. II, p. 195.

106. Ibn al-Humām, op. cit., vol. V, p. 156.

107. Baber Johansen, "Eigentum, Familie und Obrigkeit im hanafitischen Strafrecht," op. cit., p. 42 and note 162.

108. The most striking example of this reasoning is to be met with in the case, analyzed by many jurists, of the slave who has been condemned to death but who can still licitly be sold by his master. They argue that the sale concerns the *māliyya*, the exchange value, whereas the death sentence concerns the life, *nafsīyya*, of the slave. Both are the result of independent claims and do not interfere with each other. Only if the death sentence is executed does the slave's exchange value disappear with his life and only in this case is the death sentence considered to be a redhibitory vice which entitles the slave buyer to a compensation: see Sarakhsī, op. cit., vol. XIII, pp. 115-116, cf. vol. XVIII, pp. 171-172; Marghīnānī, op. cit., vol. V, pp. 178-181; Bābartī, op. cit., vol. V, pp. 178-181; Ibn al-Humām, op. cit., vol. V, pp. 178-182.

109. Sarakhsī, op. cit., vol. XIII, pp. 61, 98.

110. Ibid., p. 61.

111. Ibid., p. 58: *li'anna iqdāmahu 'ala waṭ'ihā ta'yīnun li'l-bai' fīhā wa-isqāṭun li'l-khiyār,* see also pp. 64, 97, 98, 166.

112. Sarakhsī, op. cit., vol. XIII, p. 64.

113. Sarakhsī, op. cit., vol. XIII, pp. 58-59.

114. Sarakhsī, op. cit., vol. XIII, p. 61, see also p. 96.

115. Sarakhsī, op. cit., vol. XIII, p. 64, see also pp. 46-47.

116. Sarakhsī, op. cit., vol. XVII, p. 100: the satisfaction of desire is here closely related to the coitus interruptus (*'azl*) which separates it from the sexual intercourse for the begetting of children.

117. Schacht, op. cit., Introduction, p. 127; Kāsānī, op. cit., vol. II, p. 272.

118. Kāsānī, op. cit., vol. II, p. 272; see also Sarakhsī, op. cit., vol. V, pp. 123, 129, 130-31; vol. XVII, p. 120; Qādīkhān, op. cit., vol. I, pp. 369-70; 'Aynī, op. cit., vol. IV, p. 771.

119. Sarakhsī, op. cit., vol. XVII, pp. 135-136; Marghīnānī, op. cit., vol. II, pp. 499-500; Bābartī, op. cit., vol. II, p. 500; *Tātarkhāniyya*, vol. III, pp. 157-158; *Fatāwi 'Ālamgīriyya*, vol. I, p. 331.

120. Sarakhsī, op. cit., vol. XVII, pp. 99-100, 136, 137, 163.

121. Sarakhsī, op. cit., vol. XVII, p. 100.

122. In the competition of free men over the paternity of a slave woman's children, it is an important asset if they can prove that they have been the slave woman's masters at a time when she could have conceived the children in question because their ownership of her body legitimizes their sexual intercourse with her and thus gives them a legitimate claim to her children; see Sarakhsī, op. cit., vol. XVII, pp. 101, 102, 107, 109.

123. Kāsānī, op. cit., vol. II, pp. 233-34, 236, 237; Qādīkhān, op. cit., vol. I, p. 343; Marghīnānī, op. cit., vol. II, pp. 486, 491; 'Aynī, op. cit., vol. IV, pp. 745, 753-54; *Tātarkhāniyya*, vol. III, p. 155.

124. Sarakhsī, op. cit., vol. V, pp. 113-114, 125-127; Kāsānī, op. cit., vol. II, pp. 237-238; Qādīkhān, op. cit., vol. I, p. 343; Marghīnānī, op. cit., vol. II, pp. 491-492; *Tātarkhāniyya*, vol. III, p. 156; *Fatāwi 'Ālamgīriyya*, vol. I, p. 331.

125. Sarakhsī, op. cit., vol. V, pp. 113-114, 125; Kāsānī, op. cit., vol. II, pp. 234, 236-237.

126. Kāsānī, op. cit., vol. II, pp. 237-238; Marghīnānī, op. cit., vol. II, pp. 491-492; Bābartī, op. cit., vol. II, pp. 491-492; Ibn al-Humām, op. cit., vol. II, pp. 491-492; 'Aynī, op. cit., vol. IV, p. 754.

127. Sarakhsī, op. cit., vol. V, pp. 110, 122.

128. Sarakhsī, op. cit., vol. II, pp. 121-122; Kāsānī, op. cit., vol. II, p. 245; Qādīkhān, op. cit., vol. I, p. 343; *Tātarkhāniyya*, vol. III, pp. 158, 170; 'Aynī, op. cit., vol. IV, p. 745.

129. Sarakhsī, op. cit., vol. V, pp. 114-115, 121-122; Kāsānī, op. cit., vol. II, pp. 237; ʿAynī, op. cit., vol. IV, pp. 745, 764-65; Marghīnānī, op. cit., vol. II, p. 497; Bābartī, op. cit., vol. II, p. 497; *Tātarkhāniyya*, vol. III, p. 157.

130. Sarakhsī, op. cit., vol. V, p. 121.

131. Sarakhsī, op. cit., vol. V, pp. 121-122.

132. Kāsānī, op. cit., vol. II, p. 245.

133. Kāsānī, op. cit., vol. II, p. 245; Sarakhsī, op. cit., vol. V, pp. 121-122; *Fatāwi ʿĀlamgīriyya*, vol. I, p. 333.

134. Kāsānī, op. cit., vol. II, p. 245.

135. Kāsānī, op. cit., p. 245.

136. Quoted from Avram L. Udovitch, *Partnership and Profit in early Islam* (Princeton: Princeton University Press, 1970), p. 225 (quoting Sarakhsī, op. cit., vol. XXII, p. 122). See also Sarakhsī, op. cit., vol. V, p. 122.

137. Sarakhsī, op. cit., vol. V, p. 115; Marghīnānī, op. cit., vol. II, p. 491; Bābartī, op. cit., vol. II, p. 491; Ibn al-Humām, op. cit., vol. II, p. 491; ʿAynī, op. cit., vol. IV, p. 752; *Tātarkhāniyya*, vol. III, p. 167.

138. Marghīnānī, op. cit., vol. II, p. 491; Ibn al-Humām, op. cit., vol. II, p. 491; ʿAynī, op. cit., vol. IV, p. 752.

139. Sarakhsī, op. cit., vol. V, p. 115.

140. See, for example, Sarakhsī, op. cit., vol. XVII, p. 100; B.F. Musallam, *Sex and Society in Islam. Birth control before the nineteenth century* (Cambridge: Cambridge University Press, 1983), pp. 15-23.

141. Musallam, op. cit., p. 32; see above, note 53, and also the *loci probantes* cited below, note 142.

142. Musallam, op. cit., p. 36; Marghīnānī, op. cit., vol. II, p. 494; Bābartī, op. cit., vol. II, p. 494; Ibn al-Humām, op. cit., vol. II, pp. 494 495; ʿAynī, op. cit., vol. IV, pp. 757-760; *Fatāwi ʿĀlamgīriyya*, vol. I, p. 335 with an interesting digression on the woman's right of abortion during the first months of her pregnancy, on which see also Ibn al-Humām, op. cit., vol. II, p. 495, and Musallam, op. cit., pp. 57-59.

143. See all loci probantes quoted in note 142.

144. Sarakhsī, op. cit., vol. XVII, p. 162; Qādīkhān, op. cit., vol. I, p. 374.

145. Sarakhsī, op. cit., vol. V, pp. 109, 116, 118-119, 120-121; vol. XVII, pp. 176-177; Kāsānī, op. cit., vol. II, p. 237; *Tātarkhāniyya*, vol. III, p. 167.

146. Sarakhsī, op. cit., vol. V, pp. 118-119; vol. XVII, pp. 176-177; *Tātarkhāniyya*, vol. III, pp. 167-168.

147. See above, note 53.

148. Kāsānī, op. cit., vol. II, p. 272.

149. Sarakhsī, op. cit., vol. V, pp. 111, 114; Marghīnānī, op. cit, vol. II, pp. 495-496; Bābartī, op. cit., vol. II, pp. 495-497; *Tātarkhāniyya*, vol. III, pp. 161-162; 'Aynī, op. cit., vol. IV, pp. 760-763; *Fatāwī 'Ālamgīriyya*, vol. I, pp. 332, 335.

150. Sarakhsī, op. cit., vol. V, p. 111; Marghīnānī, op. cit., vol. II, p. 495; Ibn al-Humām, op. cit., vol. II, p. 496; Bābartī, op. cit., vol.II, p. 495; 'Aynī, op. cit., vol. IV, pp. 760-763.

151. The authors cited in note 150 state that the husband acquires an additional revocable repudiation and thus can hold his wife in marital dependence for a longer time.

152. Johansen, "Eigentum, Familie und Obrigkeit im hanafitischen Strafrecht," op cit., pp. 10-12.

153. Ibid., pp. 12-18.

154. Ibid., pp. 25-28.

155. Sarakhsī, op. cit., vol. V, p. 116; vol. XIII, pp. 172-175; Marghīnānī, op. cit., vol. V, p. 163; Bābartī, op. cit., vol. V, p. 163; Ibn al-Humām, op. cit., vol. V, p. 163; 'Aynī, op. cit., vol. IV, pp. 755-756.

156. Johansen, "Eigentum," op. cit., pp. 12-18.

157. Ibid., pp. 12-18.

158. Kāsānī, op. cit., vol. VII, p. 237.

159. B. Johansen, "Der 'iṣma-Begriff im hanafitischen Recht," in *La Signification du Bas Moyen Age dans l'Histoire et la Culture du Monde Musulman.* Actes du 8e Congres de l'Union Européenne des Arabisants et Islamisants (Aix-en-Provence: EDISUD, 1978), passim.

160. Aristotle, *Ethics*, pp. 200-201

161. Johansen, "Eigentum," op. cit., pp. 31-36, 66-67.

162. The references to such problems are innumerable. The following are random illustrations: Sarakhsī, op. cit., vol. IX, pp. 58-59: the debate between Abū Ḥanīfa, Abū Yūsuf and Muḥammad ash-Shaybani on whether a man who rents a woman in order to make love to her should be punished as an adulterer or whether the rent should be considered to be a nuptial payment (*mahr*); ibid., p. 59: a man has illicit sexual intercourse with a slave or a free woman under the assumption that his payment to them was a price in a sale contract; should he be punished as an adulterer or should his payment in the case of the slave woman considered to be her price and in the case of the

free woman her nuptial payment (*mahr*)?; ʿAynī, op. cit., vol. IV, p. 766, cites legal authorities who determine the criterion for the amount of the ʿuqr, the money that has to be paid to the owner of a female slave by a man who had illicit sexual intercourse with her, in the following way: one states how much such a woman would have earned if, given her beauty, she would have rented herself out for prostitution. This amount is then defined as nuptial payment (mahr). See also *al-Fatāwi al-ʿĀlamgīriyya*, vol. I, p. 325, for a very similar definition ascribed to the same authorities. It is evident also from *Tātarkhāniyya*, vol. III, pp. 150-152, that payments to women with whom a man has illicit sexual intercourse are, wherever possible, defined as nuptial payment.

163. Chafik Chehata, s.v. *dhimma* in the *New Encyclopaedia of Islam*, vol. II (Leiden and London: Brill-Luzac, 1965), p. 231.

164. Sarakhsī, op. cit., vol. XIII, pp. 117-118.

165. Kāsānī, op. cit., vol. IV, pp. 160 ff; Marghīnānī, op. cit., vol. VII, pp. 280 ff; Patricia Crone, *Roman, Provincial and Islamic Law. The origins of the Islamic patronate* (Cambridge: Cambridge University Press, 1987).

166. Baber Johansen, "Amwāl Ẓāhira and Amwāl Bāṭina. Town and Countryside as reflected in the Tax System of the Hanafite School," in Wadād al-Qāḍī, ed., *Studia Arabica and Islamica. Festschrift for Iḥsān ʿAbbās on his sixtieth birthday* (Beirut: American University of Beirut, 1981), p. 254.

167. Lewis, op. cit., pp. 82, 167-169.

168. Norman Anderson, *Law Reform in the Muslim World* (London: The Athlone Press, 1976), pp. 103-104; Linant de Bellefonds, op. cit., vol. II, pp. 71-73; *Code de statut personnel et des successions (Moudawwana)* (Royaume du Maroc, Ministere de la Justice—Institut National d'Etudes Judiciaires, Collection de la Legislation Marocaine, Série de Droit Privé, Texte Integral, 1983) (Publications APREJ), art. 12 (4).

169. Linant de Bellefonds, op. cit., vol. I, pp. 76-77, vol. II, pp. 71 73.

Marriages and Misdemeanors: A Record of *resm-i 'arūs ve bād-i havā* [1]

AMY SINGER

Introduction

In the late winter and early spring of 1586 the wheat harvests were ripening in the foothills and plain which stretched from Jerusalem westward to the Mediterranean Sea. The preparations for this harvest and that of barley, and other winter crops probably occupied the time of many villagers, in addition to preparing food, tending livestock and all the other daily rural chores. The rains continued as the weather gradually warmed flowers and trees bloomed, filling the air with color and fragrance.

Twenty-nine couples from eight villages in the district (*nāḥiye*) of Ramle in the province (*sancak*) of Gaza had their marriages registered from late January to mid-May. During the same period thirty-three criminal or punishable incidents in these same villages were recorded. Fighting, perhaps brawling, was the most common offense, but there were incidents of lying and thefts of grain as well.

Village life in the Ottoman empire has long eluded the attentions of most scholars, especially in the pre-modern period. For, in order to consider the nature and meaning of rural existence, some evidence, some testament from the peasant world must provide the basis for interpretive discussion.[2] Peasants as individuals have begun to appear in studies which take the records of the provincial judges (*ḳāḍī sicilleri*) as their starting point. From these, the networks of relationships between peasants, Ottoman officials, and local urban personages may be traced, their complex interweaving elucidated. The *sicill*s even offer some evidence about the relations among the peasants themselves.[3]

In general, the towns of the Ottoman empire have been a more frequent focus for research than the villages. However, the extent to which Ottoman forms and practices penetrated into village life and agrarian routine is an inseparable aspect of the investigation of the towns, as they were part of a continuum. Like the towns, rural areas of the empire were affected differently by Ottoman rural administration, and local practice shaped the Ottoman agrarian regime just as it did the urban. In this regard, the Ottoman legacy to the modern Middle East is not sufficiently understood, and only a few studies have successfully explored deep into the countryside to begin to elucidate it.[4]

As so often, however, the question is how to accomplish this challenge. The most successful studies, mentioned above, have used the judicial records as testimony to rural life. These records exist for a wide variety of places in the empire, throughout its history. However, they are not uniform. And they are of necessity incomplete because they represent for the most part an urban record of rural behavior. To date, only a small fraction of this documentary record has been read and used as the basis for studying peasants in the Ottoman empire. The work published so far indicates that the *ḳādī sicilleri* should probably be a principal focus for any scholar investigating the rural world.

Another kind of documentary record may prove to rival the records of the kadis as a source of information about villages in the Ottoman empire. This record is not a single type of document but rather includes a varied typology of documents all relating to a common institution: the *evḳāf* (s. *vaḳıf*), or pious endowments. These endowments comprised properties whose revenues supported a variety of charitable foundations. The largest of the *evḳāf* founded in the Ottoman empire were set up by the sultans, members of the imperial family, and other personages wealthy enough to afford such projects. The endowments supported mosques, *medrese*s (religious colleges), *kuttāb*s (elementary schools), hospitals, poor kitchens, hospices, and caravansarays. Each endowment drew revenues from its own properties, which might include urban space such as houses or bazaar shops, and rural holdings like orchards, vineyards, or extensive agricultural lands. It is the administrative records of these latter holdings which turn out to be a treasure trove of evidence about village society and economy. As the foundations which were supported by endowment funds were very often to be found in cities, these document collections will probably also provide further materials to enrich our interpretations of urban-rural relations.[5]

The document discussed in this article—D-3528/4—is one example of the kinds of records which may survive in collections of documents pertaining to pious foundations. This particular document was found in the Topkapı Sarayı Arşivi among the papers catalogued as belonging to the accounts of the charitable foundations of the Hāṣṣekī Sulṭān in Jerusalem, Egypt, Mecca, Amman, Istanbul and Edirne. The hāṣṣekī of many of these documents is Süleyman I's chief consort and wife Hürrem Sulṭān. The document considered below was discovered in the context of a larger project on Hürrem Sulṭān's foundation in Jerusalem, and the villages mentioned there were all part of this endowment.

Hürrem Sulṭān established this large foundation in the 1550's. It included a mosque, rooms for students and pilgrims, a caravansaray, stable, and a large public kitchen (*ʿimāret*).[6] Over time, the *vaḳıf* became commonly referred to as the Hāṣṣekī Sulṭān *ʿimāret* or *takīyyat al-Sitt*, thereby emphasizing the importance of its kitchen. Agricultural revenues from the *vakıf* villages were collected mostly in kind and brought to Jerusalem to supply the needs of the kitchen; surplus produce was sold to fund the purchase of other necessary supplies.

The revenues recorded in the present document, however, are those generated by *resm-i ʿarūs* (marriage fees) and *bād-i havā* (occasional fines or windfall taxes). *Resm-i ʿarūs ve bād-i havā* defines one category of taxes due from villagers in the Ottoman empire. Like the agricultural taxes which are estimated in the *tapu tahrir defterleri* for each village, an estimated annual yield from these taxes was recorded as a lump sum in the same registers. Rarely, however, did these surveys note any details of such incidental and fluctuating fees. Even the *ḳānūnnāme*s (statute lists) which preceded many surveys elaborated on these taxes only to note that the tax differed depending on whether a marriage was of a virgin or a remarrying woman, or to specify who might rightfully receive these fees and fines. However, on this basis nothing much could be said about individual marriages or incidents which provoked the fines.

This *defter*, or register, provides a unique record of the actual marriages and misdemeanors which occurred in eight villages around the town of Ramle in part of the year 994 A.H. (early 1586 C.E.) While marriages in towns and cities had to be registered in the *şer 'ī* court, village practices have been less well-understood. The *resm-i 'arūs* and *bād-i havā* were collected as part of the income of one Ḥuseyn *ṣubaşı*. He (or his scribe) thus made a record of the individual marriages for which he expected to collect the tax.[7]

The *defter* is written on one side of a paper folded into four, forming four separate columns of writing. Coincidentally, the text itself consists of four sections: 1) a listing of *resm-i 'arūs* and *bād-i havā* by village for a period of three months (pages a-c); 2) an account of payments owed by Ḥuseyn *şubası* for various things (page c); 3) a listing of *resm-i 'arūs* and *bād-i havā* paid to Ḥuseyn for one additional month (page d); and 4) an account of the payments Ḥuseyn owed from this additional month (page d). The *defter* appears to be complete, with an initial heading, closing signature, seal, and date.

Transcription of the Ottoman Turkish text

Page a

Defter-i mevaddāt-i maḳbūżāt-i Ḥuseyn ṣubaşı-i ḳarye-i Lidd ma'a baḳıya-i ḳurā-i e[v]ḳāf-i Hāṣṣekī sulṭān tāba serāha der Kuds-i Şerīf bād-i hav[ā] ma'a resm-i 'arūs fīgurre-i şehr-i Ṣafer el-hayr ilā gāyet-i Rebī 'ül-āhir sene-i 994

'An ḳarye-i Lidd
'an resm-i nikāḥ-i Sulaymān b. Ḥātim 'alā Nuṣra bt. Qudsī *bikr* 35 pāra
'an resm-i nikāḥ-i 'Īsā b. Sulaymān 'alā Rūmiya bt. Manṣūr *bikr* 35 pāra
'an resm-i nikāḥ-i Ibrāhīm b. Ṭarīq 'alā Ṭarafa bt. Quṭub *rāji'* 18 pāra

'an resm-i nikāḥ-i 'Usfūr b. Khālid 'alā Ḥalīma bt. Gharīj *bikr* 35 pāra
'an resm-i nikāḥ-i Ḥannā b. Khalīl 'alā bt. al-Hanā bt. Muḥiyȳ *bikr* 35 pāra
'an resm-i nikāḥ-i Mūsā b. Mikhāīl 'alā Ṣāliḥa bt. 'Ūlān *bikr* 35 pāra

'an resm-i cerīme-i Mūsā b. 'Ajlūn 'an cihet-i iftirā 20 pāra
'an resm-i nikāḥ-i Mūsā b. Kadūs 'alā Sitt al-'Izz bt. Sālim *bikr* 35 pāra
'an resm-i cerīme-i Naṣr b. Niqūlā 'an cihet-i mīsāḳ bi-gayr-i ḥikr 80 pāra

'an resm-i nikāḥ-i Manṣūr b. 'Īsā 'alā Ramiya bt. Ḥajāj *bikr* 35 pāra
'an resm-i cerīme-i Maṭar b. Badīr 'an cihet-i muḳātele ma'a āhar 30 pāra
'an resm-i cerīme-i 'Awda b. Khitāna 'an cihet-i iftirā 50 pāra

'an resm-i cerīme-i Ḥasan b. ..aylim 'an cihet-i iftirā 50 pāra
'an resm-i cerīme-i Pir 'Īsā Marwān 'an cihet-i tezvīr 40 pāra
'an resm-i cerīme-i Muḥammad b. A'war 'an cihet-i sirḳat-i erz 200 pāra

'an resm-i cerīme-i 'Arīf b. Daqīq 'an cihet-i iftirā 30 pāra
'an resm-i nikāḥ-i Ṭāhir b. Hindī 'alā Diya bt. al-Dawīk *rāji'* 18 pāra
'an resm-i nikāḥ-i Ilyās b. 'Awda al-Sāi' 'alā Mūlis bt. Ilyās *bikr* 35 pāra

'an resm-i nikāḥ-i Mikhāīl b. Rizq Allāh 'alā 'Azīma bt. Khalīl Naṣrānī *bikr* 35 pāra
'an resm-i cerīme-i 'Abd al-Qādir 'an cihet-i muḳātele ma'a Muṭāwi' 50 pāra

'an resm-i nikāḥ-i Khalīl b. Ibrāhīm al-Majd 'alā Ṣāliḥa bt. Natba/Muntaba? *rāji'* 18 pāra

'an resm-i cerīme-i Muḥammad b. Maṭar 'an cihet-i muḳātele ma'a āhar 25 pāra
'an resm-i cerīme-i Marīs b. Malik 'an cihet-i iftirā 25 pāra
'an resm-i cerīme-i 'Aṭāllāh b. Quṭub 'an cihet-i muḳātele ma'a āhar 30 pāra

Page b

'an resm-i cerīme-i Ibrāhīm b. Kashka 'an cihet-i muḳātele ma'a āhar 25 pāra
'an resm-i cerīme-i Aḥmad Shāmī ma'a riḳāḳihim 'an cihet-i şürb-i ḥamr 160 pāra
'an resm-i cerīme-i Mūsā b. ... ve Sālim ve riḳāḳihim 'an cihet-i muḳātele ma'a Rabī' b. ..-lim 200 pāra

'an resm-i cerīme-i Sālim b. Salīm 'an cihet-i muḳātele ma'a 30 pāra
'an resm-i nikāḥ-i 'Alī b. Abzaḥ 'alā Fāṭima bt. Muḥammad Gharānī *bikr* 35 pāra
'an resm-i nikāḥ-i Muhanna b. Sālim 'alā Ṣāliḥa bt. Banūrā *bikr* 35 pāra

'an resm-i nikāḥ-i 'Abd al-Raḥmān b. ... 'alā Ṣāliḥa bt. ... *rāji'* 18 pāra
'an resm-i nikāḥ-i 'Umar b. ... 'alā Ṣāliḥa bt. 'Azīza ... *bikr* 35 pāra
'an resm-i cerīme-i Muḥammad b. ... 'an cihet-i muḳātele ma'a āhar 50 pāra

yekūn 1,587 pāra

'An ḳarye-i Sāfariyya
'an resm-i cerīme-i Khalīl b. al-Ṭābi' 'an cihet-i kesr-i feddān 50 pāra
'an resm-i cerīme-i ahīhi 'an cihet-i muḳātele ve iftirā 80 pāra
'an resm keşif-i Ibn al-Ṭābi' mağrūḳ fī bi'r-i ḳarye-i mezbūre 400 pāra

'an resm-i cerīme-i Khalīl b. al-Ṭābi' 'an resm-i cerīme-i muḳātele ma'a Ibn Qudsī 140 pāra
'an resm-i cerīme-i Khāṭir b. Qudsī 'an cihet-i muḳātele ma'a Ibn al-Ṭābi' 130 pāra
'an resm-i nikāḥ-i Ṣāliḥ b. Mushtanim 'alā Ṣāliḥa bt. Abū Bakr *bikr* 35 pāra

‘an resm-i cerīme-i Khalīl b. al-Ṭābi‘ ‘an cihet-i muḳātele ma‘a Ibn Qudsī 540 pāra
‘an resm-i cerīme-i Khāṭir b. Qudsī ‘an cihet-i ahz-i bint 200 pāra
‘an resm-i cerīme-i Khalīl b. Qudsī ‘an cihet-i muḳātele ma‘a āhar 200 pāra

yekūn 1,775 pāra

‘An ḳarye-i Bayt Dajan
‘an resm-i nikāḥ-i Muḥammad b. Ibrāhīm b. Abū Ḥalās ‘alā Rūmiya bt. ‘Utba *bikr* 35 pāra
‘an resm-i nikāḥ-i Aḥmad ‘an ḳarye-i mezbūre ‘alā Ṣāliḥa bt. ‘Alī *bikr* 35 pāra

yekūn 70 pāra

‘An ḳarye-i Kafr Jinnis
‘an resm-i nikāḥ-i Zayn b. Fashār? ‘an cihet Ṣāliḥa bt. ... *rāji‘* 18 pāra

Page c

‘An ḳarye-i Jindās
‘an resm-i cerīme-i b. Abū ‘Alī ‘an cihet-i muḳātele 30 pāra
‘an resm-i cerīme-i Ismā‘īl b. Abū al-Su‘ūd ‘an cihet-i muḳātele 35 pāra

yekūn 65 pāra

‘An ḳarye-i Yahūdiyya
‘an resm-i nikāḥ-i Aḥmad Shārī ‘alā Salīmā bt. Aḥmad *rāji‘* 18 pāra
‘an resm-i nikāḥ-i Majd b. Aḥmad ‘alā Ṣāliḥa bt. Rajab *bikr* 35 pāra

yekūn 53 pāra

‘An ḳarye-i Subtārī
‘an resm-i cerīme-i Abū Jamāl ‘an cihet-i muḳātele ma‘a man ṣarrafahu 20 pāra
‘an resm-i cerīme-i Muḥsin ‘an cihet-i muḳātele ‘an cihet-i ḳuṭn 45 pāra

yekūn 65 pāra

'An ḳarye-i Yāzūr

'an resm-i nikāḥ-i Ḥasan b. Sālim 'alā Ṣāliḥa bt. Aḥmad *rāji'* 18 pāra
'an resm-i nikāḥ-i Khayr al-Dīn b. Muṭawwa' 'alā Fāṭima bt. Abū Bakr [*bikr*] 35 pāra
'an resm-i nikāḥ-i Al-'Aryān b. 'Amīd 'alā Umm al-Ḥamd bt. Māḍī *bikr* 35 pāra
'an resm-i cerīme-i evlād-i 'Amīd 'an cihet-i muḳātele ve iftirā 600 pāra

yekūn 688 pāra

Minhā

el-ma'rūf der hüccet ve müseccelāt ve taḥrīr ma'a levāzim ma'a 'öşr-i ṣubaşı ve ücret-i ḥammāliyet ve gayrīhā

'an resm-i hüccet-i Muḥammad b. A'war 'an cihet-i sirḳat-ı erz 80 pāra
'an resm-i hüccet-i 'Alī b. al-Ṭābi' 'an cihet-i muḳātele 90 pāra
'an resm-i hüccet-i evlād-i 'Amīd 'an cihet-i ... iftirā 80 pāra

'an bahā-i ṣīd ma'a ücret-i mu'allim der vaḳt termīm-i dirva 20 pāra
'an bahā-i meunet-i ḳu'ūd ma'a ücret-i mu'allim der vaḳt riyāset-i fāṣıl-ı ḥınṭa 20 pāra
'an bahā-i ḥınṭa ma'a meunet-i ḥammāliyet der vaḳt-ı naḳl-ı gilāl 'an enbār-ı ḳarye-i Lidd ilā 'imāret-i Ḳuds-i Şerif 30 pāra

'an resm-i hüccet-i Khāṭir b. Qudsī 'an cihet-i muḳātele 60 pāra
'an resm-i hüccet-i Khalīl b. Qudsī 'an cihet-i muḳātele 120 pāra
[in the right margin, sum of five "'*an resm*" lines gives: 430 pāra]

'an ücret-i ḥammāliyet-i ahālī-i ḳarye-i Yahūdiyya ve Subtārī ve Yāzūr nāḳilīn-i ḥınṭa 'an ḳarye-i Lidd ilā enbār-i 'imāret-i Ḳuds-i Şerif 550 pāra

'an ücret-i ḥammāliyet-i ahālī-i ḳarye-i Yāzūr ve Bayt Dajan ve Sāfariyya el-nāḳilīn-i ḥınṭa 'an ḳarye-i Lidd ilā 'imāret-i Ḳuds-i Şerif 280 pāra

'an 'öşr-i ṣubaşı-ı mezbūr 440 pāra

yekūn 1,770 pāra

Page d

Īfā-i maḳbūżāt-i Ḥuseyn ṣubaşı fī gurre-i şehr-i Cumādā ul-evvel ilā gāyet-i şehr-i mezbūr min bād-i havā ma'a resm-i 'arūs sene-i 994

'an resm-i nikāḥ-i Muḥammad b. Aḥmad Khalīl 'alā Ṣāliḥa bt. ... *bikr* 35 pāra
'an resm-i cerīme-i Muḥammad b. Ḥuseyn b. Ibzaḥ 'an cihet-i muḳātele ma'a zevcetihi 120 pāra
'an resm-i nikāḥ-i Jum'a b. Razīk 'alā 'Azīza bt. Mamdūḥ *bikr* 35 pāra

'an resm-i cerīme-i evlād-i Nādī 'an resm [sic] cihet-i muḳātele ma'a Ibn Abū Sa'āda 80 pāra
'an resm-i cerīme-i 'Irfān Qudsī ma'a rafīḳihi 'an cihet-i muḳātele 200 pāra
'an resm-i cerīme-i 'Alī b. ... 'an cihet-i sirḳat-ı şa'īr 45 pāra

'an resm-i nikāḥ-i Muḥammad b. ... 'alā ... bt. Abū al-Naṣr *bikr* 35 pāra
'an resm-i nikāḥ-i bin Nūr al-Dīn 'alā ... bt. ... *bikr* 35 pāra

yekūn 580 pāra

Minhā
el-ma'rūf der hüccet ve müseccelāt ma'a levāzim

'an resm-i hüccet-i taḥsīn der vaḳt-ı ziyāde 60 pāra
'an resm-i hüccet-i Muḥammad b. Ḥusayn Ibzaḥ 'an cihet-i muḳātele 60 pāra
'an resm-i hüccet-i 'Irfān Qudsī 'an cihet-i muḳātele 60 pāra
'an resm-i Muḥammad 'Aṭ[ā] al-Dīn Ni'ma naṣrānī 80 pāra
'öşr-i ṣubaşı-ı mezbūr 55 pāra

yekūn 315 pāra

Taḥrīren fī hitām-i şehr-i Cumādā ul-evvel sene-i 994

El-faḳīr Ḥuseyn ṣubaşı ... [te]m[me]

Translation of the Ottoman Turkish text

[v. = virgin (*bikr*); w/d = widowed or divorced (*rāji‘*)]

Page a

Register of the matters of the receipts of Ḥuseyn ṣubaşı of the village of Lidd, together with the other villages of the endowments of Hāṣṣekī Sulṭān, may her grave be pleasant, in Jerusalem; occasional fines together with marriage taxes, on the first of Ṣafer until the end of Rebī‘ ül-āhir 994 [22 January-19 April 1586]

From the village of Lidd
from the marriage tax of Sulaymān b. Ḥatim to Nuṣra bt. Qudsī v. 35 pāra
from the marriage tax of Īsā b. Sulaymān to Rūmiya bt. Manṣūr v. 35 pāra
from the marriage tax of Ibrāhīm b. Ṭarīq to Ṭarafa bt. Quṭub w/d 18 pāra

from the marriage tax of ‘Usfūr b. Khālid to Ḥalīma bt. Gharīj v. 35 pāra
from the marriage tax of Ḥannā b. Khalīl to bt. al-Hanā bt. Muḥiyy v. 35 pāra
from the marriage tax of Mūsā b. Mikhāīl to Ṣāliḥa bt. ‘Ūlān v. 35 pāra

from the penalty tax of Mūsā b. ‘Ajlūn for lying 20 pāra
from the marriage tax of Mūsā b. Kadūs to Sitt al-‘Izz bt. Sālim v. 35 pāra
from the penalty tax of Naṣr b. Niqūlā for a contract with no ground rent 80 pāra

from the marriage tax of Manṣūr b. ‘Īsā to Ramiya bt. Ḥajāj v. 35 pāra
from the penalty tax of Maṭar b. Badīr for fighting with another 30 pāra
from the penalty tax of ‘Awda b. Khitāna for lying 50 pāra

from the penalty tax of Ḥasan b. ...aylim for lying 50 pāra
from the penalty tax of Pir Īsā Marwān for falsification 40 pāra
from the penalty tax of Muḥammad b. A‘war for stealing rice 200 pāra

from the penalty tax of ‘Arīf b. Daqīq for lying 30 pāra
from the marriage tax of Ṭāhir b. Hindī to Diya bt. al-Dawīk w/d 18 pāra
from the marriage tax of Ilyās b. ‘Awda al-Sāi‘ to Mūlis bt. Ilyās v. 35 pāra

from the marriage tax of Mikhāīl b. Rizq Allāh to 'Azīma bt. Khalīl Naṣranī v. 35 pāra
from the penalty tax of 'Abd al-Qādir for fighting with Muṭāwi' 50 pāra
from the marriage tax of Khalīl b. Ibrāhīm al-Majd to Ṣāliḥa bt. Natba/Muntaba? w/d 18 pāra

from the penalty tax of Muḥammad b. Maṭar for fighting with another 25 pāra
from the penalty tax of Marīs b. Malik for lying 25 pāra
from the penalty tax of 'Aṭāllāh b. Quṭb for fighting with another 30 pāra

<u>Page b</u>

from the penalty tax of Ibrāhīm b. Kashka for fighting with another 25 pāra
from the penalty tax of Aḥmad Shāmī together with their slaves for drinking wine 160 pāra
from the penalty tax of Mūsā b. ... and Sālim and their slaves for fighting with Rabī' b. ...lim 200 pāra

from the penalty tax of Sālim b. Salīm for fighting with [no name] 30 pāra
from the marriage tax of 'Alī b. Abzaḥ to Fāṭima bt. Muḥammad Gharānī v. 35 pāra
from the marriage tax of Muhanna b. Sālim to Ṣāliḥa bt. Banūra v. 35 pāra

from the marriage tax of 'Abd al-Raḥmān b. ... to Ṣāliḥa bt. ... w/d 18 pāra
from the marriage tax of 'Umar b. ... to Ṣāliḥa bt. 'Azīza ... v. 35 pāra
from the penalty tax of Muḥammad b. ... for fighting with another 50 pāra

total 1,587 pāra

From the village of Sāfariyya
from the penalty tax of Khalīl b. al-Ṭābi' for non-cultivation 50 pāra
from the penalty tax of his brother for fighting and lying 80 pāra
from the investigation tax of Ibn al-Ṭābi' drowned in the well of the said village 400 pāra

from the penalty tax of Khalīl b. al-Ṭābi' for fighting with Ibn Qudsī 140 pāra
from the penalty tax of Khāṭir b. Qudsī for fighting with Ibn al-Ṭābi' 130 pāra
from the marriage tax of Ṣāliḥ b. Mushtanim to Ṣāliḥa bt. Abū Bakr v. 35 pāra

from the penalty tax of Khalīl b. al-Ṭābi' for fighting with Ibn Qudsī 540 pāra
from the penalty tax of Khāṭir b. Qudsī for abducting a girl 200 pāra
from the penalty tax of Khalīl b. Qudsī for fighting with another 200 pāra

total 1,775 pāra

From the village of Bayt Dajan
from the marriage tax of Muḥammad b. Ibrāhīm b. Abū Ḥalās to Rūmiya bt. 'Utba v. 35 pāra
from the marriage tax of Aḥmad from the said village to Ṣāliḥa bt. 'Alī v. 35 pāra

total 70 pāra

From the village of Kafr Jinnis
from the marriage tax of Zayn b. Fashār? for Ṣāliḥa bt. ... w/d 18 pāra

Page c

From the village of Jindās
from the penalty tax of b. Abū 'Alī for fighting 30 pāra
from the penalty tax of Ismā'īl b. Abū al-Su'ūd for fighting 35 pāra

total 65 pāra

From the village of Yahūdiyya
from the marriage tax of Aḥmad Shārī to Salīmā bt. Aḥmad w/d 18 pāra
from the marriage tax of Majd b. Aḥmad to Ṣāliḥa bt. Rajab v. 35 pāra

total 53 pāra

From the village of Subtārī
from the penalty tax of Abū Jamāl for fighting with the one who granted him use

of the land 20 pāra
from the penalty tax of Muḥsin for fighting about cotton 45 pāra

total 65 pāra

From the village of Yāzūr
from the marriage tax of Ḥasan b. Sālim to Ṣaliḥa bt. Aḥmad w/d 18 pāra
from the marriage tax of Khayr al-Dīn b. Muṭawwaʿ to Fāṭima bt. Abū Bakr [v.] 35 pāra
from the marriage tax of al-ʿAryān b. ʿAmīd to Umm al-Ḥamd bt. Mādī v. 35 pāra

from the penalty tax of of the children of ʿAmīd for fighting and lying 600 pāra

total 688 pāra

From it
that which is known according to the document and kadi records and survey register together with necessities together with the tithe of the ṣubaşı and the cost of porterage and other things

from the document fee of Muḥammad b. Aʿwar for stealing rice 80 pāra
from the document fee of ʿAlī b. al-Ṭābiʿ for fighting 90 pāra
from the document fee of the children of ʿAmīd for ... lying 80 pāra

from the price of plaster together with the cost of the master during the time of repairing the parapet/protecting screen 20 pāra
from the price of provisions for camels together with the cost of the master during the time of managing the apportioning of wheat 20 pāra
from the price of wheat together with provisions for porterage during the time of transporting the grains from the granary of the village of Lidd to the ʿimāret in Jerusalem 30 pāra

from the document fee of Khāṭir b. Qudsī for fighting 60 pāra
from the document fee of Khalīl b. Qudsī for fighting 120 pāra

[in the right margin, sum of five "from the fee" lines gives: 430 pāra] from the cost of porterage of the people of the villages of Yahūdiyya and Subtārī and Yāzūr who transport the wheat from the village of Lidd to the granary of the ʿimāret of Jerusalem 550 pāra

from the cost of porterage of the people of the village of Yāzūr and Bayt Dajan and Sāfariyya who transport the wheat from the village of Lidd to the ʿimāret of Jerusalem 280 pāra

from the tithe of the said ṣubaşı 440 pāra

total 1,770 pāra

Page d

Payment of the receipts of Ḥuseyn ṣubaşı on the first of Cumādā ul-evvel to the end of the said month from occasional fines together with marriage taxes for the year 994 [20 April-19 May 1586]

from the marriage tax of Muḥammad b. Aḥmad Khalīl to Ṣāliḥa bt. ... v. 35 pāra
from the penalty tax of Muḥammad b. Ḥusayn b. Ibzaḥ for fighting with his wife 120 pāra
from the marriage tax of Jumʿa b. ... to ʿAzīza bt. Mamdūḥ v. 35 pāra

from the penalty tax of of the children of Nādī from the tax [sic] for fighting with Ibn Abū Saʿāda 80 pāra
from the penalty tax of ʿIrfān Qudsī together with his companion for fighting 200 pāra
from the penalty tax of ʿAlī b. ... for stealing barley 45 pāra

from the marriage tax of Muḥammad b. ... to ... bt. Abū al- Naṣr v. 35 pāra
from the marriage tax of bin Nūr al-Dīn to ... bt. ... v. 35 pāra

total 580 pāra

from it

that which is known according to the document and records together with the necessities

from the document fee of improvements during the time of surplus 60 pāra
from the document fee of Muḥammad b. Ḥusayn Ibzaḥ for fighting 60 pāra
from the document fee of 'Irfān Qudsī for fighting 60 pāra

from the tax of Muḥammad 'Aṭ[ā] al-Dīn Ni'ma naṣrānī 80 pāra

tithe of the said ṣubaşı 55 pāra

total 315 pāra

Written at the end of Cumādā ul-evvel 994 [19 May 1586]

The humble Ḥuseyn ṣubaşı ... finished.

Village profiles

The eight villages in this document were all found in the coastal plain near the town of Ramle. Wheat, barley, vegetables and fruits, sheep and goats, along with cotton and some sesame were the principal products of the region. During the last half of the sixteenth century, Lidd was something more than a village and less than a town, as it lacked the administrative functions associated with the latter but had a permanent market and other urban services to distinguish it from most villages.[8] Obviously Lidd was far larger than the other villages in the group here and the total of fees and fines collected was correspondingly greater. None of the villages, except Kafr Jinnis, might be considered very small, however. In contrast to other villages in the region, and particularly when compared with the villages in the province of Jerusalem in the hills to the east, these were quite substantial in terms of population and revenues. Numerically, their populations remained relatively stable during this period, whereas the urban populations of the region contracted.[9]

While all the villages belonged to the *vakıf*, there were other villages in the same district of Ramle such as Rānṭiyya, 'Anāba or Bi'r Mā'īn which also belonged to the *vakıf* but were not included here. From his description as "*ṣubaşı* of the village of Lidd, together with the other villages of the endowments of Hāṣṣekī Sulṭān in Jerusalem," Ḥuseyn seems to have had a wider jurisdiction than the villages listed here. So, the document may give the mistaken impression of a fixed grouping. Of greater importance and interest is the question of whether the villagers themselves had any sense of belonging to a unit larger than the village, be it district, province, region, empire or the *vaḳıf* itself.

The only clues in this regard come from the kadi records of Jerusalem and a few *fermān*s. Villagers who came before the kadi were routinely identified by the name of their village. The same was true in *fermān*s recorded in both the *mühimme defterleri* in Istanbul and those copied into the local *sicill*s. In addition, when the village belonged to a *vaḳıf*, this affiliation was also noted whether or not the affair recorded in the *sicill* had to do specifically with the *vaḳıf*. Unfortunately, we have no way of knowing whether this association was articulated by the peasants when they came before the kadi, or whether the kadi's scribe filled it in as a matter of routine.[10]

Table 1: Population and Fines & Fees

	Survey #304 964/1556-7		Survey #546 1005/1596-7		D-3528/4 994/1586
Village:	Population	*bād-i havā/ resm-i ʿarūs*	Population	*bād-i havā/ resm-i ʿarūs*	*bād-i havā/ resm-i ʿarūs*
Lidd	495 hane[11]	2500 akçe	425 hane	3000 akçe	3174 akçe[12]
Sāfariyya	58	618	53	571	3550
Bayt Dajan	115	453	115	1468	140
Kafr Jinnis	19	200	18	300	36
Jindās	39	72	35	108	130
Yahūdiyya	126	400	126	545	106
Subtārī	125	1000	122	1200	130
Yāzūr	53	700	50	1600	1376
Total:		**5973** (12 mos.)		**8692** (12 mos.)	**8642** (3 mos.!)

Table 2: Marriages (for 3 months)

Village:	virgin	widow/divorcée	total
Lidd	12	4	16
Sāfariyya	1	—	1
Bayt Dajan	2	—	2
Kafr Jinnis	—	1	1
Jindās	—	—	—
Yahūdiyya	1	1	2
Subtārī	—	—	—
Yāzūr	2	1	3
Additional month	4	—	4
Total:	22	7	29

Resm-i ʿarūs and bād-i havā

The marriage tax, known variously as *resm-i ʿarūsāne*, *ʿādet-i ʿarūsī*, *gerdek değeri*, and *gerdek resmi*, appeared in Ottoman compilations of taxes at least as early as the fifteenth century. It was imposed at different rates depending on whether the bride belonged to a wealthy, middling or poor family, and depending on whether she was a virgin or a remarrying widow or divorcée. The Ottomans introduced this tax into Syria, Egypt, and Iraq after they conquered the area early in the sixteenth century.[13] And, though the evidence of the survey registers indicates that it was regularly imposed, objections were voiced against it. In particular, *fetvā*s of *şeyhül-islām*s like Ebu's-Suʿūd (1545-74) specifically cited the pig tax (*resm-i hınzīr*) and the bride tax (*resm-i ʿarūsāne*) among the illegal prescriptions in the *ḳānūnnāme*s. Another *fetvā*, however, said that "the bride tax (*gerdek ḥaḳḳı*), though unknown to the *şerīʿat*, is not an unlawful (*ḥarām*) income for the fief-holders provided it is offered as a free gift (*teberruʿ*)!"[14] The fiction of gifts or donations was not an uncommon claim from persons seeking to impose superfluous taxes on the peasants.[15] However, the bride tax seems to have stuck fast.

Occasional fines, the *bād-i havā*, included a large range of fines and fees imposed as penalties for misdemeanors and crimes. The term was found at least as early as a *ḳānūnnāme* of Gelibolu from 925/1519, but the concept is much older. *Ṭayyārāt* in Arabic, the Greek *aerikon*, and English *windfall* all emphasize the somewhat unpredictable income represented by this category, and its catch-all nature.[16] The fines belonging to the *bād-i havā* in the *defter* here are all defined as *cerīme* (penalty taxes) except for one *keşif*, or investigation fee. Fines varied according to the crime, and, like the marriage fees, according to the status of the person paying: wealthy, middling or poor.[17]

In the six large towns of Palestine, the *bād-i havā* and *resm-i ʿarūs* were grouped together with other varying taxes in the survey register lists. These usually included *cürm-i cināyet* (fines and penalties), and sometimes also *māl-i gāʾib ve māl-i mefḳūd* (property of absent and missing persons), stray cattle, runaway slaves, and *bayt al-māl* (treasury revenues).[18] In the villages of the *sancak*s of Jerusalem and Gaza, the surveys list only *bād-i havā* and *resm-i ʿarūs*. From the evidence of the present *defter*, however, *bād-i havā* clearly included the *cürm-i cināyet* category even though it was not specified. Thus, *bād-i havā* should probably be read as a heading for all these entries, with the other taxes listed under it by way of itemization. This reading of the terminology is further supported by the meaning of *bād-i havā*, which is very general and inclusive. However, the absence of the fines on absent and missing persons, on stray cattle, etc. in this document may indicate either that there were no such fines for this period in these villages, or, that they were not registered in the villages or by the *ṣubaşı* but rather in town by the kadi or by another official. More evidence from the villages would be necessary to corroborate this speculation.

The person entitled to collect these taxes varied according to the status of the village. In *tımar* villages the taxes were shared between the *sipahi* and the *sancakbeyi*, while in the class of *tımar*s called free (*serbest*), the *tımar* holder collected them entirely. In villages which were *vaḳıf*, these taxes might be specified for an official unconnected to the *vaḳıf* such as the *sancakbeyi*. Where the villages belonged to *vaḳıf*s of the holy places in Mecca and Medina, or were in the category of sultanic *vaḳıf*s, these taxes were part of the *vaḳıf* revenues;[19] these villages were also called *serbest*. *Serbest*, in general, then, indicates that the *sancakbeyi* or other administrative official had no right *ex officio* to a part of these taxes. Such was the case with the sultanic *vaḳıf* in this document.

Ḥuseyn subaşı

The *bād-i havā* and *resm-i ʿarūs* taxes were registered to "Ḥuseyn *ṣubaşı* of the village of Lidd together with the other villages of the endowments of Hāṣṣekī Sulṭān...in Jerusalem." *Ṣubaşı*s were Ottoman officers with general police responsibilities both within and outside the towns. They might also collect revenues for higher-ranking officials under a lease or sub-contract. In the *sancak* of Jerusalem, *ṣubaşı*s had specific geographic jurisdictions. However, one also finds a *ṣubaşı* assigned to villages whose revenues belonged to the *ʿimāret vaḳfı*; its villages were located in the two *sancak*s of Gaza and Jerusalem, as well as some scattered properties further north.[20]

Ḥuseyn *ṣubaşı* may have had responsibilities in all the *vaḳıf* villages, but no description of his specific duties in the enormous foundation of the Hāṣṣekī Sulṭān *'imāret vaḳfı* was found, nor was a *ṣubaşı* specified among the functionaries listed in the original endowment deed. It seems most likely that he was one of the many *ṣubaşı*s who fulfilled policing and fiscal tasks in the town and the surrounding countryside, appointed from the corps of Ottoman military personnel stationed in the region.[21] He may have been appointed to this specific position by the kadi or *sancakbeyi*, though conceivably at the request of the *vaḳıf* manager. The villages of the *vaḳıf* were technically *serbest*, while the *ṣubaşı* was one of the *sancakbeyi*'s men. Was he imposed on the *vaḳıf* as a way of accessing otherwise untouchable revenues, or did the manager request the assistance of a *ṣubaşı*, to maintain order or impose his authority on the villages? It is not clear whether the *'imāret* had more than one *ṣubaşı* attached to it. However, the variety of activities listed in the second and fourth sections of the document provide some insights into how Ḥuseyn spent his time and efforts.

The lists of marriages and misdemeanors from sections one and three contain sixty-three separate items for a four-month period. Of these, there were twenty-nine marriages, thirty-three fines for offenses, and one investigation fee. The collection of marriage fees probably was a straightforward exercise; assessing and collecting fines perhaps a more complex process. On the other hand, in order to collect the fines, the *ṣubaşı* would have to hold some form of inquiry, requiring at a minimum the cooperation and participation of the villagers themselves. An account-book entry from the early years of the *vaḳıf* lists the customary fees and windfall taxes of the village of Amyūn (another of the endowed villages) as being the responsibility of the village leaders, which suggests the *ṣubaşı* had some active assistance from within the village.[22]

Heyd's extensive discussion of criminal law codes and their application also seems to support this understanding of how the *ṣubaşı* functioned.

> Though the Ottomans charged the cadis to establish the "rights of God" and the "rights of man" in a criminal trial, the sphere of the "rights of the State" was largely left to the sec-

> ular authorities. ...Foreign observers pointed out that criminal cases were often or even generally tried by the ṣubaşıs, while the cadis dealt with people who did not take part in the public prayers, did not fast in Ramaẓān, cursed, drank wine, etc.[23]

Ḥuseyn's jurisdiction was thus defined in two overlapping spheres: As the *ṣubaşı* he dealt with petty crimes and the fines imposed for them. In addition, the Ottoman agglomeration of marriage fees and criminal fines into one collection category added collection of the state marriage levy to his other responsibilities.

Revenues and expenditures of Ḥuseyn ṣubaşı

1 Ṣafer-29 Reb'ī' ül-āhir 994 [22 January-19 April 1586]

revenues from villages	4303 pāra
fees, expenditures, tithe	– 1770
total received	2533

1-30 Cumādā ul-evvel 994 [20 April-19 May 1586]

revenues from villages	580 pāra
fees, tithe	– 315
total received	265

Ḥuseyn's revenues for three months	2533 pāra
Ḥuseyn's revenues for one month	+ 265
	2798 pāra
	(= 57% of collected gross)

Ḥuseyn collected 4303 *pāra* for the first three-month period, and another 580 *pāra* for the additional month. From each total, he was required to pay a tithe ('öşr) as well as numerous fees connected with the criminal fines, and the costs associated with the maintenance of *vaḳıf* properties and transportation of produce collected from the villages for the soup kitchen.

Some of the fines required a *hüccet* (document) from the kadi in order that they be legitimately assessed and collected. Yet of the thirty-three misdemeanors recorded, only in seven instances was the fee for a *hüccet* recorded with the *ṣubaşi*'s expenses. All these appear to have been misdemeanors incurring fines of over one hundred *pāra*, although not every such instance required a *hüccet*. Nor are all the *hüccet*s for one kind of misdemeanor, or some systematic categorization of them. No document fees were recorded for the marriages. Fixed fees existed for entering the cases into the kadi's records (*resm-i sicill*), for a certified copy of this entry (*ṣūret-i sicill*), and for the *hüccet* itself.[24] Unfortunately, no *sicills* are extant for the province of Gaza from this period, so we cannot try to locate the kadi's version of these records.

Among the duties of "the *ṣubaşı* of the *'imāret*" was the responsibility for organizing the transport of *vaḳıf* grains to the foundation itself in Jerusalem. The statutes governing peasant obligations to deliver their grain were reiterated in numerous decrees delivered across the empire which sought to rectify abuses and ensure fair practices. These consistently stressed that a peasant had to deliver his or her taxes, due in kind from the grain harvested, to the nearest town, at no more than one day's journey from the village.[25] In the present case, the village of Lidd clearly served as a central depot for the other villages of the area. Grains earmarked for the *vaḳıf* in Jerusalem were then transported from Lidd to the *'imāret* by local peasants. But because this journey took them farther than their stipulated obligations, they were paid a wage for their work. This wage was paid by the *ṣubaşı* from the revenues he collected, as part of the obligations of his office. There is no indication of how much he paid in wages to each person, nor how many persons were hired for the task. But the porters were peasants from the villages which owed the grain to the *vaḳıf*.

Ḥuseyn had to collect the necessary men and pack animals, together with a sufficient supply of provisions for the trek up through the hills. In addition to food for the journey, he had to ensure the safety of the convoy. It is interesting to reflect on this small-scale operation when compared with the enormous caravans organized from Damascus and Cairo for the *ḥajj* pilgrimage.[26] If *ṣubaşıs* (who could be janissaries or *sipahis* appointed to this post) around the Ottoman empire had to organize such transport as a matter of course, this was on-the-job training in logistics.

Here is a small provincial chapter in a soldier's life which highlights one more duty in the repertoire of fiscal and administrative tasks which filled the military career. This specific experience would later serve well when military administrators were promoted to positions where they had to organize much larger caravans.

Finally, Ḥuseyn seems to have operated as a sub-contractor for building repairs. Though it is unclear what he was having repaired—*dirva* means either a parapet or a protecting screen—he had to organize the craftsman, workmen and the materials to get the job done.

From the 4883 *pāra* he collected, Ḥuseyn seems to have kept 2798 *pāra* (=5596 *akçe*). Compared with *tımar* sizes, which were a few thousand *akçe* per annum among the most junior *tımar* holders, Ḥuseyn's income from this source was already sufficient to place him above the lowest income ranks. If he also had the right to eat at the *'imāret*, as one of the affiliates of the *vaḳıf*, then his position was decidedly better than his *tımar*-holding colleagues.[27]

The division of the document into two periods is curious. Ordinarily, tours of the countryside by officials seem to have been spaced at three-month intervals, if the sultanic decree from 1540 may be taken to indicate the norm.[28] The additional month's revenues to the *ṣubaşı* are recorded in the last two sections, on page four of the document. The hand and pen appear identical to those which recorded the preceding sections, so that the whole was composed at one sitting. This document may have been drawn up from notes recorded separately and only subsequently compiled neatly into an official report. Perhaps the additional month was the last fraction due to Ḥuseyn at the end of his appointment.

In addition, it is not altogether clear what portion of the monies Ḥuseyn was actually entitled to keep. From another document which lists the revenues of the *vaḳıf* a year later, there are several entries which record an 'Alī *ṣubaşı* handing a lump sum of money to the *vaḳıf* without mentioning that he kept anything.[29] Did the *ṣubaşı* retain a fixed percentage of the gross or perhaps a fixed sum from the fees and fines he collected? Or was he really a salaried official or janissary whose wage was not recorded here? This small *defter* provides a more elaborate understanding of the micro-mechanics of village administration, but leaves us with questions still unanswered.

Marriages

In the villages listed in the document, the marriage fee for all virgin brides (*bikr*) was 35 *pāra*, while widows and divorcées paid only 18 *pāra*. No distinction among wealthier or poorer families was made in this record. In comparison, the *ḳānūnnāme* of Silistre from 1569 states very similar fees of 60 *akçe* for virgins and 30 *akçe* for widows and divorcées.[30]

During the period of four months from 22 January to 19 May 1586, twenty-nine marriages were recorded in these eight villages.[31] If marriages took place at an equal rate throughout the year, then the village of Lidd, for example, would have celebrated 64 marriages among its roughly 425 households.[32] The marriage list for Lidd includes both Muslims and Christians, taxed equally, despite the provision in the *ḳānūnnāme* that Christians might be taxed at a lesser rate for such occasions.

Having no comparative data, however, we do not know whether this spring of 1586 saw the coming of age of a large number of children (a "baby boom" group) or whether this was in fact a smaller number of marriages than were celebrated in the past. It does seem, though, that the rate of re-marriage was not negligible, as one in every four marriages was that of either a widow or divorcée. Unfortunately, the register does not distinguish between these two types of women without husbands. In official terms, then, their defining characteristic is that of having been married previously, and being now again legtimately marriageable. The seemingly high rate of re-marriage may reflect a social preference for women to be married. One might speculate that for the divorcées it indicated the absence of a stigma which prevented their remarriage.

We know little about the marriage practices in sixteenth-century Palestine, though, as stated above, assiduous research in the *ḳāḍı sicilleri* will certainly change this. However, the work of Hilma Granqvist in the village of Arṭās south of Jerualem may shed some light on our document. Her work on marriage conditions in the late 1920s indicated that weddings were generally concentrated in certain times of the year. People did not marry during Ramaẓān, nor during the winter months nor at harvest time. The month of Ramaẓān stretched from mid-August to mid-September in the year 1586. With the wheat harvest at the end of May and the beginning of June, this would have left the spring months, mid-June through mid-August, and mid-September to roughly the beginning of December as the optimum times for marriages that year according to Granqvist's conclusions.[33] While January was still part of the winter, climatic differences between the colder, mountain winter in Arṭās and that of the plain region where the villages in this document are located may have affected the scheduling of marriages. For the same reason, the summer months were perhaps less suitable for celebrations in the hot and muggy coastal plain region.

In short, the period recorded in our document could naturally have been one of a relatively large number of marriages in comparison with other parts of the year. However, this is purely speculative. An immediate caution against drawing such conclusions comes from the totals for marriage fees and windfall taxes given in an additional document from the year 996 (1587-8).[34] For the village of Lidd these totalled 11,298 *pāra* for twelve months. The total for three months in our document is 1587 *pāra*. If this latter were used to calculate an annual rate, the total would fall far below that recorded two years later.

Crimes and misdemeanors

Thirty-three instances of wrong-doing were recorded for fines in the four months covered by the register. Of these, twenty-one were cases of fighting or brawling. Other offenses included lying, falsification, stealing rice and barley, drinking wine, failing to cultivate, and contracting without ground rent. One fee was imposed for the cost of an investigation into a drowning death. And, in one instance, a man was fined for abducting a virgin. No incidents of murder or adultery were listed, though as suggested by Heyd above, these more serious crimes were not in the jurisdiction of the *ṣubaşı*, but rather were referred automatically to the kadi for investigation and adjudication.

No distinction between types of crimes was made in recording them in the present *defter*. They are all listed as *cerīme* in Turkish, meaning "crime, transgression," or "fine, penalty."[35] All penalties recorded for these crimes were sums of money; no other forms of punishment appear in the register. The statutes prescribed punishments of bastinado and fines for most offenses that did not require *ḥadd* penalties according to *şerīʻat*. For the most part, however "there can be little doubt that the Ottoman executive officers were much more inclined to impose fines, to which they themselves were entitled, than to inflict capital or severe corporal punishment."[36] The code from Süleymān's time cited by Heyd even gives a conversion rate of strokes-to-*akçe* according to which one *akçe* is paid for each stroke due to the aggressor in a fight while one *akçe* for every two strokes is due from the party who was attacked (and, presumably, fought back).[37]

Table 3: Fines (in pāra)

(number of instances given in parenthesis when more than one)

Fighting:	20, 25 (2), 30 (4), 35, 50 (2), 80, 120 [wife], 130, 140, 200 (3), 540
Fighting about cotton:	45 [only case with cause of fight]
Fighting and lying:	80, 600
Lying:	20, 25, 30, 50 (2)
Falsification:	40
Stealing rice:	200
Stealing barley:	45
Drinking wine:	160
Contract w/out ground rent:	80
Non-cultivation:	50
Abduction of a virgin	200
Investigation fee	400

Fighting or brawling, perhaps including the notion of offense given by creating a public disturbance, incurred a fine in this document varying from 25-540 *pāra*. Unfortunately, no description of the altercations indicates whether they led to severe wounding of the parties or the destruction of property. In the criminal statutes, fines for fighting were defined according to the severity of the injuries inflicted, starting with only a reprimand for scuffling,[38] a low fine for tearing someone's hair or beard but a higher fine for beating someone, and then the more onerous penalties of 200/100/50 *akçe* (rich/average/poor) for wounding someone with an arrow or knife so severely as to confine them to bed. Both parties to a quarrel were supposed to be fined, with the aggressor paying the heavier fine.[39] Most often, the *defter* discussed here says only that a particular person was fined for fighting with "another" (*āhar*).

The distinction between rich, average, and poor was based on the valuation of a person's property. As stated in the *ḳānūnnāme* published by Heyd,[40]

> If a person inflicts a gashing head-wound [on another] making [his] blood flow, the cadi shall chastise [*ta'zīr*] [him] and a fine [*cürm*] of 30 *akçe* shall be collected. And if a bone is laid bare and [the wounded person] needs [treatment by] a surgeon—if the person who inflicted the head-wound is rich, owning one thousand *akçe* or more, a fine of 100 *akçe* shall be collected after he has been chastised; if he is poor, [a fine of] 30 *akçe*; and if he is in average circumstances, his property amounting to six hundred *akçe*, a fine [*cürm*] of 50 *akçe* shall be collected.[41]

The fine on non-Muslims or slaves was half that for free Muslims. In the instance in Lidd where slaves were fined along with their owners for drinking, the slaves were not even mentioned by name. Their owners were responsible for the slaves' behavior, and quite possibly for their fine as well. Women could be fined for fighting, and their fines were also graded according to their status. In the case of *muhaddarāt*, or women of respectable status, their husbands were threatened and fined, whereas other women, presumably poorer, were only chastised and fined.[42] There is only one woman involved in a fight here, and it is her husband who is fined for fighting with his wife.

In the village of Sāfariyya, the fines recorded seem to indicate an ongoing feud between two families. For the three months recorded in the first section of D-3528/4, five of the seven penalites listed were for fighting. All of the men fined were either of the al-Ṭābi‘ or Qudsī families, and in three cases an al-Ṭābi‘ fought with a Qudsī. Khalīl al-Ṭābi‘ was fined 140 *pāra* for fighting with Ibn Qudsī and Khāṭir b. Qudsī was fined 130 *pāra* for fighting with Ibn al-Ṭābi‘. Quite possibly these were two men fighting each other. A few lines later, Khalīl al-Ṭābi‘ was again fined for fighting with Ibn Qudsī, but this time 540 *pāra*! Was this a continuation of the same fight with a far more damaging outcome, or did the fine reflect the frustration or anger of the *ṣubaşı* with the persistant discord? Two other cases of fighting were of an al-Ṭābi‘ and a Qudsī with an unspecified person. A further entry from the fourth month also listed a Qudsī fined for fighting, but with someone not named.

Sāfariyya was a village of some 53-58 households, so that these two families may have been the largest clans. However, compared to the larger villages of Lidd, Bayt Dajan, Yahūdiyya, and Subtārī, this was an extraordinarily quarrelsome community. Yāzūr, roughly the same size, recorded a single fine for fighting and lying together during the same period. The fines imposed in Sāfariyya for fighting were also larger than the average, ranging from 80 to 540 *pāra*. This may show how disruptive or physically harmful the disputes were in this village.

Two further fines hint at the relatively violent atmosphere in Sāfariyya at this time. An investigation was conducted into the death of one Ibn al-Ṭābi‘, drowned in the village well. No charges are recorded against anyone held responsible for this death. However, murder was probably outside the purview of the *ṣubaşı*'s authority once he had carried out the initial investigation, and hence the continuation of this story would be in the kadi's records.[43] And, Khāṭir b. Qudsī, mentioned above for fighting with an al-Ṭābi‘, was fined again, this time for abducting a virgin (*ahẓ bint*). The fine was 200 *pāra*, but the girl's name is not given. Nor is there any clue as to whether the abduction was real or staged. Neither Khāṭir nor the girl, however, apparently suffered the penalty listed for abduction in the Ottoman criminal code—his castration and her branding if she had been a willing accomplice.[44]

Only in one case was the actual reason for a quarrel stipulated. A man named Muḥsin was fined for fighting about cotton in the village of Subtārī. The survey registers specifically record cotton as a separate entry in this village, indicating sufficiently large quantities were produced there to warrant cotton not being lumped anonymously in the general "summer crops" category.[45] While cotton was the subject of the quarrel, however, no one was named as Muḥsin's adversary, nor are the details of the fight supplied. The reason for another quarrel listed in Subṭārī might be inferred from the relationship of the adversaries. Abū Jamāl quarrelled with the person who leased him the usufructory right (*taṣarruf*) to a piece of land. The two may have argued about the price of the lease or its length, or perhaps the share to which the lessor had a right from the yields.

Theft was an offense whose penalty was specified in the Qur'ān.[46] Yet the sixteenth-century code specifically set aside the *ḥadd* penalty and replaced it with a fine. "If [a person] steals (*sirke etseler*) wheat or barley from [another] person's pit or storehouse—if it is not necessary to cut off his hand according to the *sharī'a,* 40 *akçe* shall be collected as a fine (*cürm*) from a rich person, 20 *akçe* from a person in average circumstances, and 10 *akçe* from a poor person." The circumstances necessitating that a hand be cut off are not stipulated. Moreover, the code treats peasant theft of grain from the threshing floor with what appears to be relative leniency. The fine is the value of the stolen grain, nothing more.[47] It may be that the code recognized that peasants might be living at subsistence level and therefore be tempted and stressed to obtain grain in any way possible. From this it follows that if caught stealing, they could not be expected to do much more than forfeit what they had stolen. Alternatively, the code may be a comment on the responsibility of Ottoman officials themselves to oversee the harvest and ensure the proper distribution of revenues following the threshing.[48]

The theft of rice incurred a 200-*pāra* fine in Lidd, while stealing barley in an unnamed place incurred a fine of 45 *pāra*. Rice was a more precious commodity than barley, which was grown locally in great quantities. Although there are some indications that rice was grown in the greater area of Bilād al-Shām, no listing appears for this crop in the registers covering all of southern Syria at the end of the sixteenth century.[49] Thus, if some rice was grown in southern Syria, its quantities were so negligible as not to be mentioned and taxed separately in the survey registers. Most rice consumed in this area, it seems, was imported from Egypt, of which some portion was specifically destined for the storerooms of the Hāṣṣekī Sulṭān *'imāret*.[50] Thus the crime of stealing rice would naturally have been viewed more severely, although the quantity of barley or rice stolen in each instance may have determined the fine as well.

Failure to cultivate one's land was also a punishable offense in Ottoman law. Khalīl al-Ṭābi', twice fined for fighting in Sāfariyya, was also fined for non-cultivation during the same period. (Perhaps he was too busy pursuing his quarrels or laid up from an injury sustained in one of them.) The Ottomans worried about the steady and regular cultivation of lands throughout the empire. Agricultural revenues were crucial for the upkeep of the army and administration, and the steady supply of basic foodstuffs to the urban centers was a key policy concern for the central government in Istanbul. Thus non-cultivation of lands was a reason for official concern, as were its causes. Many *fermān*s recorded in the *mühimme defterleri* as well as repeated orders noted in the *ḳāḍı sicilleri* caution officials against abusing peasants. And peasants appear repeatedly before the kadi to offer guarantees that they will cultivate their lands, or to promise to work their lands in the village before tending to external plots.[51]

A peasant who left his lands fallow out of turn, or simply abandoned his lands, could be charged a penalty called *çift bozan resmi* or *kesr-i feddān*. Both expressions refer literally to the "breaking of the plot," where a plot is defined as an area plowed by a pair (*çift* or *feddān*) of animals within a certain time.[52] In "breaking" the plot, the peasant was not fulfilling his part of the contractual arrangement which gave him the usufruct of a particular piece of land as long as he remained resident in the village and cultivated that land. If a peasant left land uncultivated for three years, the usufruct right could be revoked and resold to another.[53]

Khalīl al-Ṭābi' was fined 50 *pāra* (=100 *akçe*) for non-cultivation of his lands. Although some of the *ḳānūnnāme*s mention the *çift bozan resmi*, no fixed fee is usually mentioned. Perhaps this is because the penalty charged would in some way be connected to the local tax rates and practices so that the principle of the fine would be consistent though the sum varied. However, the *ḳānūnnāme* of Serim from the period of Murad III (1574-95) specified a cash fine of 80 *akçe* for poor persons and 120 *akçe* for wealthy persons.[54] If the practice in Serim was any indication, Khalīl was a man of average means.

In the village of Lidd, Aḥmad Shāmī was fined 160 *pāra* for drinking wine with his slaves. The drinking of wine (*shurb ul-hamr*) was forbidden to Muslims in the Qur'ān,[55] and Aḥmad was thus liable for the *ḥadd* penalty of 80 strokes. As this could be converted to a fine, of one *akçe* for every two strokes, his fine should have been 40 *akçe* or 20 *pāra*.[56] If however, Aḥmad was not a Muslim but a Christian, then the penalty assessed was for some other infraction than simply drinking wine, perhaps causing a disturbance or drinking in public.

In the mixed community of Lidd, where roughly one-third of the village was Christian, wine was available to the Christian community for ritual purposes at least.[57] There was no law against Christians or Jews buying, selling or manufacturing wine amongst themselves. However, the Jews generally manufactured their own wine to ensure its ritual purity. And, in Jerusalem, specific permits for wine-making were issued to those who requested them. Stiff penalties could be incurred for drinking in public or selling wine to the Muslims. The kadi threatened a fine of 1000 *akçe* in the future to one Jerusalem Jew who had been caught drinking openly.[58]

Yet people did drink, as indicated by the fine registered against Aḥmad and his slaves. Perhaps the presence of wine was an overwhelming temptation for some; Christian wine-makers may have been negligent in denying their Muslim clients. Among the long-mixed population of Lidd, wine or other alcoholic beverages may have been a fixed part of local culture. Notably, only one case of a fine for drinking wine is to be found in these eight villages for the four months covered in the document; and this one case is in the only mixed Muslim-Christian village of the group. In theory, drinking wine was a *şer'ī* offense, and should have been handled by the kadi. The administrative treatment here may further suggest that Aḥmad Shāmī was a Christian.

Of the other crimes mentioned in this small list, lying or falsification (*iftirā*) was mentioned seven times, twice in conjunction with fighting. Falsification (*tezvīr*) appeared once. No explanations for the circumstances of these incidents were included, though from the difference in fines we understand that the gravity of the falsehood was judged in its own circumstances, whatever these were. Not surprisingly, the fine for lying together with fighting was higher than just for lying.

One crime listed, which seems to read "*mīsāḳ bi-gayr-i ḥikr*" could be translated "contract without ground rent". This might mean that someone had failed to pay the normal fee to the *vaḳıf* for use of some piece of land. In Lidd, where the fine was assessed, all the village land was endowed to Hürrem's *vaḳıf*. By the nineteenth century, *ḥikr* was one of the technical legal arrangements commonly employed for leasing *vaḳıf* properties by private individuals.[59]

Concluding thoughts

How then does this rather miniscule and fragmentary account from a handful of marginal villages inform our understanding of rural administration in the Ottoman empire? For it might be argued that this scattering of detail does not really contribute to the larger picture, being too remote and local. Yet several important aspects of the Ottoman presence in the provincial countryside are highlighted.

Estimated receipts from *resm-i 'arūs* and *bād-i havā* recorded in the Ottoman survey registers differed from the actual total fees and fines noted here. The same is true for grain revenues recorded in the surveys compared with the figures in the *sicill*s.[60] The number of marriages probably varied somewhat from year to year, and if we could measure their frequency over the course of one hundred years or more, we would probably discover more pronounced changes in marriage rates, which in turn depended on broader demographic and economic conditions. Total amounts of fines certainly fluctuated as well, as the incidence of theft rose in times of scarcity, and communities went through more and less settled periods within themselves for any one of myriad reasons.

The list of fees and fines for each village in the document is highly individual, revealing something of the character of one village as compared to another. And so the document should be some authentic reflection of village life, not a manufactured report. It confirms that villages could and did differ enormously from each other even within a very small area. Officials had to confront these variations and work with them. The *tapu* surveys thus present a misleadingly uniform sense of rural life. The differences revealed here, however, are largely those which concerned the officials whose task it was to collect a variety of revenues from the villages. Fighting, lying and other disruptions might and did impede the regular and steady production of agrarian revenues. Taxing marriages, a not-uncontroversial practice, was simply a way to make money. The state's agents probably cared little about the inevitable personal, familial and village politics and dramas surrounding the rituals of courtship and marriage. Unless, that is, they provoked real disturbances.

In the short term, Ḥuseyn *ṣubaşı* cared intensely about the events and moods of these villages for they affected the ease with which he could carry out his duties. Since the document recorded Ḥuseyn *ṣubaşı*'s revenues, and was signed by him, he was apparently the one to collect these monies, pay the kadi's fees, arrange for the investigation of the drowning death in Sāfariyya, see to the repair of buildings, and organize the transport of wheat from Lidd to Jerusalem in the spring of 1586. In order to achieve these tasks, Ḥuseyn would have been in frequent contact with the local peasants, temporarily a familiar figure around the countryside. At least in this period, his was not a long-term appointment; his successors appear in documents for the following years.

This *ṣubaşı*-villages affiliation is an example of a local tax-income "circle" or "unit" wherein someone was assigned the right to draw revenues from a unit of income which he was responsible for overseeing: calculating, collecting, paying necessary fees and buying necessary services, and finally retaining some, if not all, of the leftovers for himself. The Ottoman empire had hundreds if not thousands of such units in the premodern period, so that the collection of revenues was not unidirectional toward Istanbul, with expenditures flowing uniquely in the opposite direction. Rather, revenue was collected and disbursed in a system of micro-economies, interconnected through the command chain of authority which distributed the jurisdiction over them.

However, when carefully examined, Ḥuseyn's responsibilities seem to contradict the usual picture given of the distribution and compartmentalization of authority in the Ottoman empire. Provincial administration was managed by triumverates of kadi, *sancakbeyi* and *defterdār*, or judicial, military-administrative and fiscal authorities. Though the fiscal and military-administrative have often been found to overlap, judicial authority has been thought to be separate. Even judicial authority is divided between adjudication and administration of justice, which is often in the hands of the *sancakbeyi*. Here, Ḥuseyn *ṣubaşı* combines all of these functions, albeit within a very circumscribed jurisdiction. This, however, confirms Heyd's assessment of legal proceedings regarding criminal justice, but in the rural context which he did not specifically discuss. "All these extraordinary jurisdictions [chief of police, *muḥtasib*, *maẓālim* courts] were free from the rigid rules of the *sharīʿa* penal law and criminal procedure, and were guided in the main by customary law (*ʿurf*), the public interest (*al-maṣlaḥa al-ʿāmma*), and, in particular, the consideration of administrative and political expediency (*siyāsa*)."[61] These "extraordinary jurisdictions" seem to be of crucial importance for the smooth functioning of judicial authority, reaching places not necessarily accessible to the kadi, for whatever reason. Gerber, too, sees them as a normal and not aberrant part of the judicial process in this period.[62]

No indication exists here of the basis on which the *ṣubaşı* ascertained guilt and imposed the fines which were recorded. There can be little doubt that his actions were acceptable and legitimate, since the existence of the document itself would otherwise be curious. Moreover, in some instances it is noted that a *hüccet* was obtained, presumably from the kadi and assuredly with his knowledge. Yet nowhere is there mention of *şerīʿat*, *ḳānūn* or custom. In all likelihood, the cases dealt with by the *ṣubaşı* were uncontested incidents, wherein he had only to assign and collect the penalities, without truly entering into the business of judging. In the case of disputes or protracted proceedings, matters were perhaps referred to the kadi. Clearly, there were practical advantages to this system, for it converted recognized petty criminal acts into merely administrative incidents. In this, they become comparable to the marriages, incurring a fixed fee. All of this reduces the judicial standing of the *ṣubaşı* from what was initially suggested, but may be more compatible with the way in which the Ottoman government perceived his authority and actions.

Finally, one ought to ask about the relationships of the villagers and of Ḥuseyn *ṣubaşı* to the Jerusalem *vaḳıf* in whose name they came together. Conceivably, this connection was significant only because it allowed the fortunate discovery of the document in the Topkapı Palace archives. The configuration of villages represented by this document may have been unimportant for the villagers. The various forms of administration imposed from above were probably meaningful *only* from above, initially. Yet, the question is whether, over time, the *vaḳıf* connection imposed an identity or created an affinity among villagers who were affiliated with the institution.

Notes

This research was supported in part by the Basic Research Foundation administered by the Israel Academy of Sciences and Humanities. I would like also to thank the Directorate of the Topkapı Palace Museum Archives and Ülkü Altındağ for enabling me to carry out this research.

1. All transliterations follow the *International Journal of Middle East Studies (IJMES)* style from Ottoman Turkish, except for the names of the villages and villagers, which are transliterated from Arabic.
2. Ottoman historians have analyzed extensively the role of the village within the Ottoman economy, using the imperial survey registers (*tapu tahrir defterleri*) as a foundation for their evaluations. Sultanic orders as copied into the *mühimme defterleri* define the parameters of imperial policy regarding the peasants and the agrarian arena generally. For an extensive discussion of these sources, see A. Singer, *Palestinian peasants and Ottoman officials* (Cambridge, U.K., 1994), 17-20, 22-23.
3. For examples of peasant studies using the *ḳāḍı sicilleri*, see S. Faroqhi, "The Peasants of Saideli in the Late Sixteenth Century," *Archivum Ottomanicum*, 8 (1983), 215-250; *idem*, "Political Activity among Ottoman Taxpayers and the Problem of Sultanic Legitimation (1570-1650)," *Journal of the Economic and Social History of the Orient (JESHO)*, 35 (1992), 1-39; Karen Barkey, *Bandits and Bureaucrats: The Ottoman Route to State Centralization* (Ithaca, 1994); and Singer, *Palestinian peasants*.
4. In addition to the studes mentioned above, one can add: Haim Gerber, *Social Origins of the Modern Middle East* (Boulder, 1987); Kenneth M. Cuno, *The Pasha's Peasants* (Cambridge, U.K., 1992); Barkey, *Bandits and Bureaucrats*; Suraiya Faroqhi, "Wealth and Power in the Land of Olives" in Ç. Keyder and F. Tabak, eds., *Landholding and Commercial Agriculture in*

the Middle East (Albany, 1991), 77-95; H. İnalcik, "Köy, Köylü ve İmperatorluk," *V. Milletlerarası Türkiye Sosyal ve İktisat Tarihi Kongresi. Tebliğler.* (Ankara, 1990), 1-11.

5. R.D. McChesney's book on one Central Asian *vakıf* is the only example of a study which takes a cache of documents on a single foundation and uses them to trace its diachronic history. The variety of subjects covered in his book are a reflection of the extensive local involvements of the *vakıf;* they also demonstrate how the researcher is constrained by the chance survival of certain records. See R.D. McChesney, *Waqf in Central Asia: Four Hundred Years in the History of a Muslim Shrine, 1480-1889* (Princeton, 1991).

6. The term 'imāret (Ar. 'imāra) does not mean strictly a public kitchen but rather a "building" or complex of buildings. However, by the mid-sixteenth century, it was also used to refer specifically to the kitchen in a large complex. This usage is obvious from the context in many cases: here, most notably, in the endowment deed of the *vakıf.* The final deed is found in the Türk ve İslam Eserleri Müzesi (Istanbul), #2192. The text has been published from Vol. #270 of the Jerusalem *ḳāḍı sicilleri* by K. al- 'Asalī in *Wathā'iq maqdisiyya tārīkhiyya* (Amman, 1983), 128-142.

7. The absence of precisely this type of information in the *ḳāḍı sicilleri* has recently been remarked by Dror Zeevi, "Women in 17th-Century Jerusalem," *IJMES*, 27 (1995), 163.

8. See the comparisons in A. Cohen and B. Lewis, *Population and Revenue in the Towns of Palestine in the Sixteenth Century* (Princeton, 1978), 19. On Lidd and the district of Ramle, see A. Singer, "The Countryside of Ramle in the Sixteenth Century," *JESHO*, 33 (1990), 61.

9. On the population of the towns, see Cohen and Lewis, *Population and Revenue,* 21-22, and the tables for the individual towns. On the changes in the rural population, see Singer, "The Countryside of Ramle," 64-65, and *idem, Palestinian peasants*, 30-32.

10. See Singer, *Palestinian peasants*, 12.

11. *Hane* (household) here includes *khaṭīb*, *mücerred*, and *şerīf* in order to give a general idea of the population. On estimating the number of members per household, see Ö.L. Barkan, "Essai sur les données statistiques des registres de recensements," *JESHO*, 1 (1958), 21-23, and R.L. Erder, "The Measurement of Pre-industrial population changes," *Middle East Studies*, 11 (1975), 296-299. The population of Lidd was approximately one-third Christian in 1556-7, and this proportion had increased by the end of the sixteenth century, though it remained less than one-half.

12. The fines and fees are listed in D-3528/4 in *pāra*. 2 *akçe* = 1 *pāra*. The figures have all been given in *akçe* here to facilitate comparisons.

13. See s.v., *EI*[2], I:679.

14. U. Heyd, *Studies in Old Ottoman Criminal Law*, ed. V. Ménage (Oxford, 1973), 191.

15. For an example of a dispute based on this kind of claim by an official, see Singer, *Palestinian peasants*, 96.

16. See s.v., *EI*[2], I:850.

17. See the examples in Heyd, *Studies*, 104; and N. Beldiceanu and I. Beldiceanu-Steinherr, "Recherches sur la province de Qaraman au XVIe siècle," *JESHO*, 11 (1968), 87.

18. Cohen and Lewis, *Population and Revenue*, 102, 116, 131, 142, 152, and 169.

19. Cohen and Lewis, *Population and Revenue*, 74; Beldiceanu and Beldiceanu-Steinherr, "Recherches sur la province de Qaraman," 38. See also the *ḳānūnnāme* of Silistre in Barkan, *Kanunlar*, 285-86.

20. Singer, *Palestinian peasants*, 26-27. The *ṣubaşı* for the *'imāret* villages was appointed sometime after the *'imāret* was set up, the final *vaḳfiye* having been dated 964/1557. The first reference found to him is from that year, see Jerusalem Sijill 33:2800/p. 525. Also see s.v. in Z. Pakalın, *Osmanlı tarih deyimleri ve terimleri sözlüğü* (Istanbul, 1956), III: 502, 504.

21. See the discussion of the various roles *ṣubaşıs* played, in Singer *Palestinian peasants*, 26-28.

22. The phrase is "*der ühde-i ra'īsān-i ḳarye-i mezbūre*", from TSA D-1511, p. 2a. For a full discussion of the role of village leaders, see Singer, *Palestinian peasants*, 32ff.

23. Heyd, *Studies*, 210-11.

24. Heyd, *Studies*, 213.

25. For other examples of this stipulation, see S. Faroqhi, *Towns and townsmen* (Cambridge, U.K., 1984), 57; and H. İnalcik, "Adâletnâmeler," *Belgeler*, 2 (1965), 68.

26. For the details of such operations, see S. Faroqhi, *Pilgrims and Sultans* (London, 1994).

27. If Ḥuseyn was living in Jerusalem in those years, his food costs might be calculated based on the figures in Cohen's *Economic Life in Ottoman Jerusalem* (pp. 139, 144, 151): approximately 8 *pāra* per *raṭl* for sheep or goat's meat,

12 *pāra* per *raṭl* for olive oil, and 8 *dirham ḥalabī* per *raṭl* of bread. One *raṭl* equalled somewhat less than 3 kilograms in sixteenth-century Palestine; a *dirham ḥalabī* was a silver coin which was replaced in the later sixteenth century by the silver *pāra*, although it is not clear that they were precisely equal at that time.

28. İnalcik, "Adâletnâmeler," p.112. "*Ama her üç ayda voyvodalar il üzerine çıkub gezüb reayanın ahvalını görmek emrim olmuşdur.*"

29. See TSA-D 5707, pages a, b.

30. Barkan, *Kanunlar*, 285-86. Cohen and Lewis say that the standard *resm-i 'arūs* was 60 *akçe* for girls, 30-40 *akçe* for widows and divorcées; see *Population and revenue*, 103. Most of these figures pertain to documents from the mid-sixteenth century. By the time the present document was composed, inflation and devaluation had reduced the value of the *akçe*. However, we will not embark on a lengthy discussion of the changing values of *akçe*, *pāra* and gold coins here. For a succinct discussion of this, see Ş. Pamuk, "The Disintegration of the Ottoman Monetary System during the Seventeenth Century," *Princeton Papers in Near Eastern Studies*, 2 (1993), 71-72.

31. I assume that the fees and fines recorded for the final month were from these same eight villages, even though no village names are specified in this group of entries. This assumption is based on the fact that they were intended for the same Ḥuseyn *ṣubaşı* who collected the others, since his jurisdiction was geographically defined. In addition, Ottoman registers of this type usually specify the source-location for revenues, and since none in indicated differently from those of the main body of the document, I tend to think that no new locations were included.

32. The figures from survey #546 from 1005 (1596-7) are cited because it is the closest chronologically to the *defter* considered here.

33. Hilma Granqvist, *Marriage conditions in a Palestinian Village*, vol. 2 (Helsingfors, 1935), 30-33.

34. The comparative figures are from TSA D-1527/1, p. 66.

35. James Redhouse, *A Turkish and English Lexicon*, s.v.

36. Heyd, *Studies*, 180-82.

37. Heyd, *Studies*, 104.

38. Heyd, *Studies*, 104.

39. Heyd, *Studies*, 106-7.

40. This *ḳānūnnāme* included a criminal code, "compiled by Celālzāde Muṣṭafā

Çelebi (Beğ, Paşa), who held the office of Nişāncı in 1534-57 and 1566-7." It "seems to have orginated in the years 1539-41" at the initiative of Luṭfī Paşa, who served as Grand Vizier in those years (Heyd, *Studies*, 25, 27).

41. Heyd, *Studies*, 104-5.

42. Heyd, *Studies*, 108-9.

43. No kadi records remain for this period from the *sancak* of Gaza. There is a slight possibility that the case ended up with the Jerusalem kadi because Sāfariyya was part of the *'imāret vaḳfı*. I have not had an opportunity to check the Jerusalem *ḳāḍı sicilleri* on this matter.

44. Heyd, *Studies*, 97, 98; and 299, for the punishment of a kadi who allowed a marriage to take place in such cases.

45. TTD 546. Cotton was often subsumed into this general heading, along with certain fruits and vegetables, unless it was a predominant crop in the village.

46. J. Schacht, *An Introduction to Islamic Law* (Oxford, 1964), 13.

47. Heyd, *Studies*, 113.

48. Singer, *Palestinian peasants*, 91-97.

49. See the maps in W.-D. Hütteroth and K. Abdulfattah, *Historical Geography of Palestine, Transjordan and Southern Syria* (Erlangen, 1977), where no rice is indicated. On greater Syria, see Zohar Ammar, "Notes on Flora and Agriculture in Mamluk Palestine," *Palestine in the Mamluk Period*, ed. J. Drory (Jerusalem, 1992), 220-236; and M.L. Venzke, "Rice Cultivation in the Plain of Antioch in the 16th Century," *Archivum Ottomanicum*, 12 (1987-92), 175-276.

50. U. Heyd, *Ottoman Documents on Palestine 1552-1615* (Oxford, 1960), 133.

51. See the discussions on peasant migration and abandoning of lands in A. Singer, "Peasant Migration: Law and Practice in Early Ottoman Palestine," *New Perspectives on Turkey*, 8 (1992), passim.

52. On *çift*, see s.v. in *EI*[2] and *İA*; on *feddān* see s.v. in E.W. Lane, *Arabic-English Lexicon*.

53. See in Singer, "Peasant Migration," 53.

54. Barkan, *Kanunlar*, 312/#34. and s.v. Serim *sancak* lay between the Sava and Danube rivers, in Hungary.

55. Schacht, *Islamic Law*, 13, 175, 179.

56. Heyd, *Studies*, 111, 143.

57. Schacht, *Islamic Law*, 132.

58. A. Cohen, *Jewish Life under Islam* (Cambridge, MA, 1984), 186-187; Heyd, *Studies*, 111: "If a person drinks wine (*hamr içse*), the cadi shall, after it has been proved, punish him and a fine (*cürm*) of one *akçe* shall be collected for [every] two strokes."

59. G. Baer says that *ḥikr* was common in Egypt and Syria as a long-term lease of *vaḳıf* property, given to encourage tenants to make improvements on the property. There is widespread evidence for this type of lease by the nineteenth century, though there has been relatively little discussion of it in earlier periods. See G. Baer, "*ḥikr*," *EI*^{2}, Supplement (Leiden, 1982), 368-370.

60. See Singer, *Palestinian peasants*, 64 ff., which compares tax revenues projections in the *tapu tahrir defterleri* with tax receipts occasionally recorded in the *ḳāḍı sicilleri*.

61. Heyd, *Studies*, 1.

62. See H. Gerber, *State, Society and Law in Islam* (Albany, 1994), 69-70.